# Cargo Boat of the Southern Moons

R.H. ELLIS

**Cargo Boat of the Southern Moons**

First published by Bernard Durnford Publishing
The Old Museum, Bramber, West Sussex
BN44 3WE England.
2002



A catalogue record of this book is available from the British Library

ISBN 0 9535670 5 2

Format, design and cover by StewART

Printed and bound by Antony Rowe Ltd, Eastbourne.

# Cargo Boat of the Southern Moons

R.H. ELLIS

Published by

Bernard Durnford Publishing

# Dedication

To all those who find themselves lobbing their lonely thoughts and tossing their wistful dreams of yesterday into the enveloping and deafening silence that their lives have become, and for whom getting to yet another tomorrow seems daunting and without point.

# Contents

# Author's Note

This is a work of faction. Whilst based on an actual voyage that I embarked upon in 1997, the names of my fellow shipmates, the shipping line and the vessel herself, have been changed. The illustrations are renditions based on my own photographs with apologies to that earlier voyager to the South Seas, Paul Gauguin.

Proceeds from the sale of this book will be donated to the Charities; Cruse Bereavement Care and King George's Fund for Sailors,

# Acknowledgements

I am grateful to my audio typists Ann Eldridge and Alison Phillips for their patience and their interest in the book and to Ann Stephens and Penelope Simpson for their advice with regard to the illustrations.

I thank Bill Cathy and Emma, my children, for their support and encouragement on the long way round, without which I might not have completed the odyssey.

RHE

# About the Author

Bob Ellis was educated at Marlborough,
St. Catharine's College Cambridge and
St. Bartholomew's Hospital London.
He is a retired physician who
specialised in lung disease.

Dr. Ellis and his wife Esmé saw the World
together and vowed that, if they lost each other,
the survivor should continue to travel.

Bob's interests include sport, especially cricket, rugby
football and tennis, as well as music, current
affairs and military history. He has featured in
the BBC Radio 4 programmes "Itchy Feet"
and "Pick of the Week" on the subject of
travel in the context of grief.

## *Cargo Boat of the Southern Moons*

*You gave me time, gave me space*
*Time to think and room to cry*
*Time to wish and time to dream*
*A place to ache and wonder why*
*Scope to plan, a place to scheme*
*A way to live or a way to die.*

*You ploughed the cruel, grey Atlantic*
*You severed the neck of Panama*
*You sailed the vast misnamed Pacific*
*The current with you, the trade wind fair*
*You bore me to the little pretty lands*
*Where she was so happy long, long ago*
*You left me quayside, you went your way*
*You followed the Cross, the southern stars*
*Left me to die in the pretty lands*
*Where she was so happy long, long ago*
*I hope that you knew, you understood*
*I think I always sensed that you would*
*You Cargo Boat of the Southern Moons*

# Prelude

In 1997 two years after my wife and lover died, the special abject loneliness that the loss of an almost lifelong love and friendship brings, had become harder, not easier to bear, and I was still far from reaching the numb void which might lie beyond the pain.

The flood tide of longing had flowed into every inlet and creek of my being, so that my desire and determination to die had become the controller of all my thoughts, the theme of my continuing forced existence, truly an obsession. The small house that we both so loved, and where we had known much happiness together, became a prison cell of such sadness and hopelessness that I knew that I must try to change my scene, at least for a little while; wasting time was no longer a sin but an achievement, and I had to run away but I knew not where.

We both loved seeing the world and often told each other that when one of us died the other should try to continue to travel. With that in mind, after I lost Esmé I went to South Africa, Borneo, Vietnam, the battlefields of Gallipoli and France, and the death camps in Poland, but none of this did anything to relieve the constant ache in my heart.

I had occasionally thought of going to sea, and when I saw an advertisement in the press for cargo ship travel,

I obtained a list of available ships and selected the longest voyage I could find. It would take me around the world, across the Atlantic Ocean and through Panama, across the Pacific Ocean to the South Sea Islands and to New Zealand and Papua New Guinea, and would bring me home via Singapore, the Indian Ocean, the Gulf of Aden, the Red Sea, the Suez Canal and the Mediterranean.

The ship was a mixed cargo vessel of twenty-three thousand tons, and it would call at eleven ports on the way. There was accommodation for twelve passengers in four double and four single cabins and I would be away from my dungeon of despair for over four months.

I boarded M.V. River Tweed in the port of Dunkirk on a glorious golden October afternoon. My heart was full to bursting, beating to cadenzas new, so that I felt it must leap from my chest, the clamour of the stentorian voices of doubt filling my head and fear and foreboding knotting my gut.

I was committing myself to the dark unknown, leaving my loving family far behind; I wondered if I had finally demented and was pretty sure that I had.

*Moving away from the Dunkirk quayside on a grey November afternoon in 1997. Leaving my loving family behind for four months - I wondered if I had finally demented and was pretty sure that I had.*

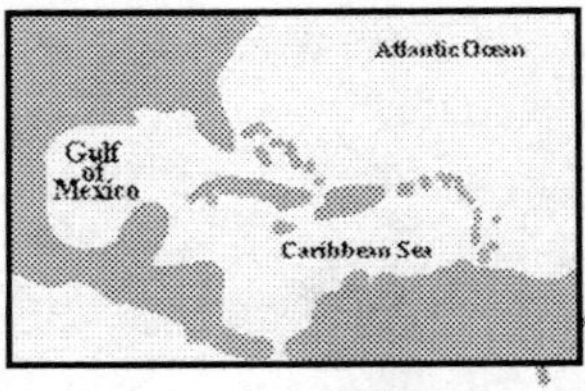


# Chapter 1

## Atlantic Ocean and Caribbean Sea

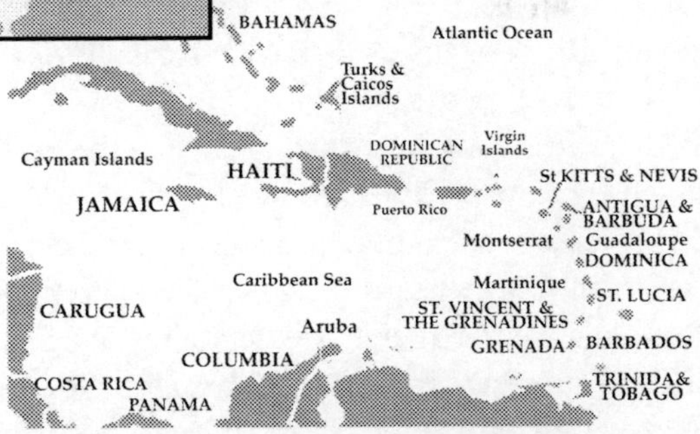


The wiry young man who came with the taxi eyed my overgravid bags, packed as they were for northern winter and southern summer, doubtfully, and said that he had just had a vasectomy and the surgeon told him to be careful for the next six weeks or so; I reassured him that the surgeon meant care in other directions, and told him to put the bags in the boot. If you are a consultant physician you can give reassurance with massive authority about things of which you may well know very little, and the more senior you are the more massive is the authority.

I was met at the assembly point in central London by an attractive girl who was the agent for River Line, together with my four shipmates, American couples, one elderly and the other in early middle age. There should have been three more English people but one of them had a coronary thrombosis the day before and they all cancelled; we were therefore down to five passengers and this was to prove a pity. I always feel that dogs have the right idea, when they want to know whether they will get on, in more senses than one, with other dogs, they sniff each others' bottoms. I am not saying that had I done that I would have turned round and gone home, and anyway it was a little too early to get that familiar, but it could have been a pointer to future developments. We were taken in a minibus through the Channel Tunnel to the port of Dunkirk, we should have sailed from Rotterdam but River Line had made a late change dictated by cargo.

Eventually finding M.V. River Tweed berthed in Freycinet 11 we were met dockside by the Purser, a very large man six feet seven inches tall and some nineteen stones in weight, with a homely north country accent. River Tweed seemed bigger than I had expected and as I hauled myself up the thirty-six steep steps of the gangway leading from the dockside to the main deck, I felt that I could be mounting the ladder to the scaffold. I was in my late seventies and I felt very old, quite alone, and scared to death; I lacked a kindred spirit with whom to share my apprehension, for the others were couples and had each other.

Purser Alec showed us to our cabins; knowing that River Tweed had four double and four single cabins and there were only five of us, I asked for and got a double cabin. I unpacked in somewhat of a daze and was summoned to the passengers' lounge to meet the Captain and Senior Officers. The captain showed scant interest in us and spent the time drooling and lusting after the girl who had brought us from London, but the Chief Officer and the Chief Engineer were very pleasant and welcoming. After the agent had left the Captain told us that when we got out to sea we could spend time on the bridge and have the run of the main deck, but that if we were injured in any way the Company took no responsibility. He also told us that the engine room was out of bounds to us at all times.

Purser Alec took us under his ample wing and introduced us to the three stewardesses, all Russian like the crew, two Olgas and an Anna and I was allotted the Anna. River Line bought the ship from a Russian company, it was built in Russia for Arctic service with ice-breaking capacity, and also the possibility of conversion for wartime use. We took meals in the dining saloon on the first deck with the Officers, and my heart sank when I realised that we must keep firmly to one table, and that for four months I would eat as a family with these two American couples. There was no bar on the ship, and I was sorry that we would not be able to have a beer with the off duty Officers; we could buy unlimited booze cheaply but could drink it only in the cabin or the Dining Saloon.

After dinner that first night I finished unpacking, sorted out my CDs and tapes and arranged my books. I listened to some music and climbed early into one of the two bunks which were built athwartships, the one nearest the window, feeling tired, utterly lonely and wondering what on earth I was doing, and I slept well.

**Wednesday 29th October** Waking for the first time in strange surroundings, and there could be fewer stranger than these, gave me quite a jolt. After breakfast we were informed that we would not be sailing until Friday 31st October because of delay in the arrival of cargo at the dockside. I spent most of the day on the top observation deck, which is seven levels up at the top of the superstructure on the top of the bridge, and which in the Merchant Navy they call Monkey Island. As you stand up there you are just eighty feet above water level, and the main deck with the eight large holds and three cranes stretches out in front of you. The dock was covered with metal of all sorts and sizes; there were large pipes with spokes at each end, each one weighing twenty-five tons and bound for the nickel mine on the island of New Caledonia, there were girders and rods and sheets of metal, there was metal netting and steel frames painted different colours.

In addition to all this there were dozens of vehicles, tractors, bulldozers, lorries and cars waiting to be driven aboard through the Ro-Ro just for'ard of the stern on the starboard side. There were piles of sacks, and of course hundreds of containers; I simply stood and watched all this activity with fascination. The noise of the forklift trucks, the container transporters, the vehicles being driven into the Ro-Ro, the clanking of metal and the shouting of the stevedores was new to me.

The pace at which the French stevedores worked tended to slow down during the day and the Captain said that they had wine stores in the sheds, and they started on this at about ten o'clock in the morning and by four o'clock in the afternoon they were not fit to do any more work. The dock and the main deck are Hard Hat Areas and injuries to the stevedores occur more frequently toward the end of the day. When I first decided to sail on a cargo vessel one of the reasons why I did so was to learn all about the workings of such ships, loading and unloading, navigation, the general ways of the Merchant Navy, the interrelationships of Officers and the Crew, the engines, none of this would I get on a luxury cruise, and I was determined that by the end of this voyage, this circumnavigation of the world, I would know all about merchant shipping.

The loading continued after dark by floodlight and I stayed on Monkey Island until late.

**Thursday 30th October** I ventured into the centre of Dunkirk to buy beer and send off letters and postcards. I had to buy the beer because the Bond on the ship remains closed until we sail out of territorial waters. Dunkirk is uninteresting and unattractive, which is not surprising when you consider what happened to it during the Second World War. The walk into the town took some forty-five minutes through the docks and there were huge ferries, anchored awaiting repair. I walked into one of them, massive doors wide open and in front of me there was a space the size of three large ballrooms.

Back on River Tweed during the afternoon the alarm bell rang, and we were instructed to put on our life jackets which were in a drawer under the bunk and assemble in the passengers' lounge. The lifebelts had a halter to go over the head, wide enough to accommodate the neck of a goitrous elephant, and a whistle and a light, and were of a ghastly bright orange dayglo colour. We were taken to the stern and they demonstrated to us how the port lifeboat was swung out on its davits; this monthly drill is compulsory by law. While he was talking to us I observed Captain Geoffrey closely, because I realised that I had placed myself in the hands of this man who would control virtually everything that I did for the next four months, where I went and when I went there; I was interested in his personality and already I felt doubt about him. His eyes were hard, and I wished that he had welcomed us properly aboard when we arrived, rather than lech after that girl from River Line. Time would tell, and I had an uneasy feeling that first impressions in his case might prove correct.

I also took a closer look at my fellow passengers. The elderly couple, Eric and Tina were from California and had made several cargo ship voyages previously. Eric had a Texan drawl from the state of his birth, and one of the longest faces that I have ever seen; his visage made the average bloodhound look as if it had just had a facelift, and a drop of sweat forming on his brow had a very long southward journey along one of the longest noses in the world until it dropped onto his chin and then his chest. He was an amusing man and I felt that I would get to like him. Tina, his wife, was very short and sturdy with cropped hair and a sense of humour. The other couple I had early reservations about.

Anthony was a large obese boomer, the more enclosed the space the louder did he seem to speak. His stomach was such that when he entered the dining saloon it appeared to precede him by several seconds; he had a beard and was ever keen to demonstrate his knowledge. His partner of twenty years was Jane, they had divorced from their spouses on the same day in order to shack up together; she was short, not unattractive and also keen to demonstrate her knowledge and her intelligence which was considerable. Eric was very deaf and his ears were festooned with hearing aides. All Americans seem to have the same way about them, the American Way, than which, in their view, there is none better throughout the World.

**Saturday 1st November** Loading was complete by 2 p.m. By 3 p.m. the pilot had come aboard, the agent took off mail for posting, the two big diesels fired and two fussy tugs attached themselves, one to the stern and one to the bow. The horn blew, the dockers waved and cheered and very, very slowly this metallic sea-going beast moved away from the dockside. The tugs took us into the main channel from the quay, turned us around and then through a lock to the mouth of the harbour; there they left us and under our own power we headed out into a grey English Channel, turned to port, increased speed, and at that point I felt that this great adventure had truly begun, there was no going back now.

The weather had changed, little or no sun all day and a dank mist and a bitter cold wind coming across Dunkirk from due north east. It was so cold up on Monkey Island that I had to come down to the cabin to swap lambswool for Guernsey under my anorak; we were told by the Officers that as soon as we pass the Azores in a little over a week we shall be in shorts, and it was difficult at that moment to believe that.

There was much traffic in the Channel and the pilot boat stayed with us for two hours. Up on the bridge Captain Geoffrey announced that minor collisions were part of the business, and so long as his ship did not have to stop he was not worried about what it hit, truly a philosophy of 'fuck the other ships, mine is alright'.

**Sunday 2nd November** Looking through the cabin window early this morning I found that we were away from all land and heading for the Bay of Biscay. There was very little rolling yet, but Captain Geoffrey's ominous statement that all containers on deck must be properly secured and we would soon know the reason why, is ringing in my ears.

The cabins have a shower and a loo and the temperature and the pressure of the water in the showers is most variable. The loos flush like those on aircraft, when you lift the handle there is a very noisy and powerful suction finishing with a violent implosion, which makes it very important to dethrone before you do anything with that lever; failure to do so might mean instant castration and radical penile avulsion.

At twenty-three thousand tons unladen River Tweed sits well in the water, almost sedately; she is capable of seventeen knots but so far I doubt whether she has exceeded twelve. Modern ships do not have the old fashioned funnels any more, there is a steel box at the stern about twelve by eight feet and thirty feet high. On River Tweed this is painted red and black and open at the top, through which ten or twelve stove pipes stick up, angled sternwards at the top. The two large pipes on each side are the exhausts of the big diesels, and when they fire them clouds of black smoke belch forth. The two engines, each with fourteen cylinders, each cylinder eighteen inches in diameter, are connected to the single shaft and screw by four clutches, two hydraulic for use in shallow water where there is a danger of fouling, and two mechanical for the open sea.

I would not call River Tweed a pretty ship, her lines are ungraceful, there is a sudden drop down from the bow to a long main deck packed high with containers. She is in contrast with the long low slender lines of the laden tankers and bulk carriers, who are surely the elegant ladies of the seas.

Standing for hour upon hour on Monkey Island with my binoculars and searching for other ships and finding them from time to time, I began to feel that I might like to do all this again; you get to feel very much a partner of the ship once you leave land, and with the reassuring, comfortable and friendly thrum of the diesels below me, and excited panting of the exhausts in the stack behind me, together with the gentle pitch of the boat, I felt half at peace.

On the bridge deck today I met Mona, the wife of Purser Alec, she is very short and overweight at four foot eleven and thirteen stone and it was difficult to imagine their union. I was reminded of a very large Australian junior doctor who was my colleague many, many years ago, and who was contemplating early marriage to his diminutive girlfriend. When I told him that they seemed to get on very well, he said that surely he got on alright but he had nobody to talk to when he did!

At 1 p.m. we passed Brest and pursued a course west south west across the Bay of Biscay at 210 degrees, and the word on the bridge is that if the weather holds we will go straight across the Atlantic on a northern route and should see the Azores. If the weather deteriorates, we shall turn southward, and then westward which will take longer. At this point I tried to imagine what it will be like to spend the next four weeks without setting foot on land, for we do not go ashore until Tahiti.

**Monday 3rd November** We have a friendly flock of gannets accompanying us and also a small land bird looking rather like a greenfinch, and I wondered if it will come all the way to the South Pacific or is merely hitching a ride to Panama.

The weather deteriorated during the night, Captain Geoffrey was called to the bridge at 2 a.m. and he changed course 20 degrees to try and avoid a bad weather system. There was fair pitching and rolling, and the westerly wind was too strong for us to stand up on Monkey Island. I spent the morning on the bridge, which is enclosed, with Captain Geoffrey telling us much; he likes to talk authoritatively and I got the feeling that he much prefers talking to listening. He is unconcerned with keeping to time schedules, and is prepared to change course at any moment depending on weather forecasts. He said that storms, cyclones, typhoons and hurricanes are all one and the same thing, and should be avoided if at all possible, even if it means lengthy diversions. I suggested that there was much less rolling and pitching in a Bay of Biscay sea as rough as this in a Force 8, than I expected, and he said that River Tweed would roll more as the fuel bunkers at the bottom of the ship got emptied.

The big radar screen has been empty all day so far, it detects ships within a twelve mile radius and Captain Geoffrey said that you rarely see other ships the whole way across, thought they must be there, perhaps twenty-five miles away. At noon today we were one hundred and twenty miles from Cape Finisterre on the north coast of Spain, but could not see it through binoculars, we were two days from the Azores and hopefully eleven days from Panama, and will have to book a passage through the canal a week in advance of our arrival.

By 4.30 p.m. we had passed through the depression and the wind relented. After spending most of the afternoon on Monkey Island clinging like grim death to the rails, I went down to the bridge deck and talked to Chief Officer Jack. He had just completed two years with P & O on cruise ships carrying up to two thousand passengers at a time, which would not be my scene at all or that of my wife, and he too prefers general cargo ships. He said that the huge modern container ships are putting smaller ships like River Lines' out of business.

We were invited to join the Captain and Officers in the passenger lounge for drinks before dinner, there were six Officers present whom I had not met and one wife, and we had a pleasant informative chat. The Officers are very pleasant people and expect us to take an interest in what they are doing and to ask them at all times if we want to know something. Scottish Bill, the Chief Engineer, has a droll outlook on life, every now and then he emerges from River Tweed's bowels to report to the Captain wearing only overalls slashed to the waist, covered in oil and with sweat pouring down his hairy chest. He is very firm that nobody but his team is allowed in the engine room, so I will never get to see those big diesels. His No.2 is Henry married to Johnny who befriended me in Dunkirk, a good looking man with bright flashing eyes accentuated by his grey beard and I shall call him Bright Eyed Bearded Henry. Scots have predominated since I first contemplated this voyage, starting with Captain Campbell of Cargo Ships Ltd., the agent with whom I booked the voyage, who even wheezes with a Scottish accent, and you feel that you can smell his Scotch malt whisky down the phone.

**Tuesday 4th November** The weather has calmed and the twelve foot waves replaced by a mild chop, and

River Tweed ploughed onwards south-westward at an immutable fifteen knots; you felt strongly that even if the Caller of the Shots, the Divine Playmaker, suddenly decided to change the salt water into treacle, the steady progress would continue just the same.

The bridge fascinated me and especially the chart room at the back where there was a long table and you could pore over the charts to your heart's content. In front of the chart annexe there was a line of free standing banks of instruments, consols, with the wheel in the centre. These included a large radar screen and a modern GPS (Global Positioning System) satellite navigator.

During the night there has been an adjustment of heading toward west at 240 degrees, and if we maintain this we shall pass close to the Azores and then ultimately breach the ring of Leeward Islands close by the Virgins, before crossing the Caribbean to Panama.

Standing on the bridge or up on Monkey Island and endlessly thinking my thoughts, I find that I am permitted occasional runs and races of half pleasant positive feelings, but such mental truancy is pretty quickly ended, and I am back to the reality that any further travel will forever be without the company of my love, and the ache in my heart overwhelmed me.

According to the large chart on the bridge we are now level with Porto on the west coast of Portugal, and diverting ever farther out into the Atlantic. The radar screen showed plenty of rain showers, but as usual no other ships. When you realise how many planes and ships cross this ocean between Europe and the New World daily and you rarely see any of them, or evidence of them, it makes you appreciate the extent of sky and sea, and how miniscule are man and his machines in nature's boundlessness. In spite of this we should perhaps now worry at the rate at which human beings and their contraptions are destroying all this bounty, but there is no evidence of this in my present situation, surrounded as I am by this limitless mass of turbulent grey water, to which the sky comes down wherever I look.

With a further adjustment of heading to 250 degrees the sun descended almost over the bow, but before it reached the sea it was wrapped in cloud like a huge precious orange jewel in cotton wool, as if to protect it, and save it for tomorrow.

**Wednesday 5th November** After the relative calm of the previous evening I awoke to a Force 7 wind and angry ten foot waves again; Captain Geoffrey announced that these conditions were known as 'High Pressure Azores' and we should be able to see San Miguel on the port bow at about 10.30 a.m. This we did, though mist obscured much of this isolated land, and we could only see the mountain skyline for a relatively short time. Later we could just make out a lighthouse on the westernmost cliff.

At this point our position was Latitude 38 degrees, Longitude 25 degrees, we had covered fourteen hundred miles averaging three hundred and eighty miles a day. An emergency signal was received from a ship just off the Gambian coast but the Captain said that most ships did not answer far off signals, assuming that other ships would be nearer. If he did answer a nearer call there might be several ships doing the same thing, and one ship would take charge, a warship if there was one, a ship with a doctor or a more modern ship, and they all had to stay until the ship in charge released them, perhaps delaying them a whole day. For this reason owners did not much approve their ships answering emergency calls.

I have mentioned the big radar screen and the automatic GPS satellite navigator on the bridge, there are also on each wing identical consols by which the ship can be manually driven. These each have three main dials, two for the engines and one for the propeller. River Line ships have the capacity to alter the pitch of the propeller blades and this can be done from the bridge to facilitate steering at very low speeds, which can become difficult. Captain Geoffrey blew a horn, the only effect of which on this lonely ocean seemed to be to make a seagull shit violently all over the window; he did it to demonstrate to us the sort of noise that it can make.

During this morning's High Pressure Azores and River Tweed's rolling response, I tried to make a cup of early morning tea as is my wont, using my electric shaver the while. This resulted in my having to field the tea bag container, and the carton of long life milk simultaneously, it was like having two balls come at you in the slips at once. I failed to field the shaver which slid across the floor and switched itself on with an angry buzz like an affronted bumble bee when it hit the wall. I failed to prevent twelve cans of beer cascading from the fridge all over the cabin.

At lunch Chief Officer Jack came in wearing clean white shorts and stockings and I suggested that he was rather anticipating the tropics. He said that he had got absolutely filthy down in the palm oil tanks which they were trying to clean ready for the return load from Papua New Guinea. Palm oil leaves behind a solid coating in the pipes and tanks, and the only way to clean them involves the use of steam under pressure and pre-heating to 65 degrees centigrade, and the oil has to be kept above fifty degrees centigrade while they are carrying it. Jack is quite fascinated by the loads in the holds and keeps going down to the hold wherein is parked the star item, the enormous truck-upon-a-truck. He says that it seems like a juggernaut lorry on top of another but more so, I cannot wait to watch the unloading of this. Jack said that it came in through the Ro-Ro, but they have serious doubts as to whether they can get it out that way. We shall see.

I have achieved my first wash and ironing. The washing machines are easy, but you have to take the iron and board to your cabin because the sockets in the laundry room are English square three pin, and the iron has a round two pin plug; I am only equipped to go the other way.

There was really quite a roll on and for the first time in my longish life, I had the experience of ironing on the run. You suddenly found yourself, iron in right hand running backwards involuntarily several steps, and then running forwards again and hopefully you got in a couple of strokes with the iron before the next southward journey. At a conservative estimate it took twenty minutes to iron a shirt, and at the end of this exercise, with three shirts, one night shirt and three pants absolutely pristine and creaseless and smelling of new-mown hay, there was a violent heave, too much for the equilibrium of the ironing board which knocked over a bowl of flowers and fruit while I kept hold of the iron. I felt that this unique effort justified between two and three beers, but after the first blew off into my face, I settled for that. As I have said earlier I am not quite sure exactly what it is that I am trying to do; I know that if my darling wife had been watching my attempts to iron, she would have asked me why I had to keep running about like that, it was much easier if you stood still, bless her dear little Welsh heart.

Life aboard ship is full of haps and mishaps, and this is the charm of it. You can mingle physical relaxation with mental alertness, which is perhaps the best combination for civilised human beings, at any rate at my time of life, or you can let your whole being descend into a state of half suspended animation; you do exactly what you wish and those about you expect you only to do just that. It is a time for thought, a time for reappraisal and a time for renewal, for those fortunate enough still to have something to renew; for those who do not have this, it can be a time for dreams and wishes and for memories of love and passion long flown.

**Thursday 6th November** The weather was warmer, the sea and the sky bluer, and Alec has put out sun loungers on the bridge deck, which is partly covered. Captain Geoffrey is now in working shorts and sandals, which he changes for white shorts, socks and shoes for lunch.

For the first time in three days two ships appeared on the radar screen this morning and passed us going south-east within six miles, a big container ship and a smaller general freighter. The Third Officer, whom I shall call Russian Iosif, was on watch on the bridge, he is rather taciturn like many of his countrymen but is always ready to explain things if asked. I noticed that Captain Geoffrey was asking him some searching questions this morning in an unpleasant tone of voice and I hoped that he had not left undone that which he ought to have done; I think he is rather nervous and perhaps the sort of person that Captain Geoffrey might like to bully.

I am surprised that the weather is so much warmer so soon; we are only seventeen hundred miles from Dunkirk and the northern winter, and yet here we are lying on the deck on sun loungers reading our books on latitude 34 degrees, but when you realise that this is level with Morocco, it is explained. All the Officers are now in shorts and I shall join them tomorrow, and hope that long trousers can be put away until we reach the Bay of Biscay again at the end of February.

Trinity House Paul, the nineteen year old cadet, eats at the next table to us; he is uncannily like one of my grandsons in looks, manner and speech. He has two more years as a cadet and if he passes his exams will become a second mate, but will start his qualified career as a third mate, probably on a cruise ship. His ultimate ambition is to be a Captain of a mixed cargo ship like River Tweed; he rejected university and decided to qualify through Trinity House all the way. Apart from his duties aboard, he has to keep up with reading and write reports, which will all have a bearing on his eventual qualification; an ongoing assessment. It is the opportunity to meet and discuss their lives with them that makes a voyage such as this so rewarding, apart altogether from the experience of the sights and sounds of far flung places in the context of merchant shipping.

I have finished an excellent book kindly given to me by a very good friend, 'Sailing Alone Round The World' by Captain Joshua Slocumb, and am now well into Marge Piercy's eight hundred page novel about some young Jewish people and their experiences during the Second World War, entitled 'Gone to Soldiers'. The war did not appear to trammel their sexual enjoyment of each other at all, which seemed to start at such a tender age. I remembered Esmé saying that the 'naughty girls' with whom she dealt as a social worker, rid themselves of their virginity with as much concern as they did the plastic around a packet of cigarettes, and, probably in many cases with about as much pleasure.

I must not read too fast because I have only fifteen books left. Obviously when we get down to the South Pacific and are calling at the islands every few days, time will pass very much more quickly. Our two periods of ocean sailing, fourteen days in the Atlantic and thirteen in the Pacific on this outward voyage, are the times for serious reading and I can always supplement with books from the ship's library. My American friends tend to watch videos of an evening, also from the ship's library, old American films, mostly three star which really do not attract me, and tonight I graciously declined to join them.

There is a total timelessness about this voyage, from Captain Geoffrey down, time is of no importance whatsoever. The cargo has to be delivered and picked up indeed, but there is no date by which this must be done. There well may be a few days slippage here, an unexpected detour there, to pick up an unexpected cargo to be delivered to an unexpected place, on the general route. All of us on this ship know that the voyage will take four months or perhaps five months, but not three months. This is the way Merchant Seamen live, with no anxiety whatever about time; if you contemplate this kind of trip, you must accept that. You must be quite free to be away from home as long as it takes and I knew when I booked my passage on River Tweed that I must be able to transfer my loneliness, cope with it under quite different conditions, and be prepared to accept the consequences of failure to do so.

In a strange way, you can preserve your individuality, immerse yourself in your problems and be seen to be doing so, without let or hindrance from others on the ship. Nobody has any responsibility to see that you are happy, they accept that you came and you will cope, and they respect you for trying to do so.

**Friday 7th November** At noon each day a notice was placed in the passenger lounge stating mileage covered and position, and at one point yesterday both latitude and longitude read the same at 34 degrees, the force of wind and water and air and water temperature are recorded, and from the Force 8 of Biscay and the Azores, we are now down to a pleasant Force 3, air temperature 21 degrees, water 18 degrees centigrade.

I spent some time at the chart table today with Third Officer Russian Iosif. He hails from Belorussia and his wife from Ukraine. He showed me that our present course will take us through the ring of Leeward Islands at the northern end, sailing over the Puerto Rico Trench, past Sombrero Island and through Sombrero Passage, leaving the Virgin Islands to port. Iosif said that on his last voyage, on a sister ship of River Tweed they entered the Caribbean through Mona Passage and went round the western side of Puerto Rico; it is all dictated by the weather.

The distance from our present position to Sombrero Island is approximately fifteen hundred miles and to Panama two thousand six hundred. Panama is almost exactly halfway between Dunkirk and Papeete on Tahiti, four thousand six hundred miles across the Atlantic and Caribbean, and four thousand four hundred miles across the Pacific, and between Santa Maria in the Azores and Sombrero Island in the Leewards there is only ocean, ocean and more ocean.

In the afternoon the tall dark good looking Russian First Officer was on watch and I shall call him Tall Dark Dem'yan. The fire alarm sounded and we had to assemble again in the lounge with life jackets. We were told that this time there was a fire in Number 5 Ro-Ro, but they were not launching the life boats right away. They asked us which boat we were listed for and it was a good thing that I knew that mine was Port 2. This proved to be another practice but I did not know that at the time. They went through all the motions in Ro-Ro 5, including squirting water all over the place, sealing the hold and pumping in carbon dioxide to create oxygen deprivation.

As I left the saloon after dinner preferring not to get into a discussion of freemasonry, I ran into a very hot and oil-stained Chief Officer Scottish Bill, who had a plate of sandwiches in his hand. The light suddenly failed and Bill plonked down the sandwiches and hared back down to the engine room. The engines then stopped, and I felt my way up to the bridge like blind Pew, which was quite dark except for some dials which were glowing. The radar was off as was the automatic GPS navigator.

It appeared that the generator had suddenly failed, and without power River Tweed lost way and began to drift. I sat at the back of the bridge out of the way and watched and listened. Captain Geoffrey, the unhurried, had stayed in the saloon to finish his Beaujolais by torchlight, thus maintaining a tradition which probably began with a game of bowls on Plymouth Hoe a very long time ago. At this point I felt rather glad that we were adrift in mid Atlantic and not the Straits of Dover in a fog, that the sea was calm and there were no twelve foot waves to buffet us, and that it was not wartime with U-boats lurking about. Somebody asked if anyone could see Venus through the window and I realised that we were now down to basics, down to being Ancient Mariners again, our modern machinery having failed us.

After half an hour they got the port engine firing and ten minutes later the starboard engine, but there was no pitch on the propeller, and although rotating at full speed we still had no way. By this time River Tweed had turned through one hundred and eighty degrees and was pointing straight back to Dunkirk. It was quite eerie in the darkness of the bridge in mid-ocean. Somebody asked who had buggered the gyro and which one of those fucking stars was Venus. Such professionalism reminded me of similar situations in operating theatres when I was a student.

The power finally returned, the pitch was increased from twenty per cent to sixty per cent and the course was corrected, though the radar was left switched off, because damage occurs if it is frequently switched on and off. Thus ended my first week at sea.

Saturday 8th November  Purser Alec joined us for breakfast and announced that we were invited to drinks before lunch with the Officers in the passenger lounge, followed by a buffet in the saloon, and this was hopefully to be a regular Saturday happening. I changed into shorts and a sleeveless shirt and my empire building stockings to the knee, because the temperature was well up. I lunched with Bright Eyed Bearded Second Engineer Henry and his wife Johnny and with the Russian Electrician Officer Pyotr, a very dishy young man behind whose eyes there were banked fires, the sexy Russian sod.

After lunch, on the bridge in the chartroom Captain Geoffrey showed us the Great North Equatorial Current, which sweeps down the west coast of Africa and then turns northward across the Atlantic and swirls up the Caribbean, often at a speed of three knots. He showed us on the chart where it joins with the Gulf Stream along the east coast of America and heads towards Scotland. This current should be behind us and Captain Geoffrey did not wish to arrive too early at Christobal at the eastern end of the Panama Canal; he wants us to go through in daylight. He warned us that the Canal has deteriorated since America withdrew. Whereas previously the locks were kept clean and free of debris, now they are all filthy, rubbish everywhere, and this can only get worse.

We learned that the income from the Panama Canal remained massive, but it had never been fairly distributed by the government. With the decrease in numbers of ships passing through, due to the concentration of cargo onto enormous modern container and bulk carrier ships which can carry the load of four smaller ships, and are not

Panama registered, the point could be reached where it may no longer be necessary for Panama to spend money on increasing the Canal facility.

There is a constant flow of interesting stimuli on a voyage like this, even in mid-ocean there is always something to keep you alert, and there are always the sunsets at sea. I have cried a river torrent since Esmé died, wept a waterfall, fathomed such depths of loneliness that I never guessed could exist, but by the end of every day something will have happened to make living just worthwhile, a new memory will have lodged itself, staked a claim on a place on the ledges in the caves of my mind.

**Sunday 9th November** After breakfast I went to the bridge deck, the air was already warm and the early morning sun shone with a bright white light on the sea with the flash and glint of a squillion sequins on a gown of indigo blue.

I felt that I was leaving the world of the morning, and travelling to the lands of the evening and the tropical nights. My beginning was astern and my ending may be ahead, and this in no way concerned me, because I have had much much more of the happiness' life has to offer than was my share.

I am enjoying Marge Piercy's 'Gone to Soldiers' but I wonder why authors who write well researched and interesting books feel such a need to sprinkle them so liberally with descriptions of sexual intercourse in every form conceivable, and some that are not. There is a curious belief among writers in the general need among their readers of unending mental masturbation, and I wondered from where this comes; I suspect that it is not the readers' need but their own. A bonk here, a shag there is all very well, but you can have too much of a good thing.

My fellow passengers fill me with admiration at meal times. They never fail to eat three full meals a day, three course breakfast, three course lunch and five course dinner, and every plate piled high. Big Boom Boom Anthony suffered a coronary thrombosis at an early age, gave up cigarettes and is now concentrating on food. He is very large and seems hell-bent on an early death. When the loos failed to flush for a day earlier on the voyage, I could well understand the consternation and anxiety among my friends, for there was a danger of us being ankle deep in excrement, not all our own.

Tall Dark Dem'Yan on the bridge this afternoon claimed that he saw some whales, and tried to alert us, but by the time we got there there was nothing to see. Dem'yan said that they were little more than a mile from the port bow; we had to satisfy ourselves with a ship four miles to port. You feel an immediate brotherhood when you sight another ship after several days, although you have no communication.

The conversation at meals today has been mainly of the crisis in Iraq, and the Americans are worried to death that things will blow up there just as we reach the Suez Canal.

Tonight we are in the tropics, we are six hundred miles from the Leewards and sixteen hundred miles, four days, from the Panama Canal.

Standing alone for hours on Monkey Island tonight, with the moon doing his best and the warm night wind of the ocean caressing my ears and whispering into them, it was almost possible to believe that this was my reality and not the imaginary, this was the peace that I yearned for, available here and now, not the impossible dream of the past two years.

**Monday 10th November** At lunch time we were told that we could have the run of the main cargo deck, and in fact the whole ship except for the engine room, and I explored. When you walk along the side of the main deck you are dwarfed by piles of containers secured on top of the hatches over the main holds, they tower thirty feet above you; there is a small fo'c's'le deck, and looking over the bow the water still seems a long way below. At the stern there is a poop deck with enormous winches and four spare propeller blades which stand six feet high. The Russian crew were painting ship and this will go on until we get home.

There is now trouble with a fuel injection pipe and we are back to the starboard engine only and ten knots, the exhaust of the port engine is silent as the sepulchre, and this is all part of this voyage without time. One freighter crossed our bow today, and for the first time since leaving the Channel I saw the vapour trail of a plane. Tonight just before dinner the port engine fired, with a muffled fart and a cloud of black smoke and Bright Eyed Bearded Henry was clapped all the way to his dinner table. He suggested in the hearing of the Captain that we should recommend a pay rise, but Geoffrey's expression seemed to indicate that the fuel injection pipe should not have fractured in the first place.

Before I left the bridge to turn in Venus shone so brightly, low over the port bow, that she cast a tentative path of light on the sea like an unsure young moon. I felt that if stars twinkle and planets shine, Venus must be the brightest and best of them all.

I have this morning completed my second wash and ironing. I have confirmed that ironing is much easier if you do it standing in one place, which I suppose applies to other activities in life like emptying your bladder and making love.

At 4 p.m. we sighted a tall pylon-like structure on the port bow, which was a tall metal tower with a light at the top, standing on a small island with some other buildings, this was much-awaited Sombrero Island, the first land since we passed the Azores, and beyond it to the south we could make out the outline of Anguilla. We were now about to enter the Caribbean Sea through the Sombrero Passage, and one hour later we saw the first of the Virgin Islands, Virgin Gorda.

I had a long talk on Monkey Island this afternoon with Johnny, she and her Bright Eyed Bearded Henry have no children by choice and they have travelled the world. They lived for some years in Florida and ultimately would like to retire to a warm climate. She is always interested in other people and I hope that I can have a beer or two with them both ashore somewhere along the way. She accompanies him on every voyage and they spend their whole life at sea.

Our first opportunity to go ashore will be when we berth in the port of Papeete on Tahiti. Perhaps the Italian woman will still be in her kiosk selling her painted shirts, and the little boutique where we bought the two pieces of branched pink coral for Esmé's tropical necklace will still be there after eight years.

After dinner I spent three hours on Monkey Island with my binoculars, the moon was full and all the world around me was bathed in a lovely white light, the wind was very soft; to starboard the lights of the Virgin Islands Tortola, St. Thomas and St. John twinkled seductively, and to port there were the lights of the larger island of St. Croix.

As I stood and watched, four very large cruise boats appeared all headed south east, three on the starboard side and one to port; Esmé used to describe them as floating wedding cakes. These floating palaces sail at night and moor at the next island of call early the next morning, and in the ocean night they shine in an extraordinary way, the whole ship is incandescent.

From tomorrow until we reach Christobal we shall see little or no shipping. When he brought my booze order tonight Purser Alec gave me a pamphlet about the Panama

Canal and I cannot wait to experience it, having been fascinated by the whole idea of it since childhood.

**Wednesday 12th November** Now that we are well within the tropics the weather is really hot and humid. I remember when we first went to Barbados twenty years ago we could not believe that the birds and the flowering shrubs, bougainvillea, oleander and hibiscus were really that colour. This morning when a small greenish yellow bird perched on the stern handrail, I was reminded of the bananaquits with whom we always shared breakfast. For these reasons I feel a little glad that I will now pass through without stopping, there are some memories which must be left unmodified, for they are much too precious, and with time and human frailty, they will become much too rare.

The vista on Monkey Island this morning was landless, just the turquoise Caribbean and school upon school of flying fish. These tiny little silver missiles seemed to hit the water with a force entirely out of proportion to their size.

A large bird, white with brown and black wings and a black head and a long pointed beak befriended us and flew along with us for quite a while. Ever imaginative and optimistic, American Tina asked was it an albatross, she is desperate to see an albatross, and I hated to disappoint her. I reassured her that when we got to the far South Pacific there would be rows of albatrosses perched on the rails, and many more queuing up for a space; she threw an apple core at me and missed.

There was a perfect plenilune tonight, it came up over the stern like a searchlight, after the sun had given way and bowed down to the sea on the starboard bow. Venus seemed to switch on rather earlier than usual, high on the port bow as if wanting to be part of this wondrous show, but she was no match for the moon. You could have read a book with small print up there tonight.

**Thursday 13th November** A fresh chart has appeared on the chartroom table showing the Caribbean and Panama in full detail. We have sailed across a sea divided up into three large basins, Venezuelan, Columbian and Clark. The depth of the Caribbean varies from eighteen hundred to five thousand metres, and the North Equatorial Current which has carried us from mid-Atlantic is replaced, as we approach Panama, by the Guiana Current which sweeps along the north coast of continental South America and then turns north until it meets the Caribbean Anti-Current coming southward. The knowledge and understanding of these currents governs our time of arrival.

We have now sailed into the rain, but before we did so we saw a small tornado, miles away to the south west. As we sailed into the rainstorm it was like driving into a creeping barrage of water, whipping up the surface of the sea in front of us to a frenzy. One never fails to be impressed by the sudden changing decisions of nature, especially in the tropics. As if by the touch of a switch the smelting furnace heat of the sun becomes a sauna or is changed into a cascading hot shower, the peace and calm of a summer day is replaced by howling wind which makes the dozing palms bend double, and their long fronds thrash like the thongs of a cat-o-nine tails; violence replaces gentleness in minutes, Wagner ousts Beethoven, but then just as quickly we hear the Pastoral Symphony again.

# Chapter 2

## Panama

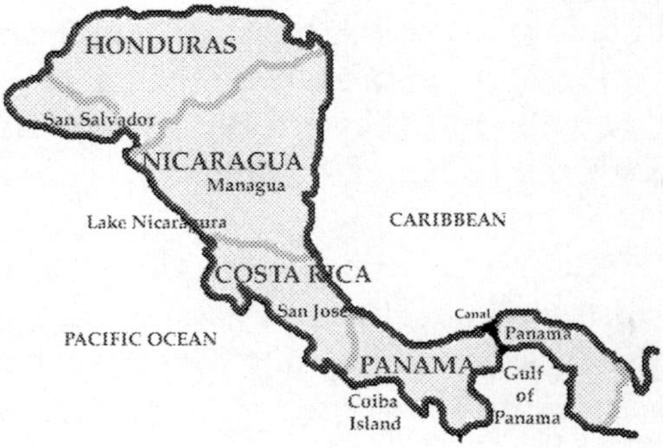


During his time off Chief Engineer Scottish Bill paces Monkey Island in his shorts and sandals; he told me he has spent time on the big container boats and he enjoys it. This ship carries six hundred and seventy containers along with all the other cargo, but big Box Boats, as they are known in the business, carry three thousand to five thousand containers and there are plans to build ships to carry eight thousand containers, to match the giant tankers and bulk carriers in sheer size and capacity. Scottish Bill loves his job, delights in the power of the machinery he controls, and is not daunted by the temperature in the engine room which often reaches 58 degrees centigrade.

**Friday 14th November** All clouds have disappeared and we should have a sunny passage through the Canal. We saw land far away to port, the northern coast of Panama, and we headed towards it, made a heading correction opposite Isla Grande, and then sailed along it some four miles from it. Our speed had fallen to thirteen knots from our average of fifteen, River Tweed was taking the Caribbean Anti-Current head on, the big diesels changed note and were like a pair of pedigree Suffolk Punches, understanding and making that extra effort demanded of them. By mid-morning we approached the port of Christobal and could see the long Western Breakwater, signifying the entrance to the Canal, and some twelve ships anchored just off it.

Standing on the back of the bridge and hardly daring to breathe, I watched the scene. There was constant talk with Christobal Signal ashore, Captain Geoffrey had switched engine room control to bridge control and we slowed to less than five knots. Christobal Signal asked him if he wanted a pilot to guide River Tweed to its agreed anchorage and he declined, turning to say to us that he had no intention of wasting seven hundred dollars and he would sail unaided to the anchorage point, equidistant from the Western Breakwater and a red tanker with a bright blue funnel. They asked what was River Tweed's draught, and he told them that it was twenty eight feet for'ard and thirty feet aft, as an afterthought he changed the clutch from automatic to hydraulic, saying that depth readings at Panama could not always be relied upon, and the last thing that he wanted was a damaged propeller entering the Canal. It seems that we shall now go through the Canal at night, and that we will follow the red tanker through, and are third in line, which pleased Captain Geoffrey, because there was quite a gang-up of ships, though it had to be remembered that Christobal is a port in its own right, and some of these ships were waiting for berths rather than the Canal.

After three hours anchored in the port of Christobal during which a cook and a crew member were disembarked to fly back to Poland to join another ship and were replaced, we very slowly followed the red tanker just ahead of us across Limon Bay toward the three Gatun Locks, which are one hundred and eight feet wide. We passed between two lines of buoys, green to port, red to starboard, and just before the locks twenty men climbed aboard from a pilot boat; these were the mule workers who would attach the hawsers from the six mules, electrically powered engines on each side of the lock which gently pull the ships and keep them straight. These engines run on rails and have a worm and cog system to drive them along the flat, and also up to the level of the next lock.

The ships use their own power to get the lock water past them, fresh water from Gatun Lake, artificially formed by dams on the Chagres River. After negotiating the locks we crossed Gatun Lake which took two hours, and entered Gaillard Cut, named after the French engineer who supervised the building of it.

At this point the ship had been lifted more than eighty feet by the Gatun Locks, and in full moonlight we slowly sailed along the Cut, five hundred feet wide and thirty nine feet deep, for eight miles, with jungle to port and terraced cliffs of rock and shale to starboard, where much work was going on with heavy earth-moving equipment, both to widen the channel and to deal with slides which have occurred on and off since it was built. At this point I tried to take in the magnitude of this engineering feat, the building of the whole Canal against tropical disease and with hitherto untried technology. Although Charles I of Spain ordered the first survey of a canal through the Isthmus of Panama in the 1530's, nothing happened for three hundred years until the French attempted, over a period of twenty years, to build a canal, but death and disease and shortage of money stopped this, and it was not until 1903 that Panama and the United States signed a treaty by which the United States agreed to construct the Canal across the Isthmus, and the French Canal Company was bought out.

It took ten years to build the Canal and over three hundred million dollars. It was not only the engineering problems but the suppression and treatment of disease which daunted the Americans, and almost brought about abandonment. The project involved digging through the Continental Divide, building the biggest dam ever built up until then, and designing and creating the biggest locks ever contemplated with the biggest lock gates. Over the years the Americans have gradually released control to Panama.

The Panama Canal Commission which was an agency of the American government would operate the Canal for twenty years commencing in October 1979, and thereafter on December 31st 1999 the Canal will be entirely handed over to Panama. Since the Canal was first opened in August 1914 the score of ships which have passed through is more than seven hundred thousand, and the time of transit does not alter from the original eight hours port to port, Christobal to Balboa.

The whole scene was utterly fascinating. There were lights of different colour every ten yards along both sides of the Gaillard Cut. Purser Alec brought three bottles of bubbly and glasses up to Monkey Island, and it was a very pleasant midnight deck party in quite unique surroundings. On Gatun Lake and in the Cut we were at the highest level of the Panama Canal, and we went down through the single Pedro Miguel Lock onto Miraflores Lake, and after a short sail we made the final descent to the port of Balboa through the two Miraflores Locks, and ahead we could see the Bridge of the Americas, which takes the Inter-American Highway through Balboa to Panama City a few miles further on. We passed under the impressive bridge and anchored out in the Bay of Panama.

In eight hours we had sailed the forty-three miles from the Atlantic to the Pacific, which is five metres lower, through six locks which had raised and lowered us eighty-five feet, had gone across a lake and through a long narrow Cut in the creation of which rivers were dammed and mountains moved. We had squeezed by other big ships passing in the night, so close that you could spit on their decks in the locks. The whole scene was lit by coloured and floodlights, and high above the full moon was the brightest and best of all of them, and knew it.

When we finally passed under the Bridge of the Americas the heavens opened and the tropical rain obscured everything, it was nature's way of bringing down the curtain on the scene of one of the finest of man's achievements, considered by historians to be on a par with the building of the pyramids, a final curtain of tears perhaps for all the people, twenty five thousand of them, who paid for it with their lives, through injury, malaria, dysentery, typhoid, cholera and, most of all, yellow fever.

**Saturday 15th November** I went early up to Monkey Island and took pictures of Panama City sprawling away to the south, and also of the Bridge of the Americas to the north, which I was unable to do last night because of the rain. As soon as I had used the camera this morning the rain lashed down again. It was very hot and humid indeed, much like Papua New Guinea when we were there in 1990 and discovered that the best way to combat high humidity was to quaff two glasses of ice-cold champagne in quick succession.

The languid pace of refuelling kept us anchored in the Bay of Panama, and it was past noon before we finally got under way and headed out into the vast Pacific. During bunkering there were three men on the flat one hundred foot long fuel barge and two on the powerful two-funnelled tug that brought it alongside. The top of the barge was covered with snaking red and blue pipes like the top of a giant placenta, and gate valves with yellow, red and green wheels on them; one of the men occasionally turned one of these, but the others spent their time sitting on the side fishing for sardines. I was surprised that they were not smoking.

It seemed now that we had fallen into one of time's bottomless ravines. The twenty or so ships anchored in the bay all swung round sedately with the currents in unison, as if Formation Dancing. Looking way across the bay through binoculars at the Bridge of the Americas, the timelessness of this ship appeared in sharp contrast to the obvious traffic snarl-up on the bridge, you could almost see the gnashing of the dentures. It was like looking at the Severn Bridge from a safe distance during extensive repairs, on a Saturday when Wales were playing England at Cardiff, with just over an hour to kick-off.

*The Miraflores Locks, Panama Canal, start of the final descent to Balboa on the Pacific Ocean.*

# Chapter 3

## Pacific Ocean

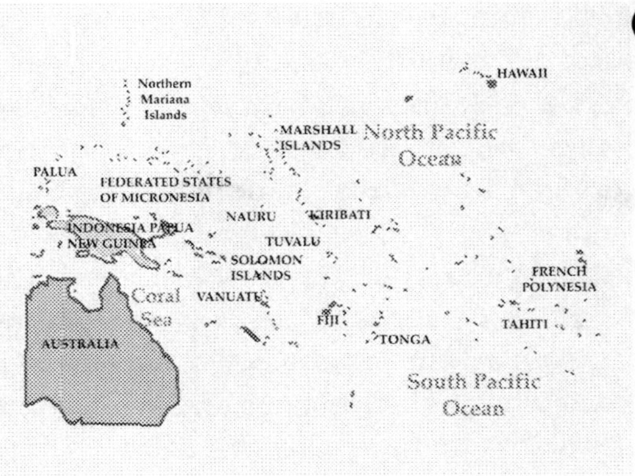


**Sunday 16th November** Painful pangs of nostalgia gripped me this morning, when five frigates appeared high above the ship. I remembered how these large birds with their forked tails fascinated us when first we saw them on Bird Island in the Seychelles and Petit St. Vincent in the Grenadines, the way they hover so high in the sky their wings seeming absolutely still and then their dive like Stukas on birds below, making them release their fish which they catch before the fish hit the water. They did not linger long before flying away.

Captain Geoffrey was very angry today because he had just discovered that the telephone in the office on the bridge could be used at any time and does not record any details and one or two of the crew have been using it. He says that he will have to answer to the owners for all such things, he has now removed the 'phone from the bridge and put it in his cabin. Captain Geoffrey is always talking about money, and I think he may be a mean man, tighter perhaps than a crab's arse, and that, as you know, is water-tight.

There was heavy rain all afternoon driving into the port side of the ship, the visibility was down to less than a mile and when Captain Geoffrey came up to the bridge he reprimanded the two Officers in front of myself for not putting the ship on stand-by; this is done when visibility drops below two miles.

A large black booby found us and flew just above the mast in the bow. Another appeared with a very young bird, and got it to perch on the cross piece of the mast, it was little more than a chick. Their swoops and sweeps and seaskims looking for fish were quite glorious to watch, and their fixed wing dives were breathtaking.

Around teatime a school of about twenty dolphins wheeled their way from port to starboard across the bow and vanished into the rain, which was whipping the surface of the sea into a foam. I stayed on the bridge until dinner watching and thinking my thoughts. In an unexpected way staring at the sea, the rhythmic movements of the ship and the complete absence of any need to consider time, brought a feeling of peace and that is what I have been searching for since I lost my love. Time ahead is the last thing I need more of, and I have embarked upon this voyage in an effort to avoid having to think about it. I just want to dwell upon the long past times of angel thoughts and sweet imaginings, when anything was possible because we had each other.

I spent an hour this evening talking to Chief Engineer Scottish Bill on the wing of the bridge. He is friendly and always willing to discuss his work, his life at sea, his family, and when I said earlier that I thought he was lonely I now know that it is because he loves his wife and children and hates being away from them; tonight he told me that his eighteen year old daughter has learning difficulties. He does a four month voyage and then has two months' leave and sticks rigidly to this, never willing to sacrifice leave to the demands of his employers.

Bill talked at length to me about the engines of cargo ships. He attributed the fact that engines on these River Line ships often had problems was due to the owners opting for cheaper inferior fuel to cut costs, and the poor servicing during Russian ownership; the engines themselves were reasonably reliable, though with fourteen cylinders moving at five hundred revolutions per minute, they were much less efficient than the modern engines in the big supertankers and container ships.

The engines in the River Line ships are two in number, each weighing sixty-four tons, whereas the engine in the modern giant tankers and bulk carriers is single, has eight cylinders, each cylinder one metre in diameter moving at the slower rate of ninety revolutions per minute, with a shorter stroke; more efficient with less wear and tear. The fact that they are single means that there is one shaft and one enormous propeller of fixed pitch, no clutch and no variable pitch mechanism to go wrong. I asked what would happen if the propeller was fouled with no facility to switch from mechanical to hydraulic drive in shallower waters, and he said that the engines were strong enough to take the shock and it was usually the propeller blades that fractured.

Having been fascinated since boyhood by ships and their engines I found this conversation very valuable. I was in fields where I knew not the flowers, but Scottish Bill respected my interest and my ignorance and I left the bridge feeling that we had more to discuss, and that he would be most happy to do so.

**Monday 17th November** The baby booby was still on his perch on the foremast and now has been joined by another. It appears that boobies often join the ship hereabouts because the Archipelago del Colon, the Galapagos Islands, are one hundred miles to port and this also explained the sudden appearance of several turtles, some basking in the sun, some swimming with the ship.

In the early hours of the morning we passed the tiny Isla del Coco out of sight forty miles to starboard, two miles by four miles, it is part of Costa Rica. It is infested with mosquitoes and red ants, and the plentiful fish around it bring many sharks; a dangerous speck in the Pacific, best not visited.

We have made a veer to the south west and are now on a heading of 250 degrees and should soon pick up the South Equatorial Current, which will increase our speed by up to two knots, across the Colon Ridge. We shall pass over Paramount Seamount, a mountain pinnacle only one hundred and fifty metres beneath us, and much further on we shall sail over the vast undersea area of the Galapagos Fracture Zone. The imagination boggles at the presence far below the ocean of this whole world of mountains and rifts and ravines, and the thought that once in time much of it may have been above the water.

The clouds of yesterday have all but disappeared, leaving just a few pledgets of cotton wool behind, and the sea is dead calm, so that we seem to be sailing over a rimless vat of bright blue milk. By nightfall the sky was absolutely clear and when I went up to Monkey Island before going to bed the moon was late on parade, perhaps exhausted by his efforts to show us the Panama Canal. The stars took their chance like extras suddenly given centre stage, stardom for the stars themselves. I cannot remember ever seeing such a crowded sky. There did not seem to be parking space for one more star, no lay-by for one more passing planet, shooting stars simply waved on. I felt that if I had a broom with a long enough handle,

I could sweep some of those diamonds from that heavenly ceiling and harvest them right there on the deck.

**Tuesday 18th November** It was announced this morning that at 10 a.m. they would start chipping rust from the aft decks where we sunbathe, with a view to re-paint. Our cabins are immediately beneath and the noise is unbelievable; there are two big sanders going, chippers, heavy hammers, all we lack is a couple of pneumatic drills. Even on the enclosed bridge, officers are wearing ear-muffs. I am sure that they can hear us on Tahiti three thousand miles away. Attempts to ascertain how long this work will take are met with hollow laughter. At one point early on there was the sound of giants playing 'toss the girder'.

I have spent some time this morning in the library and scanned the one hundred videos and the four shelves of books. I have taken the video 'Gallipoli' for tonight, having missed this at home. I did a Battlefield tour there in April and the film was often referred to. It is of special interest because my father survived the campaign as a Medical Officer and discussion of it filled much of my boyhood in the 1920's. I also saw a collection of six videos covering the history of the Pacific War, much of which was fought on and around the islands we shall call at; they should keep me occupied for a while.

By early afternoon they had finished de-rusting one deck and applied red primer; tomorrow morning they will complete the job with a coat of green paint. This is done on every voyage; there is plenty of rust elsewhere on River Tweed and I wondered whether they will manage to refurbish the whole superstructure before we get back to Le Havre.

We now have five little boobies on the foremast, and one can sit for hours watching the adults swoop down and grab a flying fish from time to time and take it up to the open beaks on the mast, more often than not they fail to get the fish. Another school of dolphins appeared today one hundred yards from the ship on the port beam, and unlike the previous school they treated us to a delightful exhibition of what they could do. There were upward leaps, backward twists, and double salkos of which Torville and Dean would have been envious.

At the end of this day, the nineteenth of the voyage, I have some observations to make concerning Captain Geoffrey. When we came aboard in Dunkirk and had a small party in the passenger lounge, and met Captain Geoffrey for the first time, he seemed an efficient professional man, but I do not remember his saying to us, and that was the time to do so, that he was glad to have us aboard. I realised that we were quite ancillary to the purpose of the voyage, but a word of welcome then would have been much appreciated, for some of us had no real idea of what we had opted for. Since then he has not at any time said or indicated that he is glad to have us aboard, and for all we know he is not.

I spend many hours on the bridge minding my own business and listening to the conversation of the Officers. Often late at night Captain Geoffrey holds court up there, and I hear of his experiences as a Master in the Merchant Navy, and the discussion is depressingly one way, but perhaps that is the norm for Captains at sea. As a student of human nature I am very interested in Captain Geoffrey, not because in our present situation he is in total command, but because I think he is a complex character. I have heard him reprimand his Junior Officers in a way that reminded me of the schoolmasters of my youth. I would like to think he is a fair man and perhaps he is, but I have no way of knowing, and I have doubts.

I have not at any time during the nineteen days of this voyage had any indication so far that he has the slightest interest in the passengers and their lives, though he is always ready to talk to us about the technicalities of running a ship such as this. He may be an efficient Captain and there may be nobody better in the Merchant Navy when it comes to getting a ship like this and its cargo round the world, but I know that he is an unclubbable man and that is unfortunate.

My family, bless them, appreciating that this voyage was big for me and much a leap into the unknown, have tried to communicate with me by fax and e-mail, and every message comes to me via Captain Geoffrey, who holds every rein when it comes to communication between the ship and the outside world. There is no Radio Officer, he does it all, and he has made me feel that the efforts of my family to get messages through to me are somewhat of a nuisance.

I suppose that my feelings were crystallised this morning when Captain Geoffrey, in the presence of two other Officers, handed me a piece of paper which recorded three attempts by my son to get a fax to me in the early hours of the morning. My son is very aware of world-wide time changes and I took it much amiss when Captain Geoffrey asked me if he had ever studied geography at school. I regretted that the Captain had been disturbed in the night, but this would not have occurred had he been able to delegate to another Officer. The fact that there was a delay in fax transmission from U.K. was not my son's fault, nor mine and I have never been prepared to tolerate sarcasm, either from schoolmasters, medical teachers or for that matter from Sea Captains, with or without the sneer.

I have a strong feeling that after thirty-nine years at sea, Captain Geoffrey is overdue for retirement, and perhaps he should work out the rest of his time on tankers and such like without the hassle of passengers; however, we have over three months to go on this voyage and things could get interesting. I have paid plenty to come on this ship and intend to use every communication facility available, for which I gladly accept the cost, without comment from the Captain.

I think that Captain Geoffrey's main problem is his unfortunate lack of charm, and if you graft onto that a lack of interest in other people and an absence of real humour in a closed-up man who cannot show warmth, you would have the answer to the whole situation. Having said that, Captain Geoffrey is in ultimate control of the lives of thirty-six people. The laws of seafaring are immutable, the Captain calls all the shots and takes the blame if things go wrong, but I blissfully have nothing to lose; I have never felt less important than I do now, not only to Captain Geoffrey, and that is quite an achievement on his part, and quite a realisation for me.

**Wednesday 19th November** We crossed the equator at 5 a.m., latitude 0 degrees, longitude 100.5 degrees, having sailed fourteen hundred miles from Panama and with two thousand eight hundred miles to go to Tahiti. There is to be a special 'Crossing the Line' buffet supper on the bridge tonight with, I hope, free booze.

They have now brought out a new instrument of torture to remove the rust on the deck; it has six metal rods sticking out of the end of it which rotate at high speed. You feel as if you had a Gatling gun two feet above your head. What this is doing to my already diminishing auditory acuity can only be guessed at. I must find out whether I should sue River Line or just Captain Geoffrey, who has probably arranged this awful racket to pay me out for being woken in the night by my son's attempts to fax me, I think I will go for Captain Geoffrey.

Just before lunch a shark was spotted on the starboard bow about eight feet long and basking in the hot sun. During the afternoon Captain Geoffrey showed me a message which he had received from a Medical Officer in Mexico asking for help with regard to an Indian crewman on a ship plying between Nigeria and Philadelphia, who had suffered a four hundred volt electric shock, was partially conscious and partially paralysed, could not speak and was not passing urine. This was an S.O.S. to all ships anywhere near, but River Tweed was much too far away to be of any help. The problem with electric shocks of that nature is damage to the heart in the first place, and then the kidneys through muscle proteins blocking the filtration system, which can lead to renal failure. We will never know what happened to that unfortunate man.

The buffet supper on the bridge deck was attended by all those Officers not on duty and the five passengers; plenty of food and cold beer in the warm Pacific night. I had another long talk with Chief Engineer Scottish Bill and he told me about the problems with his daughter who was born with a cleft palate, and deafness which they did not discover until she reached the age of six as a result of which her education has been immensely difficult. Bill is aged 50 and he very much hopes that he will be able to bring his wife on one of these voyages round the world before he retires. We discussed the question of spares should something go very wrong with the engines, and he said that there was a store of spares in Papua New Guinea maintained by River Line, and all the ships of the line carried spares, so that items could always be left in a port by one ship for the aftercoming one. Failing all else the needed spares could be flown out from the U.K. With Purser Alec I also discussed waste disposal, and it appears that all waste is incinerated as we go, and the only residual problem may be oil sludge, and this is off loaded onto road tankers in ports like Singapore and Auckland.

The party on deck went on for a long time, but I left early and went up to Monkey Island and stood by the rail in the wind of the ocean night. Ever since I lost my love I have found social gatherings painful and beat a retreat whenever I can, and surreptitiously, because lonely people can be such a bore to others still enjoying life.

**Thursday 20th November** There was a violent juddering and clanking in the early hours of the morning, and we seemed to grind almost to a halt. At breakfast we learned that a fuel pump had failed in the port engine, which had been closed down. We proceeded on the starboard engine only at nine knots which seemed very slow after the steady sixteen that we had averaged, with the help of the Southern Equatorial Current, over the previous two days. By mid-morning we had the port engine back, and speed gradually increased from seven knots to fourteen by lunchtime. We should be a little late arriving at Papeete, but these ships seem able to make up for lost time in a curious way.

Our little colony of boobies is still with us but now the young birds are accompanying the adults on fishing trips, learning to swoop and skim at the right moment to grab a flying fish. There are black boobies, light brown boobies with white heads and beaks of Cambridge blue, and also white ones with yellow beaks and the leading edge of the wings and the tips jet black. For over two days they have been the only other living things, together with the fish, that we have seen since the last ship was sighted early on Tuesday morning, far away on the port horizon. There was a high wind today blowing from the south west, and the silky calm of the ocean of the last two days, when neither ruck, rumple, ruff nor rivel disturbed the surface, has been replaced by nodding and rearing white horses, and the wind-whipped spray from their manes lashes the containers down on the main deck.

Three thousand metres beneath the waves the East Pacific Rise stretched across the sea-bed from south to north for a thousand miles and more, and if you could travel along it I wondered what wrecks you would see; there must be the graves of countless ships and men down there. Just before dinner this evening we passed the halfway point of this Pacific Ocean leg of the voyage. We now have two thousand two hundred miles ahead of us to Tahiti, with an expected time of arrival in the port of Papeete of twelve noon on the 27th November, and then we will have completed the first month of this four month voyage, all of it at sea. I am much looking forward to getting among those lovely islands of the South Pacific again, than which we saw nothing more exotically beautiful in all the years of our world-wide travels.

I had a long and interesting talk with Eric at dinner about past American Presidents. He gave a very fair and objective view of them all since Roosevelt, whom he admired immensely, although I believe him to be a Republican at heart. Sea voyages like this give plenty of opportunity to explore the minds of others if you wish, and I valued this conversation with Eric who himself is interested in the Old Country, there is nothing isolationist about him and I am glad to have met him.

**Friday 21st November** A day without incident except for the fortnightly muster with life jackets on. The temperature of the air and sea was the same today, 28 degrees centigrade and the humidity seems high, but the air conditioning is now working fully in the cabins and this makes for comfort.

I have begun a small list of things I must buy in Papeete. It is still not certain how long we will spend there, although the load for shedding is known much depends on time of arrival, availability of dock gangs and presumably there will be containers and other merchandise to pick up.

**Saturday 22nd November** I met Second Engineer Bright Eyed Bearded Henry after breakfast and joked that River Tweed appeared to be moving well now and his reply was 'Is she?'. There have obviously been major problems down in the engine room about which we are not told, it makes you wonder whether these River Line ships should have more frequent refits. At the moment we are half limping and the ship that should be a month ahead of us has also slowed down and is a week late. The ships leave U.K. at monthly intervals and ply round and round the world until something goes sufficiently wrong with one of them to compel the owners to take it out of service for a while. They are now more than fourteen years old and River Line expect at least thirty years work from them; I am not convinced that enough money is being spent on their upkeep. With fifteen hundred miles to go before Tahiti I do not fancy having to get out and push.

I have finished reading Nelson Mandela's autobiography, in which his strength is revealed as mind-blowing, I have been to Robben Island and I stood in Mandela's tiny cell, which was his world for so long. I stood in the exercise yard, surrounded by twenty foot walls and I saw the small garden by the wall wherein he buried the journal he kept. I went to the quarry where he broke stones for year upon year. His will to see the end of apartheid is unbelievable as is his lack of bitterness.

I have now started 'Wild Swans' by Jung Chang. I have put off reading this book for three years because it was the last book that Esmé ever read. Her first stroke took away her ability to read until, quite suddenly when lying on a sun bed under a casuarina tree on the beach at Galley Bay on Antigua, one year later, she told me how much she was enjoying 'Wild Swans', and she read all six hundred and seventy-six pages; always fascinated by China she loved it. Until now I have felt unable to read it myself, but now I must, because she told me that I would love it too. I can hear her describing the book as she read it, and remember her delight that she could read again. It was such a cruelly brief reprieve of her sentence, one of the more sickening mockeries of providence, a privilege given, a right restored, and then so swiftly and hurtfully withdrawn, as if she did not deserve it. I shall read this book with plangent sentiment.

**Sunday 23rd November** They appear to have sorted out the problems down in the engine room, and for the past twenty-four hours we have averaged sixteen knots which is good for this ship. This will bring forward our expected time of arrival at Papeete to 6.30 a.m. on Thursday 27th November, and should please Captain Geoffrey, if anything ever can.

In conversation on the bridge this afternoon with Tall Dark Dem'yan, of whom I have become very fond, I learned that River Line got these ships dirt cheap. Chief Officer Jack, who is also most keen that the passengers should feel at home on the ship, and enjoy everything, said that we must be very bored by now with the endless ocean, especially because, unlike him, we have no daily tasks to perform. This is his first 'deep water' voyage for years because he has been on Cruise ships. He went through the cargo lists with me and I kept looking at the door to make sure that Captain Geoffrey was not approaching, because I am sure that I was not supposed to see them.

We have a very varied cargo, many vehicles, holds full of steel frames, tubes and girders, much in the way of hazardous cargo like aerosols, oxidising agents and large gas cylinders. There are containers full of cosmetics, toiletries, detergents, alcohol, paté, and they have a lot of chocolate on board. Much of this has to be kept at an even temperature, with controlled humidity. The air temperature remained at twenty-eight degrees centigrade, the sea temperature twenty-five degrees centigrade and we worked out a humidity calculation which came to eighty-eight percent. They worry more about humidity than temperature with much of this cargo.

The air conditioning does its best in the cabins, but has given up on the bridge and the Officers on watch pour with sweat. Chief Officer Jack is looking forward to sailing into Madang, Papua New Guinea, because he very well remembers the last time he was there. He was deep in the hold when they ran aground right across the end of the little airport's runway, the airport had to be closed and it took three days to refloat the ship. I too remember Madang airport, because it was the only place in seventeen years of travel where our bags went astray, and we had to exist in the shirts and shorts we stood up in for three days.

Jack raised the question of the roll of the ship. As far as I was concerned there had never been more than a comfortable roll across the two biggest oceans of the world on this voyage so far. He said that the lower the centre of gravity of the ship when the heavy load is in the lowest holds what is known as the Calculated Righting Lever is large and this makes for a faster correction of the roll. When the weight of the cargo is higher on the ship the Righting Lever is small and the ship rolls more gently. This was what I would have guessed, that the lower the centre of gravity the more stable the ship and the smaller the Righting Lever, the greater is the likelihood of a capsize.

I look forward to many more talks with Chief Officer Jack, who incidentally already holds a Master's Ticket and who will only remain with River Line if they offer him a Captaincy. He says that there is no problem at all with regard to jobs and he is solely concerned with doing the right thing as far as his wife and three children are concerned, the shorter ferry and cruise jobs would probably be best for them all, and the pay is just as good as for the long round the world voyages. He has already functioned as Captain on the Isle of Wight ferries.

We went up to Monkey Island for a final look at the night; the moon was still busy elsewhere, and the stellar show was quite magnificent. Back in the cabin I ended another day and began another night with Beethoven's Third and Eighth Symphonies.

**Monday 24th November** The last few weeks with nothing very much to see and do have given me the opportunity to observe more closely my four fellow passengers, and by far the most interesting is Anthony; big, bearded, booming and overbearing he was well cast as a school master. Now early retired at fifty-two, since his coronary thrombosis when he gave up cigarettes, he has concentrated on over-eating to such an extent that in the dining saloon his stomach seems to sit down some way ahead of him. Not one square millimetre of plate may be served uncovered, every dish within sight must be sampled, and yesterday at lunch he spied a bowl of Russian salad after he had downed his apple and blackcurrant pie, so he had a mound of that. He has a short rest between courses when he leans back and places his arms along the arms of the chair, which gives his stomach a little more space to breathe, which it does, quite often. It is like having three meals a day sitting at table with Henry VIII. I have been in the presence of some big eaters in my time, but I think

Anthony is by some way the King of the Trough. The boredom of long spells on the open sea leads to a risk of overeating, and the Captain, Purser and Stewardesses are all overweight to some degree. Three square meals a day help to break up the time, and I am being very careful. I said earlier that Anthony seemed hell-bent on suicide and judging by the way he is going on he will not long be disappointed.

I have more time for Eric, a very pleasant elderly man, intelligent and interested in world events, though like all Americans he really considers that U.S.A. is the epicentre of all human life and I remembered Esmé asking why Americans assume that everybody would wish to live in America if they had to move from their own countries. Eric and I share a similar sense of humour. Tina, his second wife, is ten years younger and also pleasant with some wit thrown in. She and Eric firmly subscribe to the American view that only those who work should receive the spoils, and everybody can work if they wish. I like Eric and Tina and could have had worse shipmates than them.

Jane, Anthony's partner, is in her forties, she is short and dark and has a small pot, not surprising since she lives with Anthony. She has a sense of humour and is rather more intelligent than her bearded Boom Boom; she is a teacher and seems to be able to take long sabbaticals whenever she wishes. We live like a family and that will amaze my children and my friends. I knew that this voyage would provide a different way of life for a while, which was why I set out, but sometimes when I look at what I have decided to do, I surprise myself. I never doubted that I had to change my surroundings for a while or I would have lost my mind; some of my friends, and most certainly my wife, would tell me that by even thinking of doing what I am now doing means that I already have.

When you lose your love you are at once denied the chance of ever discussing that unique loss, the effect of it, with the one person who might help you to cope with the monumental task of trying to live alone.

Two disinterested dolphins passed by on the port side without so much as lifting their heads from the sea to look at us and other than an odd lone seabird, and the flying fish, they are the only living things we have seen since the boobies left us four days ago. This evening we are seven hundred and eighty miles from Tahiti and are now making good time, having averaged sixteen knots for the last two days. The first land we should see will be the coral atolls of the Tuamotu Archipeligo called the Low or Dangerous Archipelago, which caused Robert Louis Stevenson considerable anxiety when he sailed through in the small schooner Casco in 1889; over seventy islands scattered over hundreds of square miles of the eastern Pacific. Most of them rise barely twenty feet above the sea, all ringed by shallow coral reefs, and this part of French Polynesia has been a veritable cemetery for ships over the centuries.

Rangiroa is the best known of the Tuamotus, and we much wanted to fly from Tahiti and spend a night there but could not fit it into our schedule ten years ago. The lagoon at Rangiroa is over forty miles long and nearly fifteen miles wide and it is where the famous South Seas black pearl is found. If what we hear about global warming is true, these lovely little coral atolls, sunblest Edens all, where the surf sighs on the coral and whispers on virgin sands of bridal whiteness and fine as flour miller's dust, face inevitable submersion during the next century.

**Tuesday 25th November** Late last night there was an S.O.S. from a ship in trouble off the coast of Portugal and sinking. This morning we heard that it had sunk but there was no information about loss of life and I remembered that our own passage across the Bay of Biscay was relatively trouble free.

Late tonight we passed the Iles des Desappointement, Napuka and Puka Puka on latitude 14, longitude 141. They were discovered in 1765 by Admiral John Byron on H.M.S. Dolphin, with H.M.S. Tamar in support. They are the northernmost atolls of the Tuamotu archipelago, but though we passed within a few miles of Napuka all we saw were three or four flickering lights which quickly faded. Presumably the name was given to this group of islands by some frustrated ancient mariner who thought that he had found the great Southland, which Ptolemy first suggested stretched right across the South Pacific and which also fascinated Captain Cook, who could not rest until he found it.

We have been warned of storms ahead, a cyclone between the Tuamotos and Tahiti. We should catch the edge of it and it will be an interesting new experience.

**Wednesday 26th November** Last night we had inflicted upon us a two hour video of the wedding of Fat Mona to Purser Alec which occurred just before we sailed. This had been threatened for some time, but Mona has suffered almost unrelieved mal de mer since the Bay of Biscay. Poor little thing, she started out from Dunkirk so full of the joys of life and wife, giggling and cackling without cease, you only had to open your mouth to get her going. I felt that if I had told her that her mother had just dropped dead she would have rolled off her sun lounger in helpless mirth. This happy scene came to a sudden end with the sea sickness, and she did not appear for days on end.

She joined us occasionally but never for long, I spoke in sympathy to Alec and he said that it was all in the mind, but quite a lot of it was on the deck, (I nearly slipped up in it), and also over the side. Mona felt a little less sick up on Monkey Island and as she hauled herself up and down the ladder, she looked like a pregnant beach ball with vestigial limbs. I felt so sorry for them both and hoped very much that the pregnant state played no part in her problem. Returning to the video, we started with the grooming and dressing of Mona, and finished with the happy departure in the usual car festooned with tin cans. When she arrived at the church and got out of the car with difficulty, Mona knocked her head dress off and it fell into the gutter, but was happily restored and she entered the church rotund and radiant. Before he left for the church Alec was shown fortifying himself for the ordeal ahead with a plate of thick ham sandwiches; Mona said that had she known that he had done that she would have been worried to death that he would fart in the aisle.

At the altar they presented an unusual picture, Mona four foot eleven and thirteen stone in bulging white, every button and zip taking the strain most nobly, with an imitation tiara on her head, looked like an overblown duck's egg wrapped in muslin, with a silver ring on the top of it. Alec, all six foot seven and nineteen stone of him resplendent in the Merchant Navy Officers' uniform, with buttons bright and with his hat correctly under his right arm, was a fine figure of a man. I have said before that their conjugation fuelled the imagination.

They are lovely genuine people and the salt of the earth, and I hoped that the gentler seas of the south will allow Mona a complete recovery, though if this comes about the peace and tranquillity of the South Sea Islands will be rudely shattered, and the birds sent screaming, when I get Mona going again on the sun deck. After that video last night I suggested that tonight we should have another look at 'Four Weddings and a Funeral', so as not to lose the nuptial mood.

Today we shall sail through the Passe de Fakarava between the island of that name where Robert Louis Stevenson and his family settled for a while in 1886, and Toau. The Passe is nine miles wide and five hundred metres deep, and we will then have left behind the timeless open ocean and I will be among the little pretty lands that we loved so much. The cyclone has edged away to the south and by being a day late we have missed it. We heard that considerable damage had been caused on some smaller islands and the schools were closed on Tahiti. It has now been downgraded to tropical storm anyway, but I am sorry to have missed it; First Officer Jack was not sorry because this ship does not behave well in cyclones, and there is hell let loose down in the holds if cargo breaks adrift. This cargo was positioned by the stevedore teams in Dunkirk in whom Jack obviously had no confidence whatever, and remembering their frequent breaks for wine he is probably right.

I stumbled upon a meeting of the others in the passenger lounge after dinner last night. It appeared that a mutiny was afoot, they were dissatisfied with the food since the new chef came aboard in the Panama Canal. They had just had a dinner consisting of thick pea soup, Goa curry with rice, dahl, mango chutney and all the spicy extras, roast lamb, two thick slices, three for Anthony, roast potatoes and carrots, Black Forest Gateau and cheese and biscuits to finish with. I could barely manage just the curry.

As a result of this you had to assume that their problem was quality not quantity. They plan to wait until we get beyond Tahiti and then make an official complaint to Purser Alec, and I am sure that they assume that I shall join them, but they are in for a disappointment. If they were prepared to meet me over Captain Geoffrey's rude way of speaking, general charmlessness, and lack of manners, I would be first to load the blunderbuss and draw the cutlass.

**Thursday 27th November** At 9.30 a.m. I saw through binoculars, seven miles on the port beam, an island with trees, a small atoll called Taiaro and it is worth recording for it is the first land that we had seen since Panama, discovered in 1835 by Captain Fitzroy of H.M.S. Beagle, there are only a handful of residents and it is entirely tree covered with a closed lagoon. Two hours further on we passed another atoll, Kauehi, also discovered by Captain Fitzroy on the same day as Taiaro. One can imagine him planting the flag on Taiaro, having a good long lunch in his cool cabin under the poop deck, and then claiming Kauehi before dinner. I wondered if he was the Fitzroy famous for the Admiral Fitzroy mercury barometer, one of which hung on the wall in my grandfather's surgery and absolutely fascinated me as a boy, although I was forbidden ever to touch it. I am pretty sure that he was.

It is strange how certain things in your early life remain crystallised in your mind; that barometer was one such, another was the framed slogan also on the wall of my grandfather's surgery, in red, blue and gold scroll, advising his patients to 'Praise The Lord And Keep Your Bowels Open'.

My father also had a practice in the Fen Country and had a slogan in his waiting room: 'Worry Not, It May Never Happen'. Had I been a family doctor no doubt I would have followed tradition and displayed something like: 'Don't Bloody Worry Me, I've Got Troubles Of My Own' or somesuch equally redolent of the Hippocratic Oath.

My grandfather and my father were both very careful with money, and living in the times of penny-in-the-slot loos, for a suitable inscription on their tombstones we should have borrowed that well known Fen Country epitaph

'Here I lie broken-hearted
Paid a penny and only farted'.

My grandfather was arguably the most selfish old goat that ever lived. He married a little above himself for money, and drank it away in fair time and died penniless. His wife died in her fifties, presumably in order to get away from him and he drove his only daughter into the arms of a gypsy with disastrous consequences, but we were never allowed to talk about that. Having said that, he was the only grandfather I knew, and the picture of him sitting on an ornate wrought-iron bench in an apple orchard wearing a Panama hat will remain with me forever, and the way he gripped my arm and hurt me, and called me 'Young 'un'. He terrified me. I must have been taken to see him during the winter as well as summer, but he must always have been sitting in that orchard wearing that hat, perhaps covered with snow, for I remember nothing else, except his regular sending to me of cuttings from the Morning Post about cricket. We had that in common across the generations.

There were twenty-odd pubs in the High Street of Swavesey, the Fen village in which he practised, and he did his rounds in a pony and trap, starting at the top end by the church. I should say that in Fen villages the top end was so called because it was two feet six or perhaps two feet four inches higher than the other end. He paid his calls mainly sitting in the trap and shouting, he preferred to get out only at the pubs. After a couple of hours and about half way he would fall asleep, and the horse would wait a while, and then slowly and ever so gently take him home, where the groom would get him into the house. My mother hated him, only allowed him to come to lunch on one Sunday in the year and made him remove his boots before entering the house. When he died at the age of eighty-four she said to me triumphantly, 'There you are you see, I knew the drink would get him in the end'.

Once we get through the Tuamotus, scattered as they are like stepping stones across this part of the Pacific, we shall have a clear run west south west on a heading of 235 degrees to Tahiti, and the expected time of arrival there is now 5.30 a.m. tomorrow morning. The Passe de Fakarava was safely negotiated, we passed the larger island of Fakarava on the port side and then after an hour or so, Toau on the starboard beam. Few of these atolls have populations of more than a few hundred, and through binoculars they are typical tropical paradises with the ocean breaking on long coral reefs enclosing lagoons of the most brilliant blue or green or both, endless beaches of white sand and behind them spinney upon spinney of coconut palms waving in the trade winds. This scene was very much part of our souls over many happy years of travel.

I realised this evening that I had a minor beer crisis, the bond on the ship would be closed while in Papeete and as we were still some ten hours out I asked Purser Alec for a 'case just in case'. He had already completed his paper work and locked up the booze, so I told him not to bother. He has just delivered a case to the cabin because he was worried that stocking up in Papeete would cost me a fortune, and I seem to remember that he is right, bless him.

I am going to miss some people at the end of this long voyage and one of them most certainly will be Purser Alec along with Engineers Scottish Bill and Bright Eyed Bearded Henry, Chief Officer Jack, not to mention young Trinity House Paul, our upwardly mobile cadet, who has a fine sense of humour, which is quite unappreciated by Captain Geoffrey, whom I shall not miss at all.

Up on the bridge last thing Chief Officer Jack was discussing large ships, bulk carriers and likewise. His experience on these ships was on the Sir Alexander Glenn, one hundred and eighty thousand tons dead weight, sister ship of the ill-fated Derbyshire which sank in a few minutes with no survivors in the North Pacific. They were mixed bulk carriers, and the Sir Alexander Glenn carried one hundred thousand tons of tapioca on the voyage when Jack was aboard. I tried to imagine one hundred thousand tons of tapioca in one place and failed.

The Derbyshire sank in 1978 but was only found five years ago, she split into two parts the long main cargo section, and the short stern section comprising engine room and crew quarters and superstructure, and Jack said that this was entirely due to the fact that in construction the longitudinal beams stopped short of the engine room bulkhead. There were other longitudinal beams which traversed the engine room, but they were not continuous with those of the forward part of the ship, and this was where the fracture occurred. After this disaster, on the Sir Alexander Glenn the beams had to be inspected every week for cracks, a dreadful uncomfortable crawl into the very skeleton of the ship, which befell to Jack who was then a junior officer. During the construction of the Derbyshire and her five sister-ships, welders were paid by distance covered and not by time, and they tended to throw loose welding rods into the beam and weld over the top of them.

Of the six ships four have sunk, the last was the Kowloon Bridge, off the coast of Ireland. Jack said that the modern giant tankers of five hundred thousand tons were unlikely to have the same problem as the Derbyshire and her sister-ships, because of the cargo, oil was buoyant, and did not subject the ship to the same strains.

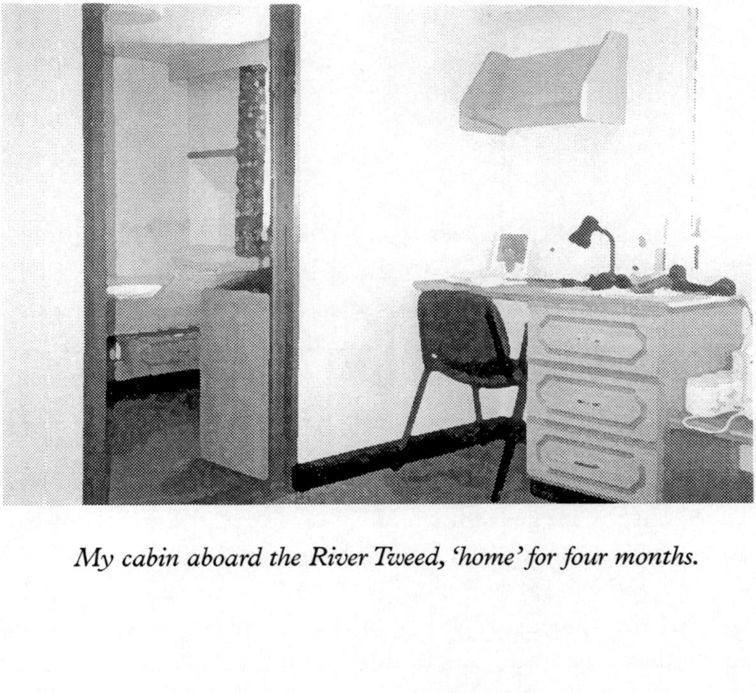

*My cabin aboard the River Tweed, 'home' for four months.*

# Chapter 4

## French Polynesia

**Friday 28th November** We glided past mountainous Moorea at 6 a.m. with the little pilot boat just off the starboard bow watching and guiding, the chick leading the hen. Papeete is a small port and the entry is between two buoys only some fifty yards apart, with the sea breaking on the reef on either side. They must have cut a trench through the coral when they built the harbour, and for much smaller ships. The harbour is only thirty-five feet deep and the bigger ships like River Tweed draw thirty feet, so there was a good deal of sand churned up.

Papeete had not changed, and as we edged gently toward the quay, nudged by a tug, I experienced such an overwhelming surge of sadness, such a tidal wave of wanting and longing that I could scarce control myself. The heavy hatches with which for much of the time I have managed to batten down my grief, suddenly sprang open and there was nothing whatever that I could do.

I spent the day in Papeete which always seems like a busy bustling little metropolis in the middle of nowhere. I found the kiosk on the waterfront where we bought shirts, hand painted to order by the friendly and talented Italian woman; she had gone, and the kiosk now sells unattractive tee-shirts with tasteless illustrations.

It was extremely hot and humid, but the cold draught Hinano Tahitian lager dealt with any problems of overheat, and Papeete has no shortage of bars. Although the ship was berthed just across the water from the centre of the town, you had to walk all round the harbour past the Naval dockyard, the yacht marina and the big ferry terminal for Moorea, and it takes a full fifty minutes. I welcomed the exercise after weeks confined to the ship, but the others went by car, and had I been Anthony I would have done the same; to carry his stomach all the way round the harbour in heat like that would have been too much to contemplate.

On return to the ship I was told that we would depart for Noumea, New Caledonia in the early morning of tomorrow. They were still unloading, and some sixty vehicles, cars and lorries, had emerged from the Ro-Ro just for'ard of the stern like turds from a hippopotamus with a colostomy.

Much of the forward and main decks were clear of containers and presumably more would be loaded on. River Tweed now stood so high in the water that you would think she was in dry dock; much of the hull was now visible and she looked a dirty rusty old girl.

**Saturday 29th November** The others have gone on an early ferry to Moorea and I breakfasted alone with Captain Geoffrey, and by way of conversation I said that I understood that we were now sailing at about 8 p.m. tonight. He asked me curtly who had told me that, and to look at the blackboard on the deck. That ended a conversation stillborn if ever one was, and I vowed not to try again. When I leave at Le Havre, but not before, I shall have the greatest pleasure in telling Captain Geoffrey what I think of his lack of manners, and that I shall make a strong recommendation to the company that he serves the rest of his time on coal barges or, preferably on ships carrying nuclear waste or blue asbestos round and round the world for ever, because nobody will receive it.

I walked into Papeete again for lunch in torrid sun and I do not remember heat such as this when we were previously here. With Rue de Gauguin, Avenue Pomare and Place de Bougainville, with his statue and two guns at his feet pointing at forty-five degrees, Tahiti tries to preserve its history. They had pollarded a row of casuarinas leading to the harbour bridge, and the trees looked strangely mutilated without their attractive fine feathery fronds, like lovely women cruelly shorn of their tresses. In the heat of that sun I wondered why anybody should wish to diminish any available shade.

Sitting in the bar of my choice and well into my second large Hinano beer, I watched the hustle and bustle of downtown lunchtime Papeete, and Les Trucks fascinated me as always. When we first saw these curious buses we thought that they were relics from the past, kept going by constant repair and cannibalisation, old lorries with a large wooden box with seats and windows behind. This is not at all the case, they have modern Mercedes, Daihatsu or Honda fronts, and shining bodies, and I realised that there were factories turning them out all the time, they filled the modern need and the same applies to the becaks of Sumatra, the cyclos of Vietnam, the motorised rickshaws of China, and the jeepneys of Manila in the Phillipines. The wide variety of vehicles and boats that you see as you travel the world, is just as fascinating as the people themselves, and emblematic of them.

There are only two berths in the port of Papeete for bigger ships and River Tweed shared with a large container ship, the Contship Ticino registered in Bremen. Initially they were nose to nose, but Ticino has turned and now presents her backside to River Tweed. Container ships which carry nothing else have the benefit always of a clean cargo, and this is why they appear spruce compared with mixed cargo carriers like River Tweed, the worse for wear behind her pristine Aryan neighbour, like a raddled old tart behind a film star.

They worked late on the unloading, a lot of the steel had been packed wrongly, and some other cargo not intended for Papeete had to be unloaded and reloaded again to get at the steel. River Tweed has much metal aboard and I watched endless crane loads of narrow strips, girders, coils and wire netting placed either directly onto lorries or onto four by two wooden planks on the dockside, to enable the fork- lifts to get beneath them. The daylong noise of the forklifts, tractors, container lifters, cranes and lorries, and the clanking of metal fascinated me and I loved the activity of it all. I shall have plenty of chance of more of it as we work our way round this oceania of the southern world. I went to bed feeling curiously like a lone foreign cell, enclosed within a tissue within an organ; the tissue my fellow travellers, the organ the ship. I was glad when they all went to Moorea for the day.

**Sunday 30th November** We left the dock at 11 a.m. and as we sailed gently across that stretch of water between Tahiti and Moorea so beautifully named the Sea of the Moon, I took a last look at Papeete. I could not see far enough round the headland to port to get a view of the Beachcomber Hotel. I left Tahiti thinking how much I would prefer being in a wooden over-lagoon bungalow at that hotel with the woman I loved, for two weeks, to being four months on this voyage round the world. If wallowing in nostalgia helps to dissipate grief, then I should be well out of it by now; but I am far from that point, and have no reason to suppose that I will ever reach it. Grief is a disease in the truest sense of the term, an ailment for which there is no effective treatment save the passage of time, though fragments of the pain will always remain. Grief follows bereavement like pain follows amputation, and it often makes the inarticulate verbose and the philistine poetic. I was surprised that one of the very first things that I did on getting home from the hospital on the night that Esmé died was sit down and write a poem about the details of her suffering. Many folk, perhaps the majority, prefer to keep the pain of their grief private; from the start of it I have experienced a mighty need to try to share it with a sympathetic audience, but after two years I have learned to expect and accept an empty auditorium.

We waved goodbye to the folk on the top deck of Contship Ticino, as we passed; she too is headed for New Caledonia, so perhaps we shall meet there.

We now have a two thousand four hundred and fifty-nine mile sail to Noumea. We shall pass within fifteen miles of Aitutaki in the Southern Cook Islands, to which we flew in 1987 from Rarotonga to spend a fantastic weekend. It was arguably the most beautiful unspoilt place we saw in all our years of travel; the crater rim of a huge submerged volcano with a lovely atoll attached, it was an idyllic haven of perfect peace.

We have a lively sea, Force 7 wind, and River Tweed has rolled around, enough to have everything skidding around on the floor that you did not have secured. This always has my American companions a little ruffled and even reduces their food intake, though only temporarily. Contship Ticino came up abaft the port beam and passed us at a good eighteen knots compared with our fifteen. She has a German Master and Chief Officer and all the rest of the crew are Filipino; she is bound for Australia after

Noumea while we divert to Auckland. I am surprised how little fraternising there is between ships' crews, information tends to be gleaned from the stevedores, who get to know much about the ships they work on. One of them told Chief Officer Jack that on the large cruise ship which tied up opposite us in Papeete single cabins cost six hundred pounds per day all in, and it was full to the gunwales with Americans cruising round the Society Islands. This piece of information made me warm to dear old River Tweed.

I had a talk with Boom Boom Anthony tonight, he and Jane travel extensively when they can, but she has to start a new job on their return, and this will be the end of far away travel for some time for him. He told me that there was no point in travelling alone; I could only reply that I entirely agreed with him and wondered whatever had happened to tact. As the years pass as a widower I have come to accept that people have to live their own lives quite exclusively, and consideration of the feelings and problems of others, though desirable has no real priority; living is often difficult enough when you have someone to share it with.

**Monday 1st December** We continued to plough our way across what seemed like the bottom of the world, with the help of a Sub-Tropical Current which added no more than 0.5 knots to our speed, but was with us. Anyone contemplating a voyage such as this must have a certain personality, there must be no need for a shape to their day, the only regular happenings are meals. There should be an interest in ships and their workings, and in those who sail them. There should be a love of sky and sea as part of your very self, and an ability to wonder at the timeless beauty of it all; for there will be endless opportunity to feel part of it and no opportunity to feel part of anything else. It is a different loneliness for me, but no more painful than I have known these past three years. There is a blessed oblivion somewhere in that night heaven with its galaxies, and below that tumultuous ocean, and I cannot help thinking that I can reach it before long.

We continued with a Force 7 wind and the roll of River Tweed was 14 degrees. On the bridge deck the sun loungers would slide to and from the rail all the time were they not tethered. Fat Mona now spends much time with us on the deck, and today her sun-lounger broke adrift and bore her to the rail screaming and cackling. I try not to get her going, because I am sure that she will wet herself; all the mattresses are the same pattern, and I might pick hers tomorrow. It is only when you saunter forth from the cloisters of your normal daily life on a trip like this, and mingle with your fellow human beings from rather different cloisters, that you realise what a mixture we all are.

**Tuesday 2nd December** We have pursued a south west course since Dunkirk but now we have turned and are sailing almost due west on a heading 265 degrees. At 8 a.m. we passed Beveridge Reef, just over the starboard horizon. We shall cross the International Date Line tonight at 10 p.m. and will miss out Wednesday and tomorrow for us will be Thursday 4th December. I think that means that I could never have died on Wednesday 3rd December. After breakfast tomorrow we will cross the Tonga Trench, nine thousand metres deep, pass south of the Friendly Islands and our expected time of arrival at Noumea is 10 p.m. on Saturday 6th December; by then we will have sailed eleven thousand one hundred and fifty-nine miles since leaving Dunkirk.

Chief Officer Jack, on the bridge this afternoon showed me the large red handle hanging down in the port wing, the emergency handle to be pulled if there is a man overboard. It ejects a raft and life belt and a smoke signal which is activated by sea water to emit dense clouds of orange smoke, and a light. It stops the ship and sends out S.O.S. signals to other ships. The Captain is statutorily bound to stop and search on penalty of imprisonment; owners' consideration of cargoes do not weigh at all. Jack said that if overboard they are taught to smack the surface of the sea with both hands for white splashes can be seen for miles. Looking out of the window at the millions of white horses created by this continual Force 7 wind, I gained little confidence from his advice. The weather may be warm hereabouts but the sharks might present a different problem.

**Thursday 4th December** The southernmost of the Friendly Isles, Eua, came and went to starboard some eight miles away before breakfast. It was a mountainous island with a sheer cliff on the eastern side and I saw giant waves hurling themselves at the foot of it in the absence of a reef for them to thrash. Just beyond you could make out the low outline of Tongatupu, the biggest of the Tongatupu group, with Cook's Point at the southern tip of it; Tonga itself lies much further north. Thoughts of Tonga brought back clear memories of the late Queen Salote in the coronation procession of Queen Elizabeth in 1953. I can picture her sitting in the pouring rain in an open carriage, a huge black mountain of a woman accompanied by a small man. All the carriages of other Royals were covered against the rain but Queen Salote wished to show her deference to Elizabeth in the Tongan way, by seeming wet and uncomfortable. In Tonga you should appear at a disadvantage in the presence of those of higher rank than yourself.

I remembered reading somewhere after the coronation, that when somebody asked who was the small man with Salote, Noel Coward suggested that he was probably her lunch.

Before the turn of the century a Hawaiian king suggested that all the island peoples of the South Pacific should unite to form one large kingdom, Australasians, Melanesians, Polynesians and Micronesians all constituting one United Kingdom, one United Commonwealth of Nations, one glorious United States of Oceania of the little pretty lands. The very thought of the possibility blows my mind, but union was never possible politically; Hawaii is now a state of America, French Polynesia is an overseas territory of France, Tonga remains a kingdom, Fiji has applied to rejoin the Commonwealth of Nations and the Cook Islands are a republic. One wondered though whether there could not be some union for the furtherance of art and culture in the whole region.

We have been told that the owners have instructed the Captain to slow down and arrive in Noumea on Sunday morning. Unloading is not to start until Monday, thereby avoiding paying the dockers overtime; this means that we should have three full days on New Caledonia.

It has become the norm for Boom Boom Anthony and Know All Jane to propound their knowledge and lecture to us about what we are seeing, should see and the meaning of it all. I suppose that if you spend your life teaching it is difficult to stop when you are with people, some of whom may have done their own research and even be more experienced than you are in areas that you may wish to teach them about.

I wondered if Anthony will set examination papers for us at the end of the voyage. If he does I shall have the greatest pleasure in disposing of them in the time-honoured way by stuffing them up his fat arse. Mind you, Know All Jane does her fair share of lecturing and I would quite like to do the same to her.

The Friendly Islands disappeared from view mid-morning, and I imagined the feelings of Captain Bligh and his loyal sailors as he too headed west in an open boat after the mutiny on the Bounty. Cook may have named them thus but Bligh must have had different memories. We have made a further adjustment and our heading to 276 degrees and tonight the sunset was over the port bow for the first time on the voyage. It was one of those lovely sunsets when immediately after the sun ball itself has entered the sea the white cotton wool of the clouds becomes uniformly pink, as if dipped in dye and the sky all around them is also pastel pink-washed. It lasts a very short time before it changes to other colours, and it is so soft after the fierce red fire of the day. We first experienced a sunset like this when we were sitting in the rooftop bar of a hotel in Lima some years ago now, looking out across the Pacific. I remember then what a lovely contrast it made with the daytime colourlessness of Lima itself, as if trying to put a better complexion on the place to take to bed.

# Chapter 5

## New Caledonia

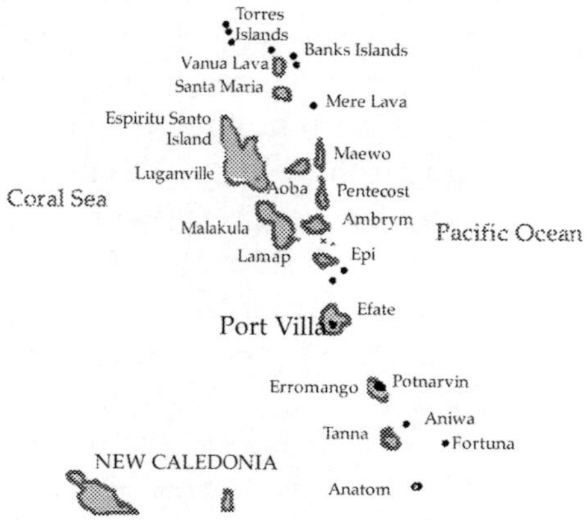


**Friday 5th December** We have left Polynesia and are Melanesia bound, and I let my mind drift freely back to the late 1980s, and nudge memories long since asleep at their moorings deep in its innermost inlets. As I left Polynesia I recalled an early evening on the island of Bora Bora, when we sat near the beach waiting for the sunset and were quite overpowered by the oleanders. We were familiar with oleanders in the Mediterranean and elsewhere but this fragrance, this noa-noa was unforgettable, as was the unbelievably sweet scent of wild vanilla. Smell can be very powerful in memory, long after other senses have faded.

Some aspects of Polynesia, the villages and the towns and the island countryside are less than attractive, some islands less than idyllic and they fall short of the image that most people have of the South Seas. I think Gauguin must have felt this, for some of his painting seems bizarre to me, as if he needed to show what he really wanted Polynesia to be like, no white beaches, but pink ones, no green fields or dark mountainsides but bright yellow or orange ones. No cruel cliffs or jagged rocks or wild seas at all. The figures and images in his paintings do not look like the tikis on the platforms and altars of the marae, many of which are ugly, but more as if they had been stolen from Borobodhur on Java or the Buddhist temples of Bangkok. Gauguin seemed to want to portray it all in a better, brighter light than he saw it; but as far as we were concerned it was spellbinding enough as it was.

My final view of Tahiti and Moorea and hence Polynesia, for I shall not come again, was of Mount Orobena towering seven thousand feet above Papeete, and the tourist named mountain of Moorea, Bali H'ai, both with nebulous pillows smothering their heads. Today is the last full sailing day to New Caledonia. This morning a clean white container carrier crossed our bows thirteen miles away sailing northeast toward Suva in Fiji. This was the first ship we have seen since Contship Ticina left us for dead out of Papeete.

At noon we were due south of Fiji only two hundred miles away. When you get among the islands the Pacific Ocean suddenly becomes so much smaller. Under us the ocean floor has undulated massively, from the nine thousand metre deep Tonga Trench we have crossed the Tonga Rise, only one hundred and fifty metres below, the Lau Basin three thousand metres below, and the Lau Ridge only one hundred and seventy metres beneath us; mountain ranges, rifts, plateaux of immense proportions, this rusty old tub blithely sails across the top of them all. We have news of a sister-ship of River Line now only twelve days ahead of us on one engine, and she encountered worse weather in the South Pacific than we did; there has been a good deal of cargo damage in her hold as a result. I wonder whether our planned route will be changed by River Line because there is now so little time between the two ships for cargoes to be assembled in the ports. If the sister-ship ahead of us breaks down altogether we shall catch her up, and may take aboard her passengers, which will crowd the accommodation here to bursting point on River Tweed and I do not want to move out of this cabin. I have come to need the space, for if I had to move to a single cabin I do not know where I would put the cases of lager; there would not be sufficient room for my wild boomerang thoughts, my empty suitcases and the grip into which I now put my dirty clothes, all of which are on the spare bunk.

**Saturday 6th December** We have reduced speed to thirteen knots as instructed and are sailing Hunter's Ridge, which forms the northern edge of the vast South New Hebrides Trench, a Pacific deep four hundred miles long, until we reach the mouth of the narrow Canal de la Havannah, where the pilot will join us to guide us into the port of Noumea at about 6 a.m. tomorrow. Negotiating the channel will take three hours and the view from Monkey Island should be fascinating.

During the morning we passed two stark dark rocks to port, two South Pacific Rocks of Gibraltar sticking up two hundred metres above the water, Hunter Island named after a ship and Isle Matthew, eighty miles apart and uninhabited except by sea birds. These rocks which have to be the peaks of under-sea mountains are very few and far between and must be a godsend for the birds. There are no coral reefs around these two islands, and the waves pound them pitilessly, as if insulted by their temerity to be there at all.

**Sunday 7th December** The pilot came out to meet us and came aboard just after 6 a.m. The land was still many miles away, but there was a smell of damp vegetation on the morning wind as we sailed on towards the sausage-shaped island of New Caledonia, a French Territory, with the second largest coral reef in the world after the Great Barrier Reef. We began to cruise through Havannah Channel, it is hardly a channel at the start for the islands at the south are discrete and miles away, but the channel gradually narrows to pass through Woodin Pass at the half-way point. As we sailed along the south coast of New Caledonia we were just above the Tropic of Capricorn and less than half a mile from the island itself, and the passing scenery was very striking. The mountains and hills are a strange reddish chocolate colour, the indigenous pins colonnaire or draucaria cover the lower slopes, and come down almost to the black rocks lining the beaches. They are tall and very slender with light grey, almost white trunks and dark green foliage, the horizontal branches on each side are like the steps on telegraph poles.

There are coconut palms here and there between the pines and the rocks, and the lush mangrove spills out onto the beaches and into the sea. We spent three hours passing by this lovely coast, with lots of inlets and pretty bays, and there were little motus off-shore crowned by pines, which looked like the heads of goddesses swimming in the blue sea. To get to the dockside in Noumea we entered the harbour between two promontories, and made a tight turn to starboard and sailed back in the direction from which we had come, making a loop as in Sydney, when you sail northward and enter the harbour between the Heads and turn to port to make for Circular Quay.

All along the coast of New Caledonia there were puffs of scarlet from the poincianas, or flamboyants as they are called in the Caribbean, and with the sun early bright it was an unforgettable scene. As it was Sunday the port was deserted save for the handful of men necessary to get the ship dockside and tied up. This was achieved with much striving, stirring up of mud and pushing by a couple of tugs. The port itself appeared unattractive and as soon as the ladder went down I made off for Baie des Citrons, one hour's walk away. I walked through the deserted and silent town up and over two steep hills and eventually saw the bay ahead of me. The white houses and bungalows on the way to and around the bay were very attractive in the bright sun. Most of them were surrounded and part-covered by breathtakingly beautiful flowers, bougainvillea varying from incandescent pink through bright red orange and pale mauve to a magical rich magenta, hibiscus which had long since opened its gorgeous red petals as if it could not wait to welcome the sun, and allamanda of the purest citron-yellow, a truly lovely shade of a tropical colour to refresh the very soul. The heady sweet perfume of the oleanders made me feel as if I was inhaling an anaesthetic from heaven itself.

It seemed as if all these beautiful shrubs had seized the light of the sun as soon as it was available, coloured it to their satisfaction and were now giving it back, improved upon, blessedly embellished. New Caledonia is known as the Island of Light and what light it can be. My walk took me past two yacht marinas where there was curiously little activity even for a Sunday, and eventually I found a restaurant that was open and enjoyed a pleasant salade paysanne with french bread washed down with plenty of cold Fosters beer. The harbour at Noumea is surrounded by low hills to seaward and high mountains to landward, and it is the high mountains that are so mineral rich. New Caledonia has almost unlimited deposits of iron, chromium, nickel, manganese, copper, lead, gold, antimony and Cobalt. The nickel deposits are probably the biggest of any country in the world, though the Philippines and Malaysia are fast developing their resources.

**Monday 8th December** Unloading went on at the pace of the stevedores, which was not fast. I saw come out of the holds the large steel frames, pipes and boxes that I had watched coming aboard in Dunkirk, and being loaded onto twelve wheel lorries for the nickel mine.

At lunch time River Tweed moved across the harbour to a berth near a huge mound of dark yellow earth brought by ship from the nickel mine at Thio, the ship was a Singapore-registered freighter, Maritime Songkhla. The thick yellow dust was choking and permeated everywhere, and although they had a water tanker spraying the dock-side it failed to lessen the dust clouds. I had forgotten what sort of industrial lung disease inhaled nickel ore can cause, and I noted that nobody wore a mask. Much of the dirt from the ship was loaded straight onto a covered over-head conveyor belt which took it to a large processing plant at the back of the dock.

My American friends, ever terrified of pollution and infection asked me what to do. I told them to take off their clothes immediately without shaking, have a shower and wash their hair, I told them to wash their clothes as soon as possible and hope for the best, because very small amounts of nickel dust inhaled, could cause very serious lung disease. They seemd to believe all this and I felt a right heel.

When earlier I tried to discuss global warming and the President's disinclination to limit further exhaust emissions by law in the United States because he was afraid of losing the automobile and oil trade vote, there was a silence, their eyes glazed as when I mentioned my trip to Vietnam and what I saw there in the way of deformed foetuses as a result of American agent Orange; on both occasions you could have heard a fly fart.

For the past two days we have blissfully been spared the presence of Boom Boom Anthony, he and Know All Jane having spent much of the time travelling to bays and hotels further away for snorkelling, and, presumably, eating. They reappeared for dinner tonight and Anthony was obviously tired as the result of his exertions, and announced that he could not eat a full dinner. He did however do fairly well with fish balls of crab meat and shrimp on a bed of spaghetti, followed by chicken Kiev, and ending with a mound of Russian salad. This caused him to have serious and prolonged eructation problems and I was glad that I was sitting beside him rather than opposite him. Know All Jane said that that they had had an unusually large lunch in a hotel, and I wondered what qualified for 'unusually large' in Anthony's capacity.

The fact that Know All Jane responds to every twitch of his finger, is sickening to behold. I suppose that you must look for the hidden gains in any situation like this, but for the life of me I could not see them. I could hear my wife saying that the answer lies within Know All Jane and with her self-image. In my situation I can only hope for an early and fatal second coronary thrombosis for Anthony, or a first and lethal stroke. That really would improve the prospects for the remaining two thirds of the voyage.

I tried to think about the reaction of the South Sea Islanders two hundred years ago, when the British and French came and went, and vied with each other over their islands. They must have thought that they were merely ringsiders at a much bigger fight between two mortal enemies from far away, with nearly a thousand years of enmity between them . I suspect that they went on with their daily living, fishing, growing vegetables, raising pigs, making love, and minding their own business, until the interference of God-bothering missionaries working out their own problems and others made it difficult for them; and in the end changed their lives for ever and surely the worse.

In much of a mixed mood, I ended the day with Elgar, who transported me far from where I was, which was what I needed tonight.

**Tuesday 9th December** Today we decided upon a full day tour and a delightful man named Johnson with a minibus picked us up at the foot of the ship's gangway, we then picked up two Australians at Club Mediterranean, and off we went. Johnson was happily fat, was born on the island of Tanna in Vanuatu, and has lived on New Caledonia for thirty years.

We took the 'motorway' out of Noumea, up the west coast with an arid plain on the seaward side and high forbidding mountains to landward. After an hour we came to a small town called Boulouparis, and turned right to cross the mountains and make for the mining town of Thio. Johnson was very voluble and keen to tell us all he knew, he laughed uproariously most of the time, Boom Boom Anthony sat in front with him because he was too fat to fit comfortably in the back, and there was just about room for the two of them. I sat on the back seat with the Australians, Lester and Nella.

There was little or no traffic and the run over the mountains was strikingly beautiful. We drove through a rain forest, round many hairpin bends with Johnson driving one handed and holding a microphone in the other, and looking round the countryside rather than at the road. Apart from pines of various sorts the commonest tree was the niaouli, a relative of the eucalyptus, though its leaves when crushed gave off a less pungent smell. They were everywhere, and there were also lush thick leafed samblon trees, and here and there, usually in a small clearing, the wide-spreading thick branched natapu trees, which bear a large nut, and many mature banyans with roots like pendent curtains and flying buttresses.

Interspersed everywhere were the glorious colours of bougainvillea, and hibiscus and many white frangipani bushes. The flamboyants seemed bigger and more beautiful than ever and were close matched by African tulip trees, with a more orange red colour. Johnson pointed out a tree with lovely blue flowers which he said was a blue flamboyant, entirely new to me, a slightly darker blue than the jacarandas.

At Thio we were still in the South Province, and had reached the east coast of New Caledonia. We visited the nickel mine by the jetty, with a long conveyor belt for the loading of ships to take the ore round to Noumea for processing, and also throughout the world. They seemed to scrape away the peaks and upper slopes of the mountains in their open cast mining leaving sore red-raw areas, they move on from one peak to the next and forty-five ton lorries run about on the mountainside like ants enshrouded in red dust. Johnson told us that they try not to stay too long in one place, in order to give the earth time to recover, and there is an extensive replanting scheme in train. Tina shut herself inside the minibus because she could not stand any more of "all that dust and dirt".

We had a good lunch in a primitive holiday camp on the coast above Thio, and began the most hazardous mountain drive I can ever remember. There is room for only one vehicle on the rough dirt road, and you were not allowed to start the run until you were given the all clear on a phone connected to the other end, for there were no passing places. Johnson regarded this part of the drive as a huge joke and bellowed with laughter every time we passed a crashed car lying in the ravine, and there were at least twenty of them. He regaled us with the number of deaths and the details of the various injuries, all the while holding the wheel with one hand and talking into the microphone in the other, and the drop beside me was sheer.

The mountains here on the east coast are quite savage and awesome, and I was glad that I was not sitting in the front. There were narrow waterfalls, the water cascading as down stairways. Johnson pointed out the native Kanak villages in the valleys below us where they live free and their villages are very private places. They farm and fish and their children catch a bus to and from school by climbing up steep slopes to the road. Eventually the road improved and we made a stop at a hot spring at Lacrouen where the Australians Lester and Nella bathed. After the spring we turned west, crossed over the island and got back to the west coast road, passed through the town of La Foa where there was a racecourse and headed for Noumea at high speed.

It was a long day with limited interest other than the beauty of the mountain scenery, and the brilliant colours of the shrubs and trees. When we returned to the ship we were told that we would not set sail for a further forty eight hours. I found it very pleasant to have Lester and Nella to talk to, different people for a change, and I felt that two or three more passengers on this ship would have been preferable from the start; those two would certainly have been an asset with their ready earthy sense of humour, and their blast of Australian fresh air to blow away some of Anthony's oral fartwind.

**Wednesday 10th December** At breakfast this morning there was an air of gloom and doom, Boom Boom Anthony had mixed himself a rum punch last night and had suffered heartburn all night, and he was very worried that he would not be able to eat any breakfast. With commendable fortitude he decided upon a 'light breakfast'. He managed to deal with a bowl of frozen melon balls, two poached eggs on toast, two thick slices of gammon, and six slices of toast and marmalade, and we all felt much better able to face the day ahead as a result. On these occasions Know All Jane's sweet smile is bravely maintained, and I could cheerfully have poured the whole bowl of frozen melon balls down the front of her shirt, inside between her silly little tits, followed by coffee, the whole jug, scalding hot.

I walked again to Baie des Citrons and found Nathalie's Bar where I had kalamari in a delightful tomato sauce with rice, and plenty of cold No.1 draught lager. When I returned to the ship, because the holds were now almost empty and she stands so far out of the water, the bulbous bow was there for all to see. It was a little like taking River Tweed's pants down and looking at her private parts. When, after a struggle I climbed the ever-lengthening gangway, Trinity House Paul told me that the stevedores had dropped a twenty-four ton steel ring back into the hold, when two ropes gave way. There is quite a dent down there and I thought of getting Boom Boom Anthony to ask Captain Geoffrey if he was getting a diver's inspection report before we sail. I would quite enjoy the prospect of that exchange; men could have been killed down in that hold today. As the ship is so far out of the water it has provided the opportunity to do a lot of painting, six men with long handled paint rollers have covered square yards of the hull during the last two days, rolling on black paint from stem to stern. I overheard Captain Geoffrey saying that River Tweed will do one more circle of the world after this one and will then go into dry dock for a complete refit. This will include improving the passenger accommodation, moving the passenger lounge up to the bridge deck and fitting larger windows, and moving the swimming pool also up to the bridge deck, where it will be in the open air.

**Thursday 11th December** The stevedores completed the reloading in the hold during a very hot morning tempered by an off-shore wind from the mountains. Opposite us on the other side of the harbour the Maritime Songkhla was still disgorging nickel ore, and another ore carrier, the Panama registered Arctic Trader, low in the water, was anchored in mid-harbour, awaiting her turn for the nickel birth like a cow much in need of milking.

The processing plant is vast, and we saw big furnaces at the back of it, presumably a smelting plant. Happy Johnson told us as we passed on our way round the island that the pay was high in this plant because of the filthy conditions, and many of the workers there were Vietnamese and Polynesian. This scene fanned the embers of my dying interest in pneumoconiosis, industrial lung disease of which, during my time as a lung specialist, I made a detailed study, and stimulated me to fax my son and ask him to consult a modern text book and fax back details of nickel pneumoconiosis, then I can read the juicy bits to the Americans, who are beginning to shed their anxiety that I fostered. I would love to arrange for a radiological survey for the workers in the nickel processing plant on the dockside in Noumea, and spend days looking at the chest films. I doubt very much whether the governors of this island are too much concerned with the health of the workers. The profits from the nickel must be the paramount consideration and the nickel plant, and the working of it, was almost Victorian. The whole situation could be relieved when nickel becomes superceded in the world, but I dread to think what that would do to this island's economy.

I was told that there would be a referendum in 1998 on the result of which will depend whether New Caledonia will finally become independent of France, and the smart money is going against independence. In the north they want it, but in the more populated south they do not.

We sailed out of the port of Noumea at 1 p.m. and headed for the gap in the reef. There was a wrecked freighter standing high and dry on the reef, which stretches to port and starboard as far as the eye can see, and the lagoon just inside the reef was the colour of Green Chartreuse in the afternoon sun. We sailed through a channel no more than half a mile wide with white lighthouses on each side, and were in the open ocean with Noumea fast disappearing over the stern.

We had just made ourselves comfortable on the bridge deck on our sun loungers when the port engine belched out dense clouds of black smoke, and 'blew up'. Just after this Captain Geoffrey came out from the bridge and handed us a list of the ports we will visit. Lautoka in Fiji and Santo in Vanuatu had been deleted, and Oro Bay in Papua New Guinea added. I was sorry about Santo because I wanted to go to Vanuatu where I hoped see Second World War relics. I must make the best of the Solomon Islands and Rabaul on New Britain, but River Line changes ports of call without warning and all I can do is live in hope. We continued on a south east heading of 155 degrees at a reduced speed of eleven knots, hoping to make Auckland on Sunday morning, where we shall spend less than a day before coming all the way back north again to Fiji, one thousand miles each way. I think that River Line are making the New Zealand diversion in the hope of getting into regular trade there; the small load we have for Auckland, five hundred tons of pumpkins in containers, and a large earthmoving machine cannot be financially worthwhile.

The sun has set on either side of the bow since we left Dunkirk, now it is setting on the starboard beam and floods into my cabin. The change of direction through 90 degrees had a definite effect upon me, I felt different but did not quite know why. My sense of direction has never been very good, and I think I must have a pile of rusty nails in the base of my brain in place of the normal iron filings that pigeons have. Now that we are going well south I must find the Southern Cross again and shall look for it low over the bow to the south west.

*River Tweed docking in Noumea, New Caledonia. Nickel processing is important to the economy but at what cost to the health of the workers?*

# Chapter 6

## New Zealand

**Friday 12th December** Bright Eyed Bearded Henry told me after breakfast that they had not diagnosed exactly what was wrong with the port engine, but at least one bearing in a turbocharger had gone, and they needed help in Auckland. I do not know whether this means that we shall be longer than a day there, but I suspect that when they have the parts they need we will be on our way, and the further work on the engine will be done at sea by the four Officer Engineers and their crew. My purpose in making this voyage was to find a better way of wasting time, and if it takes six months to complete it so be it; at present with the speed below eight knots it probably will.

We now have turned further east on a heading of 145 degrees and during the day we will sail over the northern end of Norfolk Rise and then along the eastern side of it over two submarine volcanoes whose craters will be less than seven hundred metres beneath us. We shall pass Norfolk Island and its satellite Philip Island, out of sight one hundred miles to starboard. The two Australians, Lester and Nella on New Caledonia waxed lyrical about

Norfolk Island and told me not to miss going there if and when I ever go back to Australia. I have read much about the deportation of convicts to New South Wales at the end of the eighteenth century, and of their harsh treatment and of the even worse treatment they suffered on Norfolk and Philip Islands. When reading recently about New Caledonia, I learned that the convicts sent there by the French between 1853 and 1898 had a much easier time of it, up to ten thousand of them engaged in mining the nickel and given relative freedom.

As we staggered through a Force 7 sea, the wind head on, on our remaining engine, River Tweed with several holds and main deck empty was pitching and rolling considerably and I worried for Fat Mona, who really had begun to enjoy herself. I have grown very fond of Fat Mona, she is a warm hearted girl. I have managed to talk to her at some length, but have to be very careful not to say the slightest thing that might unleash that cackle. She has more intelligence than I thought, but it is cloaked by her lack of self-confidence. Life must be a never ending strain for her, and there must be many times on this voyage when she longs to be safely back in the north of England.

She is reading Kenneth Williams' biography and seemed surprised, disappointed and even worried that by the mid forties he had never 'done it'. She said that surely by that age every normal man had 'done it'; I could only say that indeed I hoped so, and told her to read on, hope for the best and keep us informed.

I think I am going to appreciate Fat Mona rather more than my fellow passengers and the Captain. She is more of a kindred spirit, and a much more genuine unselfish person than any of the others. She truly has in abundance what many totally lack: understanding, compassion, humility and warmth.

To record adequately a voyage like this you have not only to be a patient observer but also a player, a participant as well as a writer, and it is the last of these that causes me most doubt. Sunsets, tropical islands, lagoons, mountains, the flowers, the trees and the people, must all be done justice to, and so many writers have tried and have fallen short.

I felt that there was really no new way of describing what I am seeing, it has been done before in every conceivable form and there are no new words, phrases or sentences left; but this does not at all diminish the effect of the symphony of sights and aromas upon my mind. The witness of beauty, at best, is a private and personal thing, like love, and indeed should be shared with a lover for the ultimate pleasure of it. That is now denied to me, but I want to honour my present privilege and try to do justice to what I am experiencing, and to attempt to describe it just the same.

Today has been a rainy windy Pacific day, the sea grey, but more black than white with a good chop. The squalls followed one another, the clouds wearing black cloaks, and their rain lacerated the waves like shards of glass, as if they had been hanging on too long and could wait no longer.

It was a day for books and Beethoven, for feelings and fantasies, for day-dreaming, for wishing, and wondering how and when; for scouring the hinterlands of the mind for ever more memories of yesteryear and beyond. It was a time to penetrate the outskirts of this pretence called life, this impostor of an existence, and search for and find a way to end loneliness.

**Saturday 13th December** River Tweed continued to pitch, roll and wallow, in this South Pacific chop, and Fat Mona was definitely not herself. No longer did the Dining Saloon echo to the loud smack of her hand against the bottom of the H.P. sauce bottle, or her between-mouthfuls cackle, and I missed her. She told me that she did not even feel like reading, which meant that we would have to wait and see whether Kenneth Williams met his death without 'doing it'. I want an end to this inclement weather, a smooth sea and Fat Mona back with us on the bridge deck, cackle and all.

I am glad to be able to report that Boom-Boom Anthony has had no recurrence of heartburn, and is doing full justice to all the food that is put in front of him and more besides. He was very delighted when Johnson, the bus driver on our tour of New Caledonia, referred to his mountainous belly as one of the biggest 'yam boxes' he had ever seen, and on the islands of Vanuatu, whence Johnson came, he had seen quite a few. This caused Anthony to beat his belly like a big base drum with both hands in glee, and a thousand tropical birds flew shrieking from the trees in abject terror.

Anthony told me at breakfast this morning that his cardiologist was very pleased with his last examination, which included cardiac catheterisation; this depressed me because it probably means that Anthony will not suffer another coronary thrombosis on this voyage, and I shall have to put up with him in full voice and unrelieved for a further three months. I am not at all sure that I can cope with that, and may have to jump off the stern when nobody is looking.

We crossed the Tropic of Capricorn in the early hours of this morning, and the air on the bridge deck was considerably cooler and there was a fair wind on the port bow. We have received an S.O.S. message from Noumea and are asked to look out for a missing yacht 12.5 metres long, white hulled with blue stripes, named Berenice. She set out from Raiatea in French Polynesia to sail to New

Caledonia and is well overdue. This was a realistic message, unlike previous ones in mid ocean, and all eyes on River Tweed are now skinned as a result of it. If Berenice is in our path she must be at least two hundred and fifty miles off course.

**Sunday 14th December** Nothing further has been seen or heard of Berenice, and we assume that she has been contacted from New Caledonia, or perhaps it was a false alarm anyway.

The head wind has dropped a little and the hard worked starboard engine is achieving ten knots, so that we should make Auckland early tomorrow morning where experts await to come aboard and deal with the port engine; we understand that the problem lies with the turbocharger only, and everything is now stripped down ready for those who really know.

With the drop of the wind the sea was calmer, the ship steadier and I looked forward to Fat Mona's reappearance on the bridge deck while we sail across Norfolk Basin and over Three Kings Ridge, eight hundred metres below us.

In mid morning Fat Mona did indeed arrive on the deck, and she had recovered sufficiently to wash her hair but not dry it, so that it hung down over her face and she looked like an unsqueezed old fashioned floor mop; she said that she wanted to dry it in the trade wind. She had also painted her toenails scarlet which had the effect of accentuating the smallness of her feet and shortness of her toes and legs. She settled herself on the next sun lounger and promised to tell me straight away if Kenneth Williams achieves what we are all desperately waiting and hoping for.

Today I decided to promote Captain Geoffrey straight through to the rank of Admiral, when I overheard him talking to his Chief Officer and Engineer on the bridge in such an authoritative hectoring manner, and capping everything they said in a way that only an admiral at sea could get away with. He shall henceforth then be 'Admiral Geoffrey', the only full admiral in the history of the British Merchant Navy. Bright Eyed Bearded Henry, Second Engineer, has dared me to call him 'Admiral' to his face in the presence of the other officers in the Dining Saloon; he said that they would all very much like to be there. I am beginning to think that I really could do that, any more sarcasm and I will.

The expected time of arrival for Auckland has now been advanced to tomorrow evening, five days later than on the original schedule, and there may be a delay there depending on the engine repair.

**Monday 15th December** After breakfast we had our first sight of New Zealand, Poor Knights Island, Poor Knights Rock, and a little later Sugar Loaf Rock, all to starboard. They are a marine reserve except for Sugar Loaf which is a bird sanctuary, and is as white as snow under the guano which covers it.

A little later we passed Hen and Chicken Islands to starboard and Mokohinai further away to port, all wild life sanctuaries, and were ourselves passed by a large school of dolphins going in the opposite direction, along with a sailing boat. When I said that I could see a naked woman standing in the sailing boat through my binoculars, Anthony and Russian Yosif grabbed binoculars and started towards me before they realised that I was joking; it was only a naked man.

All these offshore islands were stark and jagged with steep sides in which were caves, some large and at all levels, they were covered with vegetation on top and they had satellite pinnacles sticking up from the sea around them. All along behind them in the misty distance was the mountainous eastern coast of the mainland. Looking at this large isolated southland I felt as if I had reached the bottom of the civilised world. New Zealand was never a country that we really wished to visit, but those of our friends who experienced New Zealand always talked with enthusiasm. I now wish that I had a little more time to see for myself.

We passed through Jellicoe Channel, only fifty metres deep, with Little Barrier Island, a large verdant mountainous place and a wild life sanctuary, to port with its pure white cloud balanced delicately on its peaks, and Cape Rodney on the mainland to starboard.

We were passed by a large P&O container ship to starboard and two other freighters, one Russian out of Vladivostock and another big container ship, all making for berths in Auckland ahead of us as we crossed Hauraki Gulf at eleven knots.

The sea was an unattractive dirty green, they took a temperature reading and it was 21.5 degrees centigrade, air temperature 23 degrees centigrade. There were many small flat islands dotted about the Gulf, all lush and green with the high rainfall in these parts.

After the pilot came aboard we motored very slowly into the outer harbour where there were ships at anchor waiting for a berth tomorrow, among them the P&O container ship which passed us in Jellicoe Channel earlier in the day. She was the Mairangi Bay, London registered and wide enough to take thirteen containers side by side on deck compared with River Tweed's eight. We were closely followed into the harbour by a clean looking freighter, pale green with a red funnel, with a blue star on a white background, this was the Melbourne registered Melbourne Star, a nice looking ship with good lines

They will start unloading at midnight but will have to wait for a high tide to get the Ro-Ro onto the quay side. There is talk of a morning departure, and the necessary parts for the port engine will not be available until we reach Lae in Papua New Guinea in eleven days time. This means that we will limp back north to Fiji on the starboard engine alone.

The port of Auckland is in the centre of the city and the high rise buildings are only a spit away. It is rather attractive when viewed from the ship, less so when you are in town.

**Tuesday 16th December** Auckland is a compact port, there were ships cheek by jowl, River Tweed slept last night between Caribbean Challenger, Hong Kong registered, and Columbus California, a bright red German container carrier, the naughty promiscuous old girl.

Having got rid of the pumpkins and given birth down the Ro-Ro to an enormous green tipper lorry with wheels cubits high, we have taken on a dozen red six-wheeled trailers for Papua New Guinea, and other assorted vehicles, mainly for Fiji which is the next stop.

I overheard Admiral Geoffrey at breakfast laying down the law to the River Line agent, as usual with Admiral Geoffrey the agent was doing the listening. It appeared that there was an additional last minute load for Suva, which meant re-opening a hold which had been closed, and a two hour delay in departure. I do not know what was the nature of the load, but it was obviously important for the company, because the agent quietly got his way.

Tina has suffered an attack of the trots these last two days and appeared only occasionally looking wan, sorry for herself and reproachful. Like all good clean Americans she believes that these indispositions are the fault of others, and consumes pills by the pouchful as prophylactics, and now as treatment. Other people, not Americans, cause the problems of this world, the pestilences, the murrains, even the pollution and most certainly all the political unreasonableness. Everything would be alright if only we all did it the American Way. I think Tina blames the food; if only she ate a little less of it, she might not feel so uncomfortable at the moment.

Heaven help us if Boom Boom Anthony gets diarrhoea, because I have heard what his stomach can do at the northern end of his alimentary canal. In that awful event I really would have to jump ship, River Tweed's loos would never cope, it would be worse than the over full camp sites in the South of France all those years ago, when Esmé kept asking why men got so hysterical about the opening of their bowels, and why they did it everywhere except in the pan or the hole. I seem to remember plenty of obese Booming Anthonys in those campsites, and they were mostly Germans. I never saw an American in the discomfort of a camp site, and without iced water for that matter; it is quite an incongruous thought, like other countries bombing their cities, it would and must never happen.

Auckland was such a very clean port, there was no rubbish on the quay at all. All the containers were geometrically placed, there were no planks of wood thrown about, no dirty coils of rope lying around, no plastic or paper material flying about in the wind. I doubt whether there was a single cigarette end or loaded condom in the whole place. The hard-hatted stevedores were mostly wearing navy blue shorts, though it was not really very warm, and the Customs people were all in clean uniform.

I am sure that the ports ahead of us will present a different picture, perhaps like Papeete with the dockers bareheaded and barefoot or in flip-flops and filthy shirts and shorts, dirt and rubbish everywhere, and the tarmac a mosaic of ring-pulls and flattened cans; in the old days it was bottle caps, but now it is ring-pulls and flattened cans.

As ships around me were unloaded and rose higher in the water so did their big bulbous willies become visible and prominent; it was like watching men lying in the bath while the water gradually ran out.

It has rained all afternoon and Auckland looked little different from Liverpool under such conditions. We remain berthed and it is now four hours since we were supposed to sail. Admiral Geoffrey keeps the Officers informed of what is going on and has forbidden them to tell us passengers, so Chief Officer Jack confided in me last night with obvious disapproval. Admiral Geoffrey likes us to ask him when we shall sail, so that he can tell us to 'wait and see' or make remarks like 'What makes the world go round?', or 'What makes you think I know?'. Keeping folk in ignorance conveys power, and power is what Admiral Geoffrey so desperately fears losing, poor man.

I once worked as Consultant to a Life Insurance company whose Chief Executive insisted that those working on one floor of the block must never know what those on another floor were doing; in this way he kept all the power on the top floor, held all the reins himself. The Company went bust two years after he took control and was taken over without him. He had a lovely wife for whom I felt very sorry in more ways than one. I hope that we do not find our Admiral hanging from the yardarm before we get back to Europe because one thing that he can do is sail the ship. I do not think I need worry because River Tweed does not have a yardarm.

Eventually at 7.30 p.m. we left the dock, the latest delay due to a fractured steam pipe, and it took five hours for a replacement to be made in Auckland. A single tug pulled us out into mid-harbour and we left Auckland behind, enveloped in mist and dankness worthy of a November evening in Liverpool. We passed by Mairangi Bay who had finally got a berth with the high gantries alongside; she has no lifting gear of her own, and I was impressed with her size. First Officer Tall Dark Dem'yan told me that she carried up to four thousand containers and until the appearance during the last five years of the giant carriers she was one of the biggest afloat. Beside Mairangi Bay, Caribbean Challenger was the epitome of elegance, very long at more than six hundred feet, and low with a slender beam, she was a 'reefer', a refrigerator ship designed for speed because she carried perishable cargoes. Her stern seemed so low in the water that I felt that I could step across to it from River Tweed and I imagined twenty foot waves in a following sea crashing down on to it; Chief Officer Jack said that she was fast enough at twenty-five knots to get away from anything, but the big 'reefers' were not built for comfort, as far as crew and passengers were concerned. He said that the crew got rolled around 'like lovers in a hammock'. I said that I rather liked the idea of that, though at my time of life trying to do it on the flat would be hazardous enough, and shagging in a swaying sack was something that might well have been beyond me, not a few years ago, though I would not like my lover-girl hear me confess to that; I hoped she was not listening. I have immense regard for Chief Officer Jack, he loves the sea, his job, his family, and understands the needs of others. When I talk to him, I have a very strong feeling that were I a young merchant seaman I could follow him to the ends of the earth. That has to be what leadership is all about, not a narrow expert thing, but a broad thing, an acceptance of the need for limitless understanding of the requirements of others, as well as a total confidence in yourself, and the willingness to take the final responsibility come what may.

In a long life in clinical medicine, I have always felt that if you could not cope with the results of making a wrong decision, you should not be doing the job at all; better be prepared to make a wrong decision and learn from it, than be indecisive, but then this applies to everybody in authority from national leaders down.

**Wednesday 17th December** The rain of New Zealand is still with us and there was thick fog in the night, sufficient to bring Admiral Geoffrey to the bridge for two hours.

I talked with the turbocharger man this morning who flew out from Heathrow yesterday. The parts went to Suva and he hoped to make the repair there, our sister-ship two weeks ahead of us had exactly the same trouble, and it took six men to handle the parts, some of which weighed three hundred kilos. He said that the fact that turbochargers blew on both ships at the same time indicated lack of proper maintenance when they were owned by the Russians, and it should not happen at all.

We have now one thousand miles to Suva at a maximum speed of eleven knots and I dared not ask what would happen if the starboard engine packed up. The expert said that it would have to be stripped down anyway, as soon as River Tweed makes her home port.

I am beginning to wish that I had jumped across onto the stern of that 'reefer' Caribbean Challenger in Auckland; with one bound not only would I then be on a reliable ship, but also I would be shot of the inexorable selfishness of Boom Boom Anthony and Know All Jane and Admiral Geoffrey's rudeness, though sadly deprived of Fat Mona who has just confirmed our worst fears about Kenneth Williams. I wait with interest to see what book she will read next, and I hope that it will be a happier one with everybody 'doing it' everywhere and without cease. I have absolute confidence that she will keep me informed of all details.

You cannot be really lonely in the presence of Fat Mona; it may be that at the end of this odyssey I will want to take her home, she would certainly put an end to sepulchral silence, but her husband is a big boy and loves her very much. I have grown very fond of that simple down to earth couple and wish them all the luck in the world.

Boom Boom Anthony and Know All Jane deserve each other, they seize the best of everything, hog the only two comfortable chairs on the bridge, pick the only clean mattresses for the sun loungers, grab the first and last cans of beer from the cool boxes in the minibuses, try to arrange everything entirely to suit themselves. If there is only one of anything left Jane gives it to Anthony. They would be a match for the Germans around hotel pools, and I dearly wished that that was where they were at this living moment, or preferably under water face up.

I have sat in the Dining Saloon and had ear bashings from Boom Boom Anthony about inadequate men who cannot stand up for themselves, women who try to keep their figures by dieting and people who take the money but who are not prepared to work for it. From all this, if I were a psychologist like my daughter I would probably conclude that inside overbearing gross Anthony there is an inadequate thin man, slightly lazy, with a modicum of self control, trying to get out. Inside selfish Jane there is a selfish Jane very happy to stay in. As I have said they deserve each other and I am amazed that they score only two divorces between them along the way, but having found each other I can well understand whey they have stayed together for twenty years.

We head almost due north on 005 degrees and at ten knots. A shark appeared briefly to starboard and I am surprised at the paucity of fauna that we have seen while crossing the two biggest oceans in the world. I expected not only dolphins but shoals of man-eating sharks hurling themselves at the ship to get at us, with bits of River Tweed in their hideous teeth, whales all the way smacking the sea into boiling cauldrons of white foam with their tails, and taking it in turns to bonk with our bulbous bow, albatrosses fighting for a place on the rails, the decks slippery with their guano and making nests and laying eggs on Monkey Island, and going 'Quark Quark' all the time. All we have scored apart from the dolphins is a pair of sharks who did not want to know us, flying fish minding their own business, and a few gulls and boobies trying to catch them.

I am beginning to disbelieve those ancient mariners, and until I see it again, I shall even wonder if the Southern Cross itself was a figment of their rum-sodden imagination; if the sky is clear tonight I shall ascend to Monkey Island and remind myself that it does exist, and gaze in wonder at it in my beer-sodden reality.

I am now about half way through this voyage and am thinking about what I will say to folk when I return, who ask me whether I was glad that I made it and what it was really like. The average day starts in the bathroom, and the loo is in a tight corner so that you cannot comfortably get both buttocks on at once, you can get on only one and a half buttocks and your anus, which I suppose, must be the most important part. You have to remember two things, first tear off the paper before you start, since once on it is difficult to reach half round your back where they have screwed the holder, because there is no room beside you; if you are in the late seventies and with a rigid back like mine, the paper will be beyond you. Secondly you must train yourself to get done and away before you lift the flush lever if you want to retain your manhood, such is the frightening force of the suction; I find myself having an occasional look to make sure all is still with me. The shower is also in a corner, it mostly gives you a nice spray, but the position of the control lever bears no relation to the temperature of the water at any given time, which may change by the second from a scalding hot geyser to iceberg cold and vice versa, and the pressure varies from prostatic trickle to a circumcising slash.

If you drop the soap in the shower you risk two serious injuries, either you are knocked silly by hitting your forehead on the loo, or you get the hook, which some genius has screwed half way up the wall for hanging flannels on, up your arse. I should add that occasionally, just when you have thoroughly soaped yourself, all water flow ceases indefinitely and the shower head merely farts in your face.

With regard to the bunks, they are end to end, and very narrow with high sides half way along to stop you rolling out, and when the ship rolls heavily, you are banged hard against the wood, various parts of your anatomy may be at risk, and your fantastic sexual dream, if you are fortunate to have one, is rudely interrupted. If you are lucky enough to have a partner, and are of the age and inclination to *reliver* your voyage with a little nookie from time to time, you had better get out of your bunks which are too small for it, and do it standing up, in the shower perhaps, but please, please, be careful of that damned hook on your down-strokes, it could so easily convert imminent orgasm into a pain in the arse.

The cabin is pleasant and comfortable but the desk at which you sit to write has three drawers which should have restrainers to stop them leaving home. One of mine has not, and twice I have had to crawl about on the floor like an elderly arthritic labrador, retrieving fifty C.D.s, forty tapes, and the exercise books, parchments, pencils, plumes, rubbers and quills that I need to write this rubbish.

If you appreciate as much cheap booze as you can drink, and such beauty as you have never seen before, of ship, sea, sun, moon, stars, lands, trees, flowers and fascinating new folk, then you will vow that when you have completed your first voyage, you will somehow, some day find a way to do it all again. I know that I will, even alone as I am, and perhaps that is the best way to do it, and next time I will be ready for those bathroom hazards, that hook will not violate me ever again.

*The port of Auckland is in the centre of the city and the high rise buildings are only a spit away.*

# Chapter 7

## Fiji

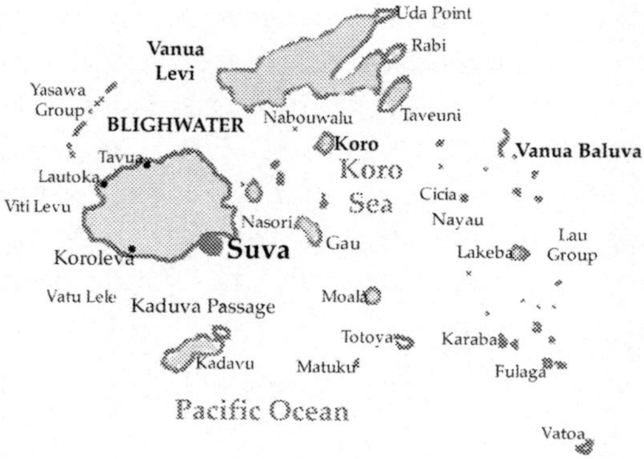


**Thursday 18th December** I fear that Tina's bowels are as unpredictably hurried as ever, and give her not rest nor peace. At dinner last night she had to leave suddenly before she could get at the Cornish pasty with creamed potatoes, courgettes and carrots, and cream of mushroom sauce, but she did manage to lower the oxtail soup with croutons and onions. Her husband thought that probably she would better have chosen the scampi with sauté potatoes and whole boiled 'termayters' and tartar sauce, which he himself chose and covered with H.P. sauce and Tabasco as a sort of challenge to the tartar sauce, and as a wake up call to those of his tastebuds which have survived, and might have nodded off thinking they were owed a rest. I am now convinced that Americans like to stuff as much as possible into their mouths at all times, Nouvelle Cuisine, as far as they are concerned, might well be the name of a film star. Each meal provides them with extraordinary sensual pleasure, and as you watch them you are convinced that, as in an act of love, they are orgasm bound.

Tina was in there pitching again at breakfast this

morning, and was doing alright, scoring apple juice, iced water melon, and bran with added raisins 'for daily whole body health', and I wondered what half body health was like, and if you could choose which half, until her choice of two fried eggs 'easy over', bacon 'all over crisp', and fried frankfurter 'long and all across' was placed before her. She beat quite a dramatic retreat, obeying yet another insistent call to stool. Eric pressed on with his two fried eggs 'sunny side up' which he perforated with a vertically held fork in his left hand, and then with some difficulty spooned with a teaspoon onto pieces of toast, which meant changing hands with fork and teaspoon, heaped marmalade upon it and got most of it into his mouth.

Watching Americans eat is like watching an intricate game. They spear everything with a fork and cut it into small pieces, change hands, play around with it for a bit like a cat with a mouse, and eventually suck it in. A meal for them is an important playtime; it has nothing whatever to do with taste or palate or true nutritional needs. Bulk is of the essence, no course must be missed lest the table is vacated with some small gastric alcove, nook or cranny, or diverticulum or pouch in those lucky enough to have them, is left unoccupied.

The bottle of Thousand Island Dressing became void last night, and I woke this morning with beads of the sweat of anxiety upon my brow lest it had not been replaced in time for breakfast. I tried to imagine eggs of any sort, done any way, bacon, sausages, even with marmalade, but without Thousand Island Dressing, and my brain rejected such sacrilege, and I felt that I must seek expiation immediately, nay flagellation, for my sinful thoughts.

Admiral Geoffrey has let slip the information, I am sure unintentionally, that we are after all calling at Santo on the Island of Espiritu Santo in Vanuatu. There will be a load of five hundred tons of copra for River Tweed, and we shall be there for one day, which could be long enough to get ashore and see some Second World War relics. There was never fighting on Espiritu Santo during the war, and it became a gigantic forward base for the Americans as they pushed the Japanese back across the Pacific to Japan. While we are there I hope very much to get to Champagne Beach and Million Dollar Point, but I must not tell that to Admiral Geoffrey because he would probably then forbid all shore leave, or steam right past the whole bloody island.

Fat Mona has started reading a new book, a horror book and it frightens her to death, but she cannot put it down. She told me that it is about a Beautiful Defenceless Girl held prisoner by a Drug Crazed Robber who plans to indulge his Perverted Sadistic Lusts. Fat Mona's eyes are lovely and big anyway, but when she tells me about the book, and behind her pebble glasses, they seem to be positioned several inches in front of her sockets. I think she really should get back to reading Stephen King as soon as possible, he only gave her nightmares, and stopped her getting any sleep.

She talked to me at length this afternoon about her life, and she is much more intelligent than I had thought, I think it was the nervous cackle that put me wrong. She was a hairdresser, then worked as a nanny before joining a travel company and was a representative for eight years in Spain, Italy, Greece and India and then spent three years working in travel agencies. She is now in her mid-thirties and they want to have a family, having bought a house in the north country. She and Johnny, the other travelling Officer's wife, together with their husbands are sick of the bad manners of Admiral Geoffrey, though they are very careful not be to overheard complaining. It embarrasses them that he ignores them, I assured them that they are missing nothing by that.

Tina has recovered sufficiently to have her hair cut by Anna, the youngest of the stewardesses. Tina's hair was already of the short American curly variety, a bit like trained steel wire, and now it looks just like an old-fashioned hard bristled lavatory brush, short, straight and quite rigid; any hedgehog would love to swap with her. I shall place my own head under Anna's scissors after Fiji, because I dare not risk the alternative, Big Vanya's lawn mowers and garden shears with which he offers a 'No 1' cut to all comers - it is the only one he can do. He is a much larger and uglier edition of Krushchev and they tell me that he has the gentlest of dispositions but he frightens me to death, the great Russian bear; he is big enough to play bowls with fifty gallon oil drums, full, and probably does, every Saturday night with vodka up to his shaven Russian cranium.

A large school of dolphins came and played about in front of the ship this morning and in her panic to avoid missing anything, and to be first to see it if at all possible, Know All Jane rushed upstairs, fell and dropped her binoculars and damaged them; Anthony grudgingly will buy her a replacement in Fiji. The only other minor anxiety this evening concerned Tina's 'hormone pills', I did not like to ask what was their nature, perhaps they are Hormone Replacement Therapy but if she misses out on her hormone pills she gets migraines, although she also takes anti-migraine pills. She is worried that she has not brought enough of either but I am sure that she has, because like food, Americans rarely go short when it comes to medication.

Of the others, Eric has enough thyroid replacement pills, Anthony is well-stocked with blood pressure and coronary dilator pills and Jane with her anti-histamine pills. As for myself I have a supply of pills for gastric relief when I drink too much beer, I have brought plenty because I have no intention of stopping drinking too much beer.

**Friday 19th December** A beautiful day has dawned, air temperature 24 degrees centigrade, and sea temperature a surprising 25.5 degrees centigrade. Purser Alec came and passed the time of a lovely day with us on the bridge deck. He is usually so busy and has little time to chat to us, which is a pity because he is an amusing man with much sea-going experience, and he has a gorgeous north country wit. He told us of a large red and green parrot which a sister-ship of River Tweed brought back from Papua New Guinea a couple of years ago; it was much at home on the ship and loved by everybody. By the time that they reached Europe, the Cadet Officer had taught it to say 'Fuck the Captain, silly old Fart', which was much appreciated by one and all, especially, to his credit, the Captain. Alec wondered how that would have grabbed Admiral Geoffrey. The parrot was discharged from the Merchant Navy at Rotterdam and now resides at the home of the second cook in Kent, where it greets every visitor to the house with the same advice that it gave to everybody on board ship.

We still have many containers on board and some trailers, but everybody now waits for the palm oil and copra. We have crossed the South Fiji Basin at our sedate speed of eleven knots, and are three hundred and twenty miles from Suva on a flat sea. There was a sharp storm earlier, which caused the drawer in this desk to do another Cresta Run round the walls of the cabin, and I was surprised by how much I had put into it when, for the third time, I did my crawl of retrieval.

I was reminded of my dear mother, the queen of this world's hoarders, who never allowed anything to be thrown away, and packed a sizeable house where I was born and bred, to the eaves with rubbish, as well as three stables, and a barn big enough for a loaded haywain to pass through, and the ultimate problem of clearing it all out when she died.

In one bureau, the drawers cannot have been opened for thirty years, and were a five star hotel for generations of mice. I could imagine one mouse asking another whether they should finish off for supper that letter that little Bobby wrote to his Mummy, at the end of the first day at public school in 1935, or should they try the Last Will and Testament of Charles Hayden Cox, dated 1910, or leave that for tomorrow and make a start on that enticing wad of share certificates at the back with Duplicates Cannot Be Issued Under Any Circumstances written on them, followed by some of those Boer War medal ribbons for sweet; then after supper all scamper down to the bottom drawer through that big hole they gnawed, and have a lovely communal crap in that cardboard tube containing the M.D. Diploma of Robert Ellis, dated 1919.

There were two cupboards in the house which were never opened because if you did you were buried under an eight foot mountain of used wrapping and tissue paper, envelopes, letters, cardboard boxes, and bombed by rolls of string in one case, and a similar pile of mildewed suitcases and rolls of cloth, so moth-eaten that they looked as if they had been used for machine gun practice, sufficient to kit out a regiment for overseas service, in the other.

The stables and barn were a heaven for a growing boy, containing everything from tables and chairs, and sofas with rats' nests, decayed sacks, old lawn mowers, rollers, cat skeletons, and pieces of ancient motor car circa 1915, to a machine gun from a German Fokker warplane, along with trunk after trunk of aerial photographs of the trenches on the Western Front, circa 1916, not to mention bayonets, aerial darts, tin hats, a German rifle and a Gurkha's kukri.

Knowing of my mother's disinclination to part with anything at all, I have often wondered how she gave birth to me, but apparently she resented my presence within her almost as much as she resented having to accommodate my father, for the very much shorter length of time necessary for my conception.

There was a third cupboard in the bathroom, bigger than the other two, for old newspapers, old evening dresses, a wedding dress reeking of camphor and lavender bags, and all sorts of hats invaginated one into the other in big round boxes with locks and handles, and I remember looking in there one day and finding a copy of the Morning Post reporting the start of the First World War on 14th August 1914.

I have digressed from this voyage, and perhaps I am dementing, people do dement at sea on long voyages, and the tell-tale sign is often a return to dwell in the distant past. In fact the immediate future here holds the prospect of Boom Boom Anthony, and curry is on the menu and he loves curry. Every time we have curry his stomach makes noises like a bubbling beaker and retort in the laboratory of a mad chemistry professor making another Frankenstein, or the hot geysers of Rotorua on a very colly-wobbly day. I dread to think what happens after he gets to his cabin, but of course I know. I find my dear mother's anal retention rather preferable.

**Saturday 20th December** We had our monthly emergency drill this morning; we were given twenty-four hours notice that it would occur, which should be enough time for anybody to prepare themselves to abandon ship, after all they had only two and a half hours on the Titanic.

We sat in the Passenger Lounge, wearing our big dayglo orange life belts; my whistle will not work properly, and a dolphin swimming three feet away would not hear it. It is a good thing we have not actually had boat drill, because I know that I could not get my leg over high enough to get in the boat. They would have to leave me crying at the rail, and anyway I would not want to spend a month and more in an open boat with Boom Boom Anthony; Captain Bligh might have coped with that, but I know that I could not. I shall stand at the rail and go down thinking of England, and what the Australian cricketers are going to do to us next winter, and my ears shall be filled with Tchaikovsky's Fifth Symphony and Fat Mona's fading cackle from across the waves; I know that she would find a sinking ship absolutely killing.

**Sunday 21st December** We arrived a little early outside the reef, and had to wait for the pilot to take us through the gap. I remembered Suva very well from eight years ago, and little had changed. I walked from the dock into town, through very pleasant gardens with poincianas and bougainvillea, I found the Chinese restaurant where we had possibly the best Chinese meal of our lives, and holed up at Travelodge Hotel; it was Sunday and Suva seemed totally closed down, but the hotel put on a good lunch. In the evening, after a few beers with Trinity House Paul and Chief Officer Jack, we were joined by Anthony and Jane and found another Chinese restaurant, and had a pleasant meal together, and we learned much of what was going on behind the scenes on River Tweed. The officers talked freely and she is not a happy ship, and all fingers seem to point in the direction of Admiral Geoffrey.

There is trouble with the Russian crew because a twenty gallon drum was discovered full of alcohol, which they had distilled and were drinking, but were never found drunk. Because of this Admiral Geoffrey banned all alcohol for the crew, including beer, and mutiny was very close. Purser Alec managed to persuade Admiral Geoffrey to lift the ban on beer; it is very hot and the men really need a cold beer from time to time. Geoffrey should remember that it was lack of imagination which led to Captain Bligh having to make a very long and uncomfortable voyage in an open boat.

When I got back to River Tweed I had a long talk with Fat Mona and Alec. Mona had left her Barclaycard in a shop in Auckland, and had only just realised it, and had phoned to cancel it. We discussed the voyage and the people and they are very guarded in what they say; Fat Mona told me that she was keeping a diary of the voyage and wanted my address so that she could write a letter to me after we get home. There is a ferment afoot on this ship, and I cannot think that this situation is normal in the Merchant Navy.

**Monday 22nd December** Tropical rain descended upon us this morning and I delayed my visit to town until after lunch. Purser Alec had himself made his special chilli chicken dish aboard and it was quite delicious.

There is a shortage of pleasant bars in downtown Suva and I found myself again at the Travelodge in the poolside bar. After a little while and before I had finished my first draught Fiji Bitter, I became aware of a child at the next table staring at me; so unblinking was it, that I wondered if it had a congenital absence of the eyelids. It then got out of its chair and came round and stood behind me, so that I could feel its hot breath on the back of my neck. I prepared to do a backhand swipe, the sort of stroke you use when quelling squabbling kids on the back seat of the car, when you are driving in heavy traffic, but it ran round and went back to its chair and I felt that it had lost interest in me, but do you know what it then did? It put its hand up its shorts and pulled down its willy stretching its foreskin like a piece of Blu-Tack and proffered it at me. I felt like reaching for my glass in order to break it and grind it into that horrible little face, when it made to point at me and knocked over its father's beer. This earned it a left hook to the ear hole of which Mohammed Ali would have been proud in his prime, and there followed the shrieking of a hundred banshees in an enclosed space, during which its mother and father started a steaming, yelling row. As I left the bar I gave it a mouthfart, and I am quite good at mouthfarts.

It is strange how you find things to grab your attention when you are sitting alone in bars, quenching non-existent thirsts.

I looked in a bank on the way back to the ship, thinking perhaps to change a little money, but there were long queues at each window with people jockeying from one to the other; at least at home there is only one queue for all the windows in Post Office and bank, though there can be frustration with that system. You join the queue and when you finally get to the head of it, and your turn comes to approach a window, just as you get there wearing your winning smile, at least you think it is a winning smile, but actually it makes the *risus sardonicus* of end-stage tetanus look attractive; she slams the window shut, and you assume, you poor deluded git, that she has gone to the loo momentarily to relieve herself or change her Tampax, usually both. But no, she has gone to have a long relaxed coffee in the office of that loin-thudding under-manager, with whom she finally got something going only last Friday, the day his wife left for two months to see relatives in Australia. You return to the head of the queue, but a dozen pairs of malignant eyes signal you to the back, and you wonder how long this stupid bloody game of snakes and ladders will continue.

We sailed at 6 p.m. powered by two engines for once. We left behind a Suva oppressed by black sky and a paralysing humidity, but ahead to the west the sun's golden sovereign had done its plummet and plunge, and the white puffs of the cloudlets low down looked like bursts of anti-aircraft shells, and above and behind them the cloud tendrils had become linear and layered and dappled a lovely salmon pink. I stayed up on Monkey Island until all light had gone; to leave before would have seemed ungrateful somehow, like walking out before the end of one of the great concerti which was being wondrously performed.

*Chinese fishing boats alongside in Suva, Fiji. I had visited Suva eight years earlier and little had changed.*

# Chapter 8

## Vanuatu (New Hebrides)

**Tuesday 23rd December** We have a nice short run west north west to Santo to arrive tomorrow, Wednesday, around midday, six hundred and seventy-nine miles from Pilot Suva to Pilot Santo; and we will have the South Subtropical Current with us. We must be careful to avoid a drifting derelict steel vessel, seventy feet long and sticking ten feet out of the water in the West Fiji Basin; it was discovered only in August 1997, and I wondered what happened to its crew. I suppose there must be ships like this floating about the oceans, they will sink ultimately of course, but many must drift on empty and lonely and unwanted for years.

It was extremely hot and humid still, and if you put on a clean shirt it was soaked in sweat almost before you could do the buttons up, your manly private parts stuck to the inside of your thighs, the air conditioning was minimal and sometimes felt more like hot breath on your neck. There was only hot water in the shower, and the loos had stopped working again.

The good news after lunch was that we shall be in Santo for six nights because the cargo at Port Vila has been brought overland to Santo; this means that I can spend five nights ashore, hopefully in Hotel Santo, the only reasonable pub on the island of Espiritu Santo, which will cover Christmas and enable me to escape the forced hilarity on this ship, and telephone my loved ones.

Aristophanes would have approved of Monkey Island as a suitable phrontistery and I had it to myself and my thoughts for three hours this afternoon. There was nothing but the ship, the sea and the sky to occupy my mind and embroider my memories. There was no wind, the sea was almost flat with only a long languid swell and, above, the sky normally ever changing and usually in a hurry seemed to be waiting for instructions, arrested even. The wads of cloud had assembled in a discrete pattern so that the impression was of a gigantic pavement, the close-set white slabs embedded in a blue matrix as far as the eye could see.

Vanuatu, which means 'Our Land' obtained independence in 1980 and dispensed with Cook's unimaginative name of New Hebrides. Cook was not the first navigator to find these islands, the first was the Spaniard Pedro Fernandez de Quiros, who set foot on Espiritu Santo in 1606, and like all of them he thought that he had found the Great Southland, whose existence was originally suggested by Ptolemy and Marco Polo. Quiros killed plenty of natives in the name of the Church of Rome and claimed the island for King Philip III of Spain. He broke their taboo by shaving their heads, he stole their food, he raped their women like a good man of his God, and kidnapped their little boys to convert them to Catholicism, but I fear they may have had other uses.

So sure was Quiros that he had found the great southern continent that he named it Terra Australis del Espiritu

Santo. The Spaniards, as everywhere, were brutal to the natives and did unmentionable things in the name of their god. More or less voluntarily Quiros left for Spain after seven years and died later in obscurity and in poverty, and one can only hope that his death was long and agonising; like Pizzaro in Peru, if ever a man deserved to be crucified it was Quiros.

Bougainville sighted the islands of Vanuatu without landing in 1768, and then Cook came and charted all of them in 1772, and named them the Archipelago of New Hebrides, which was rather more acceptable than Quiros' New Jerusalem.

In the nineteenth century the French and the British argued about ownership, as they have about everything on earth, and then came together with an agreement in 1888. The Germans muscled in, and to keep them out the Franco-British Condominium was formed, known in the islands as the Pandemonium, which really did not work very well; you cannot have one small country with two different sets of laws, education systems and two separate languages.

The First World War had little effect but the Second brought the Americans, and the islands, specially Espiritu Santo became a huge forward base in the campaign to kick the Japanese across the Pacific back to Tokyo, which they did ultimately though with great loss of life on both sides, as this was achieved island by island. The loss of life would have been very much greater if the Americans had had to invade the Japanese mainland, but thanks to Harry Boy Truman having the guts to grasp the nettle, and authorise the dropping of the atom bombs on Hiroshima and Nagasaki, seventy-eight thousand killed in Hiroshima and twenty-four thousand in Nagasaki, but a million lives were saved; that was the score.

I telephoned ahead to Hotel Santo from the ship, because I feared that with only twenty-two rooms it might be full over Christmas, but the extremely laid-back woman who spoke to me said that the hotel was completely empty, and I could have the Bridal Suite whether I had a bride or not, and if not they would gladly find me one or more depending upon how long I stayed.

I have heard that this hotel is a meeting place for seafarers with much local atmosphere, and has tasteful and artistic decoration by a Frenchman, Marcel Monton, renowned for this. However it is decorated, and whoever drinks in the bar, it will be a very welcome change after eight weeks on River Tweed. I have strongly advised Boom Boom Anthony and Know All Jane to stay at the Hotel Bougainville, all of five kilometres out of town, and they have taken my advice.

When I booked this voyage with Boozy Wheezy Captain Campbell, of Cargo Ships Ltd., I asked him what would my fellow shipmates be like, and he said that they would be exactly like myself, lonely sad old folk with the money to go. With room for twelve passengers, I wondered what it would be like if the other eleven were lonely sad old folk like me. I reckoned that it would be perfectly alright, we would respect each other's situation, be prepared to talk about it, work out how to cope with it, and get maudlin pissed together every night. I really think that it might be an improvement on what I have here, but how can I find a shipping agent who deals solely with lonely old men or women?

If there were eleven other lonely single people here, tomorrow we could half fill the Hotel Santo, and all reject Christmas together, and have a marvellous non-Christmas party with no paper hats, and if anybody produced a cracker we could stuff it up their arse in true non-Christmas spirit. Mind you, I have been to quite a few Christmas parties in my time, where if somebody had stuffed a cracker up somebody else's backside it would have saved an otherwise dubious evening. We could have a cry together, because that is what we would really want to do, without any embarrassment. Purser Alec and Fat Mona would fully understand and Fat Mona would weep copiously with us, bless her big fat sympathetic heart.

I shall therefore go to bed and hope to dream that I am in the Seafarers Bar of Hotel Santo and have just been invited to join Robert Louis Stevenson and Joseph Conrad at the other end of the bar, and we have a grog or four together, and I listen rapt while they talk of these islands and the seas between them. I said earlier that being at sea for months on end can bring forth madness, and it may have happened.

**Wednesday 24th December** At 9 a.m. this morning we entered the Vanuatu group of islands by sailing through Selwyn Passage, four hundred metres deep and five miles wide, with the southern tip of the long sausage of Ile Pentecote to starboard and the ankle of boot shaped Ambryn to port. When we emerged from the Passage we could see Espiritu Santo away to port and made a 5 degree turn towards it. The islands we have passed seemed flat and virtually uninhabited, and had no coral reefs around them that we could see.

As we got nearer, the islands seemed to come up almost alongside to inspect us, densely covered green mats, no mountains, just sea-level shrubberies. We entered Scorff Passage, the air temperature over 90 degrees Fahrenheit and there was no wind. This led us into Segund Sound, and we sailed along the long promontory which started with Million Dollar Point, where all the lorries, jeeps and bulldozers were dumped into the sea at the end of the

Second World War. This was done because the French governors did not want their trade in vehicles from France upset by a lot of cheap second hand war supplies. I think that the Americans should have just left it for the islanders.

We must have motored over the top of the President Coolidge, the thirty-five thousand ton cruise liner adapted to be a troop and vehicle transport in 1941. She hit an American mine in the Sound, the Captain tried to ground her on the coral, but she turned over on her port side, slid off the reef stern first and sank. The scuba divers love it, because the bow and first two holds are only eighty feet down and packed with vehicles.

When we reached the little dock in Santo, or Luganville as it is also called, there was room for only one ship the size of River Tweed. She was turned by the current, and nudged into the dockside and her bulbous bow now has a large dent. Eventually they got her tied up and I caught a lift with the agent to Hotel Santo, where I was greeted by Joyce Graham who manages it for the Vietnamese lady owner, and who said that they were really closed for Christmas but she was delighted to have me, and had given me her best room.

It was all very friendly in the bar, a bunch of men with straggly beards and wearing dirty yachting caps. You see men looking exactly like them in every bar on every island in the South Seas and I sometimes feel that they are the same men, and they fly ahead of us from island to island. Perhaps they are all Humphrey Bogart reincarnated. Joyce told me that she is English and she was widowed six years ago when her husband was drowned in Telekula Bay. She said that life stopped for her then, and that only a short time ago she surprised herself by teaming up with another partner, also in his sixties, who is the island vet.

I liked it here, it is a nice little place with a character of its own. I went out to change money at the Sports Club which is the official money change place for Santo, bought some beer, Victoria Bitter VB in tinnies, had some fish and went to bed. That Christmas Eve 1997 apart from the night guard I was the sole occupant of the Hotel Santo, Espiritu Santo, Vanuatu (New Hebrides), South Pacific and that suited me fine.

**Thursday 25th December** Joyce arranged for a tour of the east coast of Espiritu Santo for me, and I was picked up by Glenn who does most of her tours from the hotel. She took the trouble to come and see me off, we had a bit of a chat about sadness and pain and she really wanted to talk to me at length. It is strange how I find myself talking much more to strangers than to my friends at home; perhaps the reason for that lies with me. While I am here I would like to talk to Joyce Graham about many things.

Glenn has a more than clapped out minibus, and he put me in the front beside him and said that I was second -in-command for the day, we picked up two young Frenchmen in their early thirties and began to bounce our way north.

I had read about the state of the one main road on Espiritu Santo, but I can honestly say that in all our experience of travel only one other road was worse, and that was the road to the Ngorongoro Crater in Tanzania, though the 'National Highway' from Saigon to Hanoi, which I survived with my daughter last Christmas came a very close second. That road in Tanzania might have given me testicular cancer, and Esmé complained of temporary paralysis of all four limbs following alleged displacement of cervical vertebrae, though I noted at the time that she was able to hold a glass of wine. I distinctly remember her saying, after an hour on that road, that if I really loved her I would not have planned that stupid bloody trip, and what were we going to see in the fucking crater that we had not already seen? My wife's plain manner of Welshspeak was often a clarifying factor in our marriage, I have to say that.

It is at moments like I have just described that you need resources to fall back upon, but I had such a pain in my orchids that all I wanted to do was get out of that Tanzanian minibus, take the weight off them, and dangle them in a bowl of iced water. The road to the north of Espiritu Santo was built by the Americans in 1942, and Glenn said that not one pothole had been filled since they left. He was very skilful at trying to avoid the bigger holes, but a lot of little ones eventually had the same effect.

This was a marvellous non-Christmas Day, and I do not really know why I have gone on about bad roads. This is a little country so poor that it cannot afford things like road maintenance, and what use would they have made of all those bulldozers, J.C.B.s, diggers, earth movers, road rollers, lorries, trailers, and all the building material, thousands of tons of it, that the Americans decided to give to the sea, and rust till kingdom come, because they could not get their price from France, low though it was.

Our first call was at the point where the President Coolidge slipped off the reef into the deeper Sound. There were pieces of bottle on the beach and some rusty metal, the bottle worn smooth by the sea, mostly coca-cola bottles, the Americans never go to war until the coca-cola supply is ensured; guns, shells and tanks all come a poor second. I found it arresting that a huge, fully loaded liner was just below the water off shore one hundred yards in front of me.

Our next stop was Million Dollar Point, where all was given to the sea. Glenn said that the bulldozers went first, they were started up, steering wheel lashed, put in gear, and off they went; bulldozers will travel quite a distance under water. Then came the lorries and tractors, but things got congested close inshore so they had to take vehicles and supplies further out in landing craft to sink them. On the beach there was plenty of rusty metal, radiators, axles, wheels, windscreens, engine blocks, but this was nothing compared with what must lie under the sea.

Glenn took us on a jungle walk to see a crashed Flying Fortress; there was never any fighting here, it was a large forward supply and air base, and got larger and larger as the American campaign developed. Before they landed here the Americans sent over planes from New Caledonia to see if there were Japanese present; when they were not fired upon the decision was made to land, and we stood on the bay where this happened. The place has no name but since James Michiner died last October, they have decided to call it the James Michiner Memorial Park Bay.

Michiner was a serving American officer on Espiritu Santo, and Glenn was very proud to show us the giant banyan tree under which he wrote 'Tales of the South Pacific'. He told us at length about the two famous prostitutes and Madames of their establishments, Madame Carmen who was French, and Madame Cardelle who was Vietnamese. Both their brothels still stood in a derelict state. Madame Carmen's consisted of a small corrugated iron building, which was the 'Officers' Club' and attached to it was a long Nissen hut, and presumably when the need for a shag became paramount, the mounting was done on two long lines of beds in the hut.

Madame Cardelle's brothel was smaller, and all that remained was a little tin house on Peterson Bay next to Michiner's banyan tree; it appears that they had a 'special relationship', so I presumed he got it free when he wanted it. Madame Cardelle was the 'Bloody Mary' of Michiner's books, and she lived on until 1993 when she died aged

103. She was quite a girl, she wore riding boots, and carried a stock whip. The girls for these brothels were ferried over from the island of Bali Hai which we saw in the misty distance, because they were the most beautiful in this part of the South Pacific. We should therefore add to the American prerequisites for war a guaranteed supply of pretty little girls for between-battle bonking.

Finally we reached Champagne Beach, held to be the most beautiful beach in the whole Pacific. I hoped that the 'eskie' that Joyce had kindly prepared for me had managed to keep the tinnies of VB cold, and indeed it had. A long baguette, packed with chicken mayo and salad, and three tinnies restored morale and helped me to forget the discomforts of touring in faraway Vanuatu, the 90 degrees Fahrenheit heat, and 80 per cent plus humidity. This really was a very beautiful place, the sea turquoise, the very best and most brilliant of the colours blue. It looked as if the sunlight was underneath the water trying to get out, rather than beating down on the surface.

Joyce had said that Glenn was well versed in the fauna and flora of Vanuatu, and he pointed out many trees that I had never seen before; most of them big and with dense foliage. When you stood under these trees looking up, you saw a canopy of sunbright green, the leaves almost transparent, their veins etched most starkly. The nakatanbul with a trunk that becomes curiously fluted just above the ground, and makes a big boom if you hit it with a stone, is very common in these islands; the natives used to communicate in this way. The tamanu, the biggest of all, rather like the takamaka in the Seychelles, branches horizontal and spreading up to thirty yards from the trunk, the napirpir, with a bright coloured trunk which they use to build canoes, the naval wood tree which grew poisonous nuts which can kill humans in a short time, and which they used to catch fish, and the lush lau bush which came right down to the beach with its small, white fruit, were all here around Champagne Beach.

I was interested in the parasite plants which grew on the branches of these majestic timeless trees, many looked like ferns of different sorts, some hang down long ropes, and many of the trunks and branches were garlanded with entwined bromeliads and wild orchids, as if adorned especially for our visit. I saw one tamaru tree which had been struck by lightning and was black and apparently quite dead, and fallen across the silver white beach into the surf, but at the endmost dead branch there sprouted a long-leafed green plant; death after life, and life after death.

Before we left this beautiful place and while the others had gone snorkelling, I sat alone on the beach, and apart from the soft whisper of the far distant surf on the reef, there was silence. It was the sort of comfortable and reassuring silence into which you can lob your thoughts, toss your dreams and cuddle memories of happiness long gone; memories so precious and vulnerable as fine porcelain, memories which must never die until you can die yourself, and only then.

We bumped for what seemed like an age through coconut palm plantations. Most trees were fifty to sixty feet tall, and anything up to ninety years old, but much research has been carried out on Espiritu Santo to produce a hybrid squat palm with a higher fruit yield, and they have succeeded, for under the tall trees there are short ones laden with many more nuts. Palm oil, wood and copra, together with some beef, are the only exports from this island. We saw many cattle, originally imported to control weeds, they are now an industry; initially all charollais, they are now mixed with other breeds from France and Australia, such as  limousin and brahman.

We saw one large forestry factory owned by Malaysians, and Glenn was quite disgusted that they fell the forests without any plans at all for replanting; these poor little countries sell their very soul and get so little in return that would help them improve their standard of living in the long term.

We saw birds, but they were not as striking as those in the Caribbean and Seychelles. There was one extraordinary flash of brilliant malachite green, two Green Pigeons, bodies green, tails black with white edges, and there were the usual mynah birds. We saw quite a few small red birds, Pengali, smaller than sparrows, and the red colour very dark, almost as venous blood.

On the way back to Luganville, Glenn took us to an old Second World War air-strip from which fighters flew to shoot up the Japanese planes and ships around the Solomon Islands where the real battles were fought, and to the Blue Hole, a sixty-five feet deep pool filled by springs, and the water is a deep blue, because of the depth and of the limestone around it. People were jumping and diving into it, often from quite a height, swinging on creepers like Tarzan. Glenn proudly told us that Dorothy Lamour swam in the Blue Hole in 1943, watched by crowds of G.I.s. To Coca Cola and South Sea Island beauties, we must now add a supply of film stars in the field, as essentials for Americans to make war.

When I got back to Hotel Santo I was tired, sore and soaked in sweat, and longing for a cold shower, more cold beer and air conditioning, all of which I had. Joyce had left a plate of ham and salad, which was all I needed, and I rated non-Christmas Day 1997 as enjoyable as non-Christmas Day 1996 in Vietnam, and non-Christmas Day 1995 in South Africa, but I asked myself why must I cope with any more non-Christmas Days at all?

**Friday 26th December** I have not told my family that tonight I am planning a mutiny upon M.V. River Tweed, willingly assisted by officers and crew. Purser Alec and Fat Mona are coming to sup with me this evening, and perhaps Bright Eyed Bearded Henry and Johnny; they are two officers much pushed around by Admiral Geoffrey, so there may be big news, big headlines:

STAND BY FOR IMPORTANT
ANNOUNCEMENT
MUTINY ON ENGLISH CARGO SHIP
IN SOUTH PACIFIC
CAPTAIN SET ADRIFT IN DINGHY BOUND
HAND AND FOOT
NO WATER AND BRICK ROUND NECK
AUSTRALIAN RESCUE SERVICES
SCOUR PACIFIC
BRITISH CRUISERS H.M.S. UPYOURS AND
H.M.S. PRETTYPRAT JOIN SEARCH
AIRCRAFT CARRIER H.M.S. WINDFART ON
STANDBY IN AUCKLAND
RIVER TWEED BELIEVED HEADING
FOR SOUTH POLE
BAR CONVERSATION IN SANTO HOTEL
OVERHEARD
'WHY DON'T WE JUST CUT HIS BALLS
OFF AND DROWN THE BASTARD?'

At least it would make a change from:-

QUEEN MOTHER INDISPOSED
FERGIE TO WRITE HISTORY OF
ROYAL FAMILY
CONSERVATIVE EX-CABINET MINISTER

## ADMITS TO BEING IN HOTEL
## FIVE CHINESE GIRLS IN BEDROOM
## SAYS HE ONLY WANTED TO LEARN ABOUT CHINA

It is amazing what you find to occupy your mind when sitting in a small hotel with tropical rain hurling down outside.

On my way to the beer shop this morning I ran into Fat Mona, and we had a couple of beers, and then a baguette lunch by the pool. I enjoy talking to her when she is being sensible, and we discussed many things other than Alec's problem with Admiral Geoffrey. She has hidden depths, and told me about reviving a tourist in Spain on a bus when he had just suffered a heart attack, by mouth to mouth respiration, and her subsequent friendship with the couple for three years, until he had a second fatal attack. She also told me that Alec has had an offer of a new job by a friend in another shipping line, which he will take on his return; they are sure that he will get a bad report from Admiral Geoffrey for no good reason, and must leave River Line and he has written about the Admiral to his union.

Mona told me that Admiral Geoffrey has put it about behind my back that I am 'not a proper doctor, only a physician', which intrigues me; perhaps he thinks that only surgeons are 'proper doctors'. I have no intention of disabusing him, the arrogant ignorant berk.

In her experience as a hairdresser, Mona assured me that Admiral Geoffrey's mat of jet-black curly hair is artificial, the colour not the hair. I suppose I could have proved the point by taking down his trousers and looking at his pubic hair, but he may well soot that up as well, I would not put it past him, the lecherous Lothario.

While I was down in Wongze Sing's supermarket I spied some bottles of Tsing Tao Chinese beer, and it brought back some very happy memories of our China tour in 1993, when we had a bottle or two in the White Swan Hotel overlooking the Pearl River in Guangzhao as we watched the ships plying up and down. I shall enjoy the four bottles of Tsing Tao which I have brought back for the fridge here very much indeed, in fact I am half way through the first of them as I write this.

Sitting in the poolside bar with Fat Mona this morning, I thought about the people I see in bars like that when quenching non-existent thirsts; usually I am alone, and I have said earlier that it is surprising how you find things to claim your attention. If you have been a clinician all your life you are obviously interested in folk with discernible disabilities, and you have fun trying to diagnose them; but you must not approach them if you cannot diagnose them. You must not, for instance, go up to that woman at the bar with a hideous naevus or somesuch, and say 'What is that awful mark on the right side of your face? You must terrify the children to death'. You must not go up to that man sitting at the table by the door making wild involuntary movements, and say 'Why do you keep jerking about like that ? In a minute you will knock those glasses all over the floor', any more than stand in front of that woman who walks across the bar bent almost double, and say 'Why do you walk with your bottom stuck out like that? You look as if you need the loo all the time', or walk up to that man sitting by the window with a severe facial tic, and say 'Why do you keep winking at people all the time? They will think you are trying to proposition them and you may get more than you bargain for'.

Dinner here tonight at Hotel Santo was excellent; spaghetti for Alec, followed by coconut crab, steak for

Mona, sushimi for me, and right good it all was, I had not had sushimi since we were in Japan in 1988. I followed up with garlic prawns, and it was a very pleasant meal with pleasant people. I have come to accept that you will always need people, even though you may feel that you can only play the game on your own, and the right people will always understand that you need to play it on your own, but they are prepared to be there and listen when you can manage to get out of yourself a bit.

The difference between love and close friendship is minimal; it is the magic of love that makes the difference, the magic that you cannot replace. You can be with people, strangers, for a very short time and know that they have it right, their values are right, and you wish that you could have known them longer; there are many others whom you wish you had never met at all. This all applied without reservation on a voyage like this that I am making, but after two months I know that I have met people like Mona and Alec who have enriched a life that I do not much want, and I am grateful to them for that.

**Saturday 27th December** Sandy and the minibus arrived at the Hotel Santo at 9.15 a.m., to take us on a tour arranged by River Line, and it covered most of what I saw with Glenn on Christmas Day. New for me was Fanafo Village, a custom village with strong traditions and all living in straw huts, the men naked but for the namba, and some with just gourds over their penises; they were building a water tank, and seemed to want us to look around and photograph them. It was from here that the famous Eddie Stevens, a white man, began the Santo rebellion for independence in 1980, under a huge banyan tree; I was unaware that banyans grow on other trees, overwhelm them and kill them, and that is why they have those extraordinary hanging roots.

We passed a large field of geometrically planted narare trees, very tall and dignified, which were planted to provide shade for coffee bushes below. Now that the coffee bushes have gone, they look like forgotten soldiers who failed to hear the order to dismiss, on a parade which ended years ago.

Before lunch at Champagne Beach one of the Americans confided to me that she had two problems. Firstly she had become unexpectedly accursed, and secondly that she overslept and had no time to achieve her normal eliminations before leaving the ship, and to Americans this is a very dire situation. Fortunately she had the wherewithal to deal with the first, and using all my experience as a senior consultant physician, I advised her to take a walk into the bushes to cope with the second. It is strange how people think that if you are a doctor you have an ever-ready interest in these things, when they are the very last that you wish to hear about.

This all reminded me of a gynaecologist colleague many years ago in Gloucester, who told us one lunch time, doctors talk about strange things over meals, about a patient who that very morning had sent him her period through the post; he had never had this before. An envelope arrived containing a sanitary towel with a note saying 'Dear Mr. Brand, this is what I mean.' Sydney Brand had a sense of humour, but unfortunately had to leave Gloucester in a great hurry because he was unwise enough to interfere with the young daughter of a police officer. If he had not done that he would still have had to go because of his method of convincing women who came to him complaining that they had no sexual feeling, that they had. I remember that we gave him a good-bye present of a set of suitcases, because he had to go on a very long world-wide lecture tour before it was safe enough to return to England to set up abortion clinics. The last I heard, twenty years ago, was that he was in a Paris gaol. Poor Sydney, he really had a great sense of humour.

We very much enjoyed our tropical island picnic under a very old part fallen nakantura tree, a hardwood with sap like oil and burning like it. The afternoon was spent swimming and snorkelling in that lovely lucid lagoon.

On the way back Tina did not complain about the road surprisingly, and had regained her sense of humour. She did say that although her suspect back was reasonably comfortable, she now had joggers' boobs without ever having jogged. She told me that she hoped that when the bumping finally stopped, both her boobs would come to rest at the same level; I reassured her that there was every chance that they would.

The longer you live, the more you realise that things of vital importance to other people matter sweet nothing to yourself. I was able to reassure Tina that it did not really affect the health of your skin if you could not shower after swimming in the sea, I was able to reassure Boom Boom Anthony that he was unlikely to develop bilharzia if he swam in the freshwater Blue Hole, although of course I prayed that he would, tomorrow, and die from bladder haemorrhage also tomorrow.

Dinner tonight with Bright Eyed Bearded Henry and Johnny was pleasant indeed, and they told me that Admiral Geoffrey dared not come ashore unless he had three of his officers with him, perhaps he has heard what the Russians will do to him if they get the chance; serve him right, for he has treated them badly on board. I learned much from Henry about cargo shipping, the cracks that appeared on decks, the welding over, the painting over of faults. He has watched from the bridge of a bulk carrier of two hundred thousand tons while the deck 'waved and rippled in a typhoon like a lilo'. Because of the failure by owners to service ships properly, and also because of faulty design and construction to cut costs, the lives of thousands of seamen are constantly at risk. I looked at this man aged nearly fifty who has spent his life at sea as an engineer, and who loves his Johnny, and always calls her 'darling', and I wished them luck. They will continue to sail together until he retires at sixty, and I very much hope that they can continue to enjoy each other in love and friendship long thereafter.

**Sunday 28th December** There is a nice soft breeze today, and I breakfasted outside under the big straw sunshade. The breeze had brought down many petals from the flamboyant which dominates the whole garden, and it seemed that the tree had laid down a scarlet carpet over the grass to welcome me down to breakfast.

I wondered what will happen to this little country, Espiritu Santo is the biggest of the islands of Vanuatu with only twenty two-thousand inhabitants, and all they have is copra, palm oil, timber and a little beef to export. Tourism may develop, but is barely existent at present, and there is really no infrastructure for it. From the early days there have been two companies running the island, the British Burns Philp, and the French Ballande; they have taken their profits and mostly departed for New Caledonia, and Glenn told me on Christmas Day that local people had little time for them and the way they did their business and exploited the island folk.

Yesterday we passed big lorries carrying tree trunks to the Malaysian-owned timber factory. Even if there were a co-ordinated replanting programme, it would take a generation and more for the forest to regrow; the trunks on the lorries were all of slow growing hardwood but they are not even replacing with conifers of any sort, perhaps for climatic reasons. Glenn felt strongly that the present government was corrupt, and those in power had their hands in the till and were stacking money away in foreign tax havens.

I went out for a stroll, and to replenish the Tsing Tao beer at Wongze Sing's, which was next door to Leung Ah Pow's General Store and Whole Sale, advertising Long Botel Lemonade; as with the whole body health of the Americans' corn flakes, I wondered what half sale would mean. I passed a shop window in which there was a notice announcing a Fancy Dress Ball for New Year's Eve: PIRATES AND WENCHES. DRESS NOT ESSENTIAL. In another shop, a paper shop, I read of Dr. Pratt Erwin, a general practitioner on the island who had just been struck off the register in Australia for having a five year affair with a heroin addict female patient. The main accusation against him was the fact that he failed to pass her on to another doctor, but it did not state whether for treatment or five years' more sex with a new partner. I felt that Dr. Pratt Erwin was aptly named.

I have found relative peace in this little hotel because of the staff here; they are people with nothing, people born into and destined to remain in the fourth division, but they have shown me more sense and understanding than I have experienced in a long time, and they are so much happier, like most coloured folk, than I am or ever would have been, if I had not met my wife. Their god gave them the ability to be happy regardless, but gave them little else of life's goods and chances

While I was enjoying my chopped ham and cheese baguette and a can or two of the VB young Paul, the cadet, appeared looking wan. He has had vomiting and diarrhoea for all of three days, and has been most poorly, though he can now drink fluids again. He wonders if he picked up some infection from the filthy water sloshing around in the holds, but I thought that more likely he must have eaten infected food in Suva. He told me that Admiral Geoffrey visited him in his cabin on Christmas Day and told him that his cabin was a mess, and that if you lived in a shithouse you would feel like a shithouse. I wondered if I had really misjudged the Admiral, and that he is simply trying to be funny all the time and I am being unappreciative. During the hot afternoon a couple of young men, obviously lovers, came to the pool. They were so happy together, and I got to thinking about the comments of some of my witty friends in the pubs and clubs of home, 'fucking queers' and such like; I felt that all queers are not necessarily fucking, and if they are it is nobody's business but their own, and that with both sexes 'loving' and not 'fucking' is probably the more attractive verb. What they do, how they express their love, is no business of anybody else, and if they love each other they have a golden situation which some of my witty deriding friends may never have experienced. As a burned out, shagged out, half-dead heterosexual, I feel very strongly about sexual intolerance, and those who decry homosexuality loudest and longest could well be 'protesting too much', as the Bard saith.

I dined alone with Richard Clayderman, and I remembered so well the first time that I heard Richard Clayderman in a delightful restaurant in Provence. We were enjoying a holiday in a luxurious villa owned by a wealthy patient, which was tax efficient for both of us, and we were dining with my daughter and a friend, and they played tapes of Clayderman. Memories are laid down half hidden in your mind, and you must not expect them to be hanging in front of you for the picking when you open your mental door. You often have to dredge, delve and grapple for them in a sediment of time and happenings.

**Monday 29th December** I had a beer with Eric and Tina by the pool, and after a light lunch returned to the ship. It was raining and this did not seem to relieve the heat and humidity in any way, Boom Boom Anthony and Know All Jane went fishing and Jane caught a nine pound fish, which we are to share tomorrow.

I shall see this voyage through to the end, I want to see the Solomon Islands and I want to go back to Papua New Guinea and wallow in memories. I suppose the alternative option would be to fly home from Singapore, but then I have never seen Suez, and may never have another chance; so I will go on with it in spite of the Admiral's dislike of me; I just hope that he doesn't shanghai me on some tiny South Sea Island.

**Tuesday 30th December** Back aboard I woke in a dreadful sweat in the middle of the night for two reasons, firstly because of the air temperature, and secondly because I realised that I had left my wife's photograph in the Hotel Santo. I legged it to the hotel after breakfast with the thermometer already reaching over 85 degrees Fahrenheit, and when I went through the door I was greeted by my friends of five days, Lydia, Leila, Anna, Bernadette, and John Behind the Bar, he appears to have no other name. I felt that I was the Resurrection and the Life to Come, it was indeed my Second Coming, from the way they all welcomed me. Leila went upstairs to retrieve Esmé, and though it was early, John Behind the Bar persuaded me, and it took all of thirty seconds, to have a beer. It was as if the seafarer had finally come home again; I wanted to cry, because I would never see these lovely folk again and I walked back to the ship clutching my dear old puss to my sweaty chest.

During the afternoon I spent two hours watching the loading of the copra and cocoa. The copra is coconut meat, part-dried on racks above ovens fired by coconut shells. It was brought to the dock in sacks, the lorries grossly overloaded, and emptied out onto the floor of a large warehouse; it was then shovelled into containers with mechanical shovels, and fork-lifted to the shipside. The containers are hoisted into the holds by the ship's cranes and emptied, a bulldozer swung in to distribute the copra over the floor of the hold. The whole process was very labour-intensive, and you would think that they would have some sort of conveyor-belt system to get the copra from the warehouse to the ship. If it rains everything stops, for copra must not be allowed to get wet or it will deteriorate. The cocoa came shipside in lorries, and the sacks were packed into the holds, swung aboard on pallets.

I watched all this going on with Fat Mona, who will let me have an edited copy of the video film of the whole voyage that she is making. She really has had a rough time since Dunkirk, seasickness, very swollen legs in the heat, insomnia, and now she tells me cystitis, presumably of the sort that we used to call 'honeymoon'; she is supposed to be on an extended honeymoon, bless her. She also has been badly bitten, and some of her bites went septic, she thinks her white legs attract the insects, and I must say that landing must be easy for them, and there is certainly plenty to bite on after landing.

I should say here that I have bought a black seafarer's cap in Luganville, with a raised crown and a piece of gold nylon rope stretched across and just above the peek. I did this because after they have put Admiral Geoffrey into the dinghy, with or without his balls, I intend to captain this ship, and a cap like that is bound to command respect; the Russians are saluting me already. It has 'Santo Vanuatu' in white letters on the front of it; to tell you the truth I rather fancy myself when I wear it

**Wednesday 31st December** It was very pleasant up

on Monkey Island watching the end stages of the copra and cocoa loading, very hot in the early morning sun, but then a nice sea breeze rose and blew in along Segund Sound. The stevedores stopped work at 1 p.m. for the New Year holiday, and Admiral Geoffrey has insisted that we leave after lunch, even if all the cocoa is not aboard.

I now have to report an extraordinary happening, an event more shattering than the Queen insisting on paying back tax to 1953, or the Duke of Edinburgh making a public promise not to drop any more clangers, more shattering than the Pope announcing from St. Peter's that condoms are now O.K. and that he has arranged for £20 billion of the Vatican's hoarded riches to be made available immediately, to build condom factories in every Third World country where he has preached against contraception, more shattering even than Lady Thatcher agreeing that her son Mark should not inherit the title that she secured for his father, or Jeffrey Archer insisting on giving back his Lordship because he feels that he really does not deserve it; this day, New Year's Eve, Admiral Geoffrey spoke to me without my speaking first to him. I ran into him in the passage, and he said 'Hello', such intimacy must be watched, you never know what might happen next. There are no special arrangements aboard to celebrate this New Year, and I am glad about that, because I did not want the previous two, and I certainly do not want this one.

We edged away from Luganville dock at 2.45 p.m., turned and went back northwards up Segund Channel and Scorff Passage, the way we came in. We passed the three buoys marking the wreck of the President Coolidge, then Million Dollar Point, and hugged the east coast of this big island of Espiritu Santo. We shall pass Quiros Point, named after the island's discoverer and first plunderer, and then turn westward.

We have now come to a sudden stop because one of the clutches has failed, and there is evident increased activity in the engine room, with frequent calls to the bridge. While we drift, the bosun has tipped a skipful of black plastic bags containing stinking food waste over the rail, and they float away slowly astern like the heads of Negro slaves in the sea. This is illegal, and if he was working on a cruise ship, Chief Officer Jack told us, he would be off at the next port. I asked why the food waste could not be tipped into the sea and the bags incinerated, and got no satisfactory reply. On a cruise ship one tin can overboard, if seen, is enough to get a crew member the sack, but not on dear old River Tweed. There were many island beaches a short distance away, and that was where most of these bags will end up pretty soon; if every sizeable ship did this sort of thing in these sea passages, you can imagine what the beaches, though remote, would be like.

**Thursday 1st January** I am currently reading an excellent book. It is well written and researched by an expert in his field, and with a right good tale to it as well. It depresses me that every ten pages or so he introduces a new character, and then in a further ten pages another new character of the opposite sex, and within yet another ten pages they are bonking their bums off, having ecstatic sex with no relevance to the story whatsoever, the women making love with the fervour of nuns at communion to men they hardly know.

I am sick of reading, not only in this book, about how he 'slid into her' or how she 'inhaled the whole length of him'. Now there has to be an anatomical doubt about that one; if his willy is down her windpipe for any length of time she dies of asphyxia, if it is down her gullet she will retch repeatedly, and I honestly cannot think that either of those two situations can possibly enhance an act of love, but then we are probably not involved with that.

I remembered in the nineteen-eighties we were reading and enjoying the books of Noel Barber, from 'Farewell to France' through 'Tanamera' and 'A Woman of Cairo' to 'The Daughters of the Prince', which he never finished because he died, and asking ourselves how could an author think up such well informed stories and paint such ridiculous characters. I also remembered that we asked ourselves why the sex in these books always had to be dynamic, forceful and penetrative almost to the point of perforation to be ecstatic, because that is not really what ecstasy is all about; we felt that it was more about taking time for loving, and wondered why so few authors wanted to describe that. Why could they not write about the exquisite ache of anticipation that could go on for ages, the deliciousness and delight of sure and confident delay for as long as you both may want it, and only then the come, together each to each and one and the same, with a breath and a sigh, sleek as satin, and smooth as silk?

In a very amateur way I have tried to think of all the ways possible to describe love and grief, and they are equal parts of the same equation. It is much easier to describe a single sex act, you can wrap it or unwrap it how you wish, embellish it, magnify it, distort it, you can really do anything you want with it, that is all so easy. To try to describe adequately loving and losing from personal experience is beyond me.

By 7 a.m. we have left the northern tip of Espiritu Santo behind. From Santo Pilot to Honiara Pilot is five hundred and ninety-one miles, and we are due there later tomorrow. Our present course on a north-west heading of 320 degrees took us over the North New Hebrides Trench, the sea was utterly tranquil, the sun already well up his daily climb, and on one engine this lame old tub is achieving just ten knots.

We stopped and drifted mid-morning to enable the engineers to attempt to mend the clutch bearing in the starboard engine, and we observed maritime law and ran up two black balls, so that they hung vertically on the mast on Monkey Island. This must be done when the ship goes 'out of command' so that other ships who may be able to see us will know that we are drifting without power.

While we drifted a peace descended on the ship, everything seemed very quiet, and if somebody dropped a spanner it sounded like a girder falling from a height into a hold. The repair was completed in a couple of hours, and we were off with both engines throbbing at a speed of thirteen knots and increasing.

News came through to the bridge that a British ship with twenty eight people aboard had sunk off Miami. The loss of life was not known, but U.S. coasters had taken people off; this happened in a typhoon, and we looked at the dead calm South Pacific all around us and felt that we had been very fortunate with the weather all the way so far.

I found myself on the bridge alone with Russian Iosif, and for the first time on the voyage he opened up a little about his problem with Admiral Geoffrey, who has bullied him all the way; like a true bully the Admiral goes for those whom he considers the most vulnerable. Iosif said that the only way that he can survive this voyage is to give Admiral Geoffrey the widest possible berth, and at all costs keep his mouth shut. We both, then, had the same plan; I just hoped that my natural paranoia would not get the better of me and that I can keep out of trouble until I get home, when I can do most damage to him by writing and talking to River Line.

I am convinced that Admiral Geoffrey has a mental problem which goes beyond mere constitutional psychopathy, but it would be most dangerous to stir that sort of mud while he is in legal control of us all.

*I spent Christmas Day 1997 on Espiritu Santo, Vanuatu (formerly the New Hebrides). This is the village Chief of Fanafo Village, it was from here that the Santo rebellion for independence began.*

# Chapter 9

## Solomon Islands

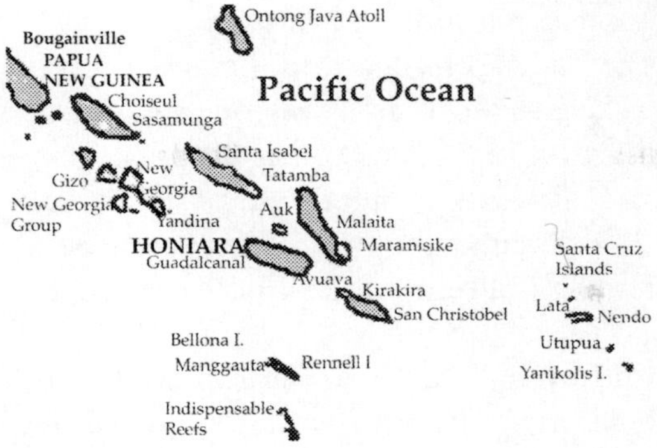


**Friday 2nd January** Know All Jane did not appear much yesterday because of her cold, but at breakfast this morning she was a little better. She appeared on deck after breakfast, knowing all again, and pontificating about the Solomon Islands ahead. She had obviously felt well enough to read it up in the South Pacific Handbook before lecturing us and so had we.We crossed the South Solomon Trench, eight thousand metres deep, and saw Santa Cuia Island fourteen miles to port, and the enormous San Christobal Island beyond. At lunch we passed within four miles of three small islands called Three Sisters, and should make Honiara late tonight.

Apart from Second World War relics which interest me greatly, the Solomons have spectacular mountains, coral reefs, lagoons and beaches. The first Europeans came here in 1568, and the islands got their name because Alvaro de Mandana, who saw them first on a voyage from Peru, suggested that here was where King Solomon found his great wealth. The renowned Abel Tasman came here, but nobody stayed until the end of the 19th century, when traders and missionaries settled the islands.

There was the usual cruelty and brutality for the natives, many hijacked to work as slaves on sugar plantations in Australia and Fiji. The British stopped this in 1893 by making the islands a protectorate based at Tulagi on Guadalcanal. It remained thus until the Japanese and the Americans virtually obliterated the whole area in 1942 and 1943.

The three hundred and fifty thousand mixed people, Melanesians, Polynesians, Europeans and Chinese, were given independence in 1978, and the first Prime Minister, Peter Kenilorea was New Zealand educated; the capital was then moved from Tulagi to Honiara.

I found it interesting that the Solomon Islands lie on the rim of the Indo-Australian and Pacific tectonic plates, which accounted for the smouldering volcanic activity, and hence the relative newness of some of the islands in the group, which have hills and small mountains with lumps of coral and shell masses, part fossilised, on the very top of them. I am looking forward to sampling Solbrew, the locally brewed lager; in Vanuatu they also brewed their own lager called Tusker, but it tasted rather vinegary, much like the Indian Kingfisher beer, the worst beer I have ever experienced anywhere in the world.

More clutch problems have now slowed us down further, and at this speed of nine knots we will meet the Honiara pilot at 5.30 tomorrow morning. The last final straight on this leg is Indispensable Strait. We have come from Espiritu Santo on a bent course, starting with a heading almost due north, and ending on 260 degrees, almost due west, and this was achieved by making three separate corrections at intervals of about one hundred miles. It has rained for three hours, the clouds black and seeming to join the sea all around us, sealing us in. Visibility was down to two miles, but there was only a mild Pacific chop, which barely moves the ship. The water, so blue and iridescent for weeks is now a glowering, gloomy grey. It was another night for books and music, and it will be Sibelius instead of Beethoven; he will better fit with what I see out of my cabin window this early-year South Pacific vesper. I shall enjoy the music so much more than joining the others to watch yet another thirty year old two star American movie, the sort of movie that starred Ronald Reagan.

**Saturday 3rd January** I devoted last evening to music. I played Sibelius' First Symphony, and that was fine, my favourite among Sibelius' symphonies, and then I played a tape called 'Classical Ecstasy', given to me by one of my daughters after her mother died, a selection of gentle emotional music she knew would feed my feelings.

Most of the time I plod on solely because I cannot escape this life. Real Men Don't Cry, Real Men Manage, in the same way that I managed at the public school at which I was lucky enough to be educated. In places like that you learned that you must never 'blub'; if you 'blubbed' it tended to be unwise, and if you ever showed discomfort when you were beaten you could get a couple more from the nasty little sadist who was my housemaster; a devout middle aged bachelor, he was well placed to work out his own problems; truly a man among boys and a boy among men.

I am not, and never have been in this context a Real Man, and I have never been able to understand that if you must not show the emotion of sadness, how could you ever truly show the emotion of love, because they are the deepest human emotions and so close. Perhaps those of my friends who are embarrassed by displays of emotion have never needed to bare their souls to their wives, their children, their friends, to anybody; I do not blame them for that, but they must be made of stern stuff indeed.

We entered the port of Honiara sailing over Iron Bottom Sound, that graveyard of fifty ships, American Japanese and Australian, and thousands of men slaughtered in the prime of their lives, and we eventually tied up at the little dock which can take only one ship of this size at a time; we had to wait for a container ship to get out of the way before we could go in. As we approached the dock, we passed through a tuna fishing fleet anchored, the fishing ships with black nets piled high on the stern, and the bigger mother ships, refrigerator ships registered in many different countries. Tuna are being fished out of the oceans, and soon will be an endangered species unless something very firm is agreed and kept to in the way of yearly quotas. There must have been fifty ships in that fleet, and along with timber fish is the main export from these islands, together with copra and palm oil. Admiral Geoffrey arranged a minibus to take us on a tour of Guadalcanal, and I was able to see the Second World War sites that I wanted to see, the War Museum containing guns and crashed planes, mostly American, Edson's Ridge (Bloody Ridge) where there was an immense and crucial battle for the airstrip, Henderson's Field now an 'international' airport. The Battle of Edson's Ridge, on Guadacanal and the sea Battle of Midway were the two battles which finally turned the tide against the Japanese. We went to Red Beach where the Americans first landed, and more such. History was made here, and it seemed such a small corner of the world.

It was a good day with a truly delightful guide named Pio, a short thickset man with a huge head, made bigger by a baseball cap with the longest peak I have ever seen, more like an awning. It seemed that his head was an afterthought, for he could never have made the journey down the birth canal with it in situ. He had a great sense of humour and spoke excellent English, a really lovely man.

We have taken on board fifty empty containers, two large containers full of helicopter parts destined for Hamburg, and I wondered where they came from, two thousand tons of palm oil and fifty tons of cocoa. We are off at midnight, with the next stop Rabaul on the island of New Britain.

I think that to compose my mood for this night, I will listen to Haydn. It is easy to listen to Haydn, but apart from that it is very rewarding. I shall listen to his Missa Sancti Nicolai, and then his Missa Brevis. I can think my thoughts so easily with that music filling my ears, and after that I shall listen to his ninety-fourth and ninety-sixth symphonies. You do not have to address the music of Haydn as you do, say, of Mahler, it is a lovely background for your thinking, a delightful happy continuum.

**Sunday 4th January** Leaving Honiara just before midnight, we took a northwest course over Iron Bottom Sound, past Savu Island to starboard and Pavuvu, of the Russell Group to port. Ahead of us, as we ploughed through New Georgia Sound, otherwise known as The Slot, there were the islands of the New Georgia Group with lovely names like Vella Lavella, Kolombangara, and the large New Georgia Island.

From Pilot Honiara to Pilot Rabaul is five hundred and seventy-nine miles, and averaging only ten knots on the one engine, we will get there the day after tomorrow. I suspect that the people of New Britain will resemble those of the main island of Papua New Guinea, dark with thick fuzzy hair. The people of the Solomons were less dark, many of them had light blond hair, and when first you see this, especially on the children, it seems rather incongruous. The people of French Polynesia do not look like the Melanesians of Fiji and Vanuatu, and those folk do not look like the Solomon islanders; that is the spice of travel, new faces, new people under new suns, new stars and new moons.

It is now mid-afternoon, and we have almost passed by the whole length of the enormous island of New Georgia, and just past it to the west is the extinct volcano of Kolombangara, one thousand seven hundred metres high. I wondered when that shot up through the surface of the Solomon Sea, for now we have finally left the Pacific and entered the Solomon Sea, with the eight thousand metre Planet Deep beneath us; I love that name, it conjured up in the mind a cut to the very heart of planet earth itself. As we approach New Britain we shall cross the New Britain Trench.

I was foolish enough last night to ask Admiral Geoffrey why we did not get the usual free lunch on our free tour yesterday. He told me that I was nit-picking and asked how I dared to discuss things like that in the Dining Saloon, but when I suggested that we should continue the discussion in his cabin, he declined and told me to write to the company. Most certainly I shall write to the company when I get home, but it will not be about free lunches, it will be to tell them that after four months' study of Admiral Geoffrey at close quarters, I am convinced that he is verging on paranoid psychosis.

My brown-nosed companions sit tight and say nothing, but they tell me that they are going to write to the company as well, I doubt they will. The way that they humour this bully of a man with their mealy mouthed talk, nauseates me. I must however be careful, because the Admiral may refuse to let me send faxes, he says he has that power, and that would effectively cut me off from my family and the outside world. By the look in his eyes last night, I will be advised to lock my door without fail; his cabin is next to mine.

FRAIL ELDERLY DOCTOR ATTACKED IN
SOUTH PACIFIC
MAD CAPTAIN LOSES CONTROL
OFFICERS AND CREW COME TO RESCUE
CHIEF OFFICER TAKES OVER COMMAND

In the late afternoon we could see the enormous island of Choiseul to starboard, with its satellite islands around it, and we were joined also on the starboard side of the ship by a school of what looked like small dolphins, but which actually were porpoises. I was, for once, able to correct Know All Jane on that point.

Discussion at dinner tonight ended with everybody being asked to say what they would do if told that death was inevitable next Friday. Eric said that he would like an old-fashioned Texan barbecue, the sort where you spoon out the hot brains from the calves' heads onto your plate as a starter, and then after the barbecue, he would go up into the mountains and wait. Tina could not make up her mind, and will tell us later, which means that she does not want to think about it. Boom Boom and Know All, said that they did not want to die anyway, and refused to make a serious decision, the self-satisfied sods; I said that I would not want to have to wait until next Friday and would have preferred yesterday, or last year, or the year before that.

I felt very lonely tonight and Tchaikovsky's Sixth Symphony did not help. I followed that with Elgar's Second Symphony, which normally uplifts me; perhaps I should have gone to bed with Beethoven, it is usually best to go to bed with Beethoven when you are at your lowest.

*A Screw Pine, the "walking" Pandanus tree, James Michiner Memorial Park Bay, Espiritu Santo, Vanuatu.*

*Fanafo Village has strong traditions – the residents all living in straw huts, the men naked but for the namba.*

*Guadalcanal. History was made here - now marked by the debris of war.*

*The spice of travel, new faces, new people. It came as something of a surprise to find that these children of the Solomons had light blond hair.*

*Loading Copra at the little dock in Santo - room for only one ship the size of River Tweed. The copra is coconut meat, part-dried on racks above ovens fired by coconut shells the trade plays a vital role in the economy of these islands.*

# Chapter 10

## Papua New Guinea

**Monday 5th January** During the night we have passed between the fringe of Shortland Islands at the southern end of huge pear-shaped Bougainville, with its stalk of Buku Island at the northern end, and to port the small Treasury Island with the Mona Mountain dominant. As we plodded on at 300 degrees over the Solomon Sea, Bougainville dropped gradually away to starboard, and when we passed the Shortlands we crossed the line of demarcation between the Solomon Islands and Papua New Guinea. From now until we head north for Singapore in just over a week, we shall be in Papua New Guinea territorial waters.

Before breakfast Chief Officer Jack got out the Meteorology for Mariners book, and told me about prevailing winds. I could not understand why we have a head-on westerly wind straight on the bow, when we should have the prevailing south-east trade-winds astern, Jack said that winds veer from the normal pattern for days on end.

Watching River Tweed sitting lower in the water again with the two thousand tons of the Solomon palm oil in her forward tank, she was quite head down, and Jack said that this would be more so after the next four thousand tons of oil comes aboard in Kimbe. In next stop Rabaul there will be a load of five hundred tons of cocoa, and plenty of empty containers, but no palm oil.

We shall sail all day without sight of land, unlike yesterday when we had islands in view much of the time. I did this morning's watch with Russian Iosif, you cannot converse much with him, because of all the Russian Officers his English is the poorest, but he does seem to understand well enough when Admiral Geoffrey ticks him off, I can see it in his face. I wondered which of the Russians will be the first to castrate Admiral Geoffrey at the end of the voyage; I reckon Big Vanya will get to him first, with Russian Iosif a close second. If I was Admiral Geoffrey I would arrange for a chopper to lift me off before the ship docks in Europe; he is a hard and vicious man, a nasty bit of work, and I was glad that I was a passenger and not an officer or a crewman under him. During a war Admiral Geoffrey would long since have had a sad accident, like falling over the side and made mincemeat of by the propeller.

At lunch today the conversation ranged from the oil platforms we may see after leaving Papua New Guinea to energy production generally, and Eric, who is really an engineer at heart whatever he did in life, told me a lot about tide and wave power, and how to harness it. He knew about harnessing wind power, and he was fascinated by turbines, and has been down in a lift on the Hoover Dam in Colorado to view the turbines three times. I wished that we could have seen the turbines in action when we visited the Aswan Dam in Egypt, and the Itaipu in Brazil, and for that matter the Hoover, but we were not given the chance; I would have loved it.

We should make Rabaul at 6 a.m. tomorrow morning, sailing through St. George's Channel separating New Britain from New Ireland, thirty-five miles wide at it's mouth and seventeen miles wide at its narrowest. Rabaul is on the north side of Gazelle Peninsula, New Britain is shaped like a sitting man and Gazelle Peninsula is his head; about thirty miles to the north was the long slender curved island of New Ireland, with a bulge at each end and a small one in the middle, like a big over-sized cap over the top of Gazelle Peninsula. St. George's Channel is narrowest just below Rabaul, and right in the middle of it is the Duke of York group of islands, seeming almost to block a clear way out into the Bismarck Sea to the west; all these islands, the Admiralty, New Britain and New Ireland form the Bismarck Archipelago.

At dinner I had a consultation, Tina had found some black mould on the bottom of her shower curtain, and she asked me if she would avoid infection if she did not touch it; I assured her that there must be every chance. She was also worried because she had got grease and dirt all over her hands when a door-knob came off, and I was able yet again to reassure her that she could well get away without serious skin disease.

I wondered what Americans would do if they had to live life in the real like the rest of us. They were quite terrified of being ashore after dark, they were scared stiff even to walk down a well-lit main street for fear of mugging and rape. Any local island man who wanted to rape these women would have to be pretty hard up for a bit of nookie. They go into shops and flash their money about and talk about it in a way that just invites trouble; they would more likely get mugged in California or Florida than in these poor little islands.

In order to re-focus my mind from my immediate

company, as usual I resorted to music and I listened tonight to Chopin's First and Second Piano Concerti, and I remembered during a tour of the death camps in Poland last summer, I listened to a man playing Chopin under a canopy beside a lake in a park on a warm spring Sunday afternoon in Warsaw. There were hundreds and hundreds of people sitting and listening and I wanted to stay while he played the tunes from the Concerti and more. Chopin seems such a gentle composer who never seeks to make the big effect. I wish that he had written more concerti, he had the time, but I am glad that he did not write symphonies because they might have led him away from gentleness and tenderness, as they do with many composers. The larghetto, the second movement of Chopin's Second Piano Concerto is the very talk of love, of his unrequited love for the singer Constanta Vakovska.

**Tuesday 6th January** The sail into St. George's Channel was impressive, with New Britain and Gazelle Peninsula four miles away to port, the outline of New Ireland twenty miles away to starboard. We passed the Duke of York group on the starboard side, and saw ahead the Crater Peninsula with four volcanoes on it; Mother, South Daughter, Matupit and Mount Tavurvur, and Tavurvur was smoking ominously. On the port side was Blanch Bay with the enormous pink mound of Mount Vulcan, with its north-east dent and collapsed holes. On 17th September 1994 at 7.30 a.m. both Vulcan and Tavurvur erupted together, as if prearranged, and covered a large part of Rabaul with volcanic ash in no time at all; together they virtually destroyed the port, but fortunately nobody was killed. The other large town of Kokopo to the east was unaffected.

After docking I walked down the main street of what must have been a very pretty little port, found the

Hamamas Hotel and renewed acquaintance with South Pacific Export Lager, of which we drank plenty in Papua New Guinea in 1990. After a salad lunch I went down Mango Avenue leading to Sulphur Creek Road and towards Crater Peninsula, once very busy streets, and I could only describe the whole area as like the pictures of Hiroshima that I have seen after the atom bomb in 1945. There was ankle deep black volcanic ash everywhere, the twisted metal skeletons of buildings and broken lumps of concrete, there was total devastation. The vegetation, destroyed by the pyroclastic flow and black ash, was beginning to grow again, but very sparsely.

I found the Second World War bunker of Admiral Onishi, in which Admiral Yamamoto spent his last night before being shot down by the Americans on a flight from Rabaul to Bougainville in 1943, cruel infamous man that he was, he would have been hanged for atrocities committed in the Philippines if he had not been assassinated.

At the bunker I made two friends, Henry and Frederick, both with red teeth from chewing betel nuts. They told me all about the eruptions of 1994, and pointed out the ruins of the buildings along the street, two banks, a pharmacy, Air Niugini offices, schools, a supermarket, an hotel, a club, and many shops; there was even a golf course which was destroyed. This was a busy thriving end of town before the disaster, and there is an ongoing dispute with insurance companies as to reparation, and until this is settled no rebuilding can start.

When I got back to the ship I sat down and tried to sort out in my mind the things that I had seen here; I have never witnessed such destruction on my travels previously, except perhaps Pompeii, but that happened so long ago, and is therefore less stark. Mount Vulcan previously erupted in 1937 and now looked dead, but Tavurvur looked far from dead, and I would not want to be living near it right now, with all that smoke pouring out of the top of it, it looked as if it could erupt again any minute.

Rabaul is at the top end of lovely natural Simpson Harbour, easy to defend in a war, and the Americans never took Rabaul from the Japanese, who stayed here until the end. I left thinking about all that devastation, the black ash, the twisted metal, the dust everywhere, and I wondered how could the likes of Henry and Frederick have rewarding lives; they are educated young men who speak perfect English, but they have been so handicapped early in their lives, as were their forefathers by the Japanese occupation, and the complete destruction of the port by American bombing.

We sailed out of Simpson Harbour across Blanch Bay, and at one point Crater Peninsula with its four volcanoes to port, and Mount Vulcan to starboard were only two miles apart, two miles between Sulphur Point and Vulcan Point. Sulphur Point was aptly named; as we approached this morning there was the pungent sulphurous smell from Tavurvur on the morning wind when we were still miles away. The stink of hydrogen sulphide took me back to the chemistry laboratories at school.

Tonight as we left Tavurvur was lit by the moon, the white smoke from its crater glowed rufescent from time to time as red hot rocks shot up into the cloud capping it; it looked like a huge giant's bonfire, presently banked but ever ready to burst into flame. There was something very awe-inspiring about this place.

**Wednesday 7th January** At breakfast the menu is scanned carefully by my American shipmates for some combination that is not on it, and they ask for that, to keep the stewardesses and kitchen staff on their toes. This day every conceivable combination was there, and they had a problem. I tried to help by suggesting the combination of 'termayter and termayter' on fried Ryvita, but did not get a laugh.

I tried to equate American overendowment and overindulgence with Russian poverty and misfortune, and I failed.

During the night River Tweed had rounded the northern point of Gazelle Peninsula and entered Bismarck Sea, she was now half way across on a south-west heading of 224 degrees, and around lunch time we should cross Kimbe Bay and reach Kimbe, after a short run of one hundred and seventy eight miles along the coast of New Britain, from Rabaul Pilot to Kimbe Pilot.

On our way across the Bismarck Sea, we had to be careful to keep west of the unsurveyed Banham Reefs around Loloban Island, an active volcano, separated from the mainland by Expectation Strait. I loved these names, and wondered what led ancient mariners to use them. What was the deception about Deception Point, the disillusion about Disillusionment Isles? What troubled Cook about Cape Tribulation in Queensland? Two of Banham Reefs are named Father Reef and Son Reef, so we have Mother and Daughter Volcanoes, and Father and Son Reefs in New Britain, I liked that.

Kimbe Port lies in Stettin Bay and the German influence in Papua New Guinea is considerable. I hear Admiral Geoffrey asking that we dock before dark; the one jetty is occupied by an oil tanker, and he wants to get in before dark because the jetty in Kimbe keeps getting knocked down by ships, and it is an expensive sport. The jetty is approximately half the length of a ship like this, and we are taking on board four thousand tons of palm oil and one thousand five hundred tons of copra, so we need to be parked about right as far as the holds are concerned.

I had a good look at my clothes, because at lunch I learned that the washing machine is spinning far too long, and the drier was too hot, and my shipmates' clothes were getting ruined. I run on four shirts, four pairs of shorts, four pairs of pants, and four pairs of socks, and do a wash and iron about once a week, and I have to get into the laundry room and hog the machines before the other passengers, and the Admiral. He is usually first in, but I have found out from his stewardess that she wakes him at 6.15 a.m., so I get my stuff in the washing machine at 6 a.m. Once you have possession of the washing machine you control the whole game.

I honestly hope that my men friends will never, never, never find themselves in my position, and manage to die before their wives; they probably will, most of them, but one or two will not, and their only alternative seems to be to forage abroad and hunt for a quick replacement, but that can be fraught with peril. If you found somebody younger, which obviously you will want to do as a better investment, you could be presented with tests which could daunt you, and this problem could outweigh the witty comments in your pub or club: 'Look at old So and So, he didn't wait long, the old dog.' 'Wo-wo' and 'Phwarrrrh', and that sort of inane male bar talk.

If you found somebody older she could already have a health problem and you would not want to go through another terminal illness which is not your own. Your own may not be far away, you pray, if you are myself. No, I will bat on alone, even if it means dealing with washing machines that spin too long and dryers that are too hot, and trying to avoid all those other ghastly old drooling decrepits at the 'meals for one' shelf at Sainsbury's or Tesco, or wherever. I am very glad to do this, because I would never have wanted my darling old puss to have to do the same thing, and now she never will; she is safe from that.

We sailed into the wide-mouthed Stettin Bay, the headlands twenty-five miles apart. This approach was different from Rabaul, Honiara, Santo, Suva or Noumea, no Passages, Sounds or Channels to traverse, just straight in from the Bismarck Sea. We anchored a mile from the port, because a long red tanker still occupied the jetty. The depth here was forty metres and the anchor chain was one hundred metres long; Admiral Geoffrey said that you should never be in a hurry when dropping anchor, just take it easy until the anchor bites and the chain tightens, and let the ship swing as she goes. This was only the third time on the voyage that we had anchored off-shore; the others were at either end of the Panama Canal.

It has rained hard most of the way from Rabaul, the rain spearing at the windows of the bridge like silver skewers. When we reached the wide bay mouth, Admiral Geoffrey let Know All Jane take over the bridge controls until the anchor was dropped. She has been currying his favour since we started out, and giving him the eye, there are very few more unattractive experiences in this world, than watching a hard bullying tyrant enjoy having his bum tickled, and one of them is watching a woman enjoy doing it. We have both on this ship and they will continue until Le Havre to their mutual satisfaction, and my total disgust.

I told you some while back that in rushing up the stairs to be the first to see some dolphins, Know All Jane fell and damaged her binoculars; sad to say Admiral Geoffrey has mended them for her. I wondered whether we have reached the stage where the sneaky little devil will pop down the passage of a night time to the Admiral's cabin, for a bit of legover while that fat pig Boom Boom Anthony snores off the daily intake from the trough.

We finally docked tonight at 8 p.m. the pilot boat collected hawsers from fore and aft of River Tweed, five of them, and took them one at a time to the little jetty where they were looped around metal bollards, and we were gently winched in. Mostly we have docked in the early morning, only a couple of times at night, and the yellow floodlights on the docks, and the ship's floodlights made night docking rather exciting, I enjoyed watching all the activity from high up on Monkey Island in the warm tropical night air, with the heady scents of the lush vegetation concentrating as they do after sunset, filling my nostrils

**Thursday 8th January** I had hoped that this ship would call at Tarawa in the Gilberts, because I wanted to see where a mistake in the time of high tide killed thousands of American marines when the amphitraks got stuck on the coral, but I have already seen most of the relics of the Second World War that I wanted to see on this voyage. I have asked myself why I wanted to see them. I felt that if I went to these places of suffering I could share in the suffering in some tiny way, and if I could share in it, I could diminish it; the more people there are to share in suffering, the more it will be diminished, even long after the event. If a veil is drawn over it all, and it is consigned to history books, then it can never be diminished, it will forever be as it was. We must try to go on living it for the sake of those people who failed to live through it.

I find it very hard to explain this but it is all about feelings for people who suffered. I am so appalled by their suffering, and I feel very guilty that I escaped it. That is why I have come to the South Pacific Islands like Guadalcanal in the Solomons, why I needed to go to Gallipoli and Passchendaele, to the Somme and Verdun, and the death camps in Poland. I needed to stand on that railway line outside that awful gateway with the watchtower over it at Birkenau. I needed to walk through that gateway and try to imagine the terror, the stench and the death in the wagons. I had to walk along the lines to the ramp where my medical colleague Dr. Joseph Mengele made his diagnoses when they opened the doors of the wagons; those with a bit of work left in them to the left, the elderly, the children and most women to the right, and straight on to the birch wood, after which Birkenau is named, at the far end of the line.

I walked along the dead straight track to the birch wood, turned left and down the steps into the first of two long concrete chambers half below ground, derelict now but the walls still standing. Into the first, 'the changing room', and then into the second, 'the shower room', where those with any sense stayed close to the floor and got enough cyanide quickly, while those who were unwise, climbed up high on the backs of others, women holding children near the roof, to try to escape the fumes, but none did. I tried to picture that scene which the guards saw, peering through small glass windows. I walked round the wrecked crematorium building, where they could burn only five thousand of the eleven thousand they murdered each day, and had to build outside biers, where they found that if they put the women on top, their extra body fat would drip down on bodies below and make them burn faster.

Morbid curiosity played no part in my motivations to visit these places; I felt very strongly that I owed it to those who suffered. Why did it happen to them and not to me and mine, or for that matter to you and yours?

I went ashore this morning to communicate with my family from Palm Lodge Hotel. I had some beers and lunch there, it was primitive but interesting, especially the gents loo. On the wall there, showing you the way to go, was a painting of a naked man with an impressive willy, though drooping to the south as if weighed down by the large red heavy-looking strawberry on the end of it. It was quite artistic, and I could hardly wait to go into the ladies to see what was there, but I was disappointed, the wall was bare. This confirmed previous experience that they are only really interested in willies in the South Pacific, you rarely see illustrations of the portals of paradise.

I settled my bill at the desk in Palm Lodge, under the notice 'You No Pay, You No Stay' and returned to the dock where I had a long talk with Urban the dock boss, and Max and Tom and several other stevedores, also a large grinning Alfonse, who drove the fork-lift now and then and here and there. They were most interested in where you came from, what you did for a living and what family you had, and they were anxious that I should take photographs of them in action with the containers; I did that, though there was not too much action. While I was with them they loaded just one container.

When we leave Kimbe, we leave the island of New Britain, and head for the main island of New Guinea, hopefully tomorrow, it really depends on Urban and Max and Tom and Alfonse and their friends. I spent the evening back in Palm Lodge with Toothless Jimmy, who was behind the bar, Big Mary with quite superb legs made to appear more so by an immense and impossible superstructure, and Jean, who is deeply in love and told me that trust was what mattered in any relationship. I got to thinking that if these lovely people who have very little know that, why did not some of my friends and acquaintances in upper middle class England know that as well, or if they did, why did they not honour it.

When I came back aboard tonight, Boom Boom Anthony met me at the top of the ladder, and asked where I had been. He seemed in a state of acute anxiety that I had done something which he had missed. I told him that I had spent a most enjoyable evening with good friends, and he asked if they were ex-pats. I told him that they were natives and this seemed to relieve him somewhat, it was beyond his comprehension that I should want to do that, and he was much relieved that he had really not missed anything.

**Friday 9th January** The word echoing along the passages and stairways this morning is that we will make two extra calls before heading for home. They will both be in Indonesia, at Ternate and Manado near the Northern Cape of that weirdly-shaped island of Sulawesi, in order to take on board more copra. These will be our last ports of call until Le Havre, except to refuel in Singapore, but this may be done from bunker boats without having to dock. There has been much shouting and arguing on the dock here this morning, which necessitated Admiral Geoffrey going down to the dock and walking with firm strides to the Port Office, presumably to telephone the owners, to find out whether to wait another day in Kimbe and take on more copra, or cut loose and run on to Lae.

There was the usual compromise, and we will now leave at 2 p.m. instead of the planned 9 a.m. One of the features of our stop here has been the plethora of gorgeous butterflies. I have never seen any as big and beautiful before, they are almost as big as birds, some kingfisher blue, others green, a lovely colour mix; reds and browns, yellows and blacks. They made up for the scarcity of pretty birds.

The extra few hours here gave Boom Boom Anthony and Know All Jane the opportunity to pack in another visit to the 'shopping centre', and as I watched them walk away from the ship I realised what it was about Know All Jane that had been puzzling me, and it was her figure. She is a small woman, has a nice turn of ankle, good long legs leading up to a confident bum indeed with a right good tilt to it, a pert little podex if ever I saw one. It had a sway that made the possible presentational permutations indeed a pleasure to ponder, but there it all went wrong because her trunk is very short and she has no neck; her head sits between her shoulders like a big coconut on a Turkish saddle, with rather similar hair. This has the effect of making her legs appear to end in her armpits, and gives her the general appearance of a misshapen dwarf; but Admiral Geoffrey does not seem to be put off by that, the lecherous sod.

She plays him like an ugly pratstruck pike, and I am going to keep close observation, my cabin door will be ajar all night, my ears skinned for the sound of her little feet in the corridor and the click of his cabin door. I would love to catch them in mid-bang, I really would, it would restore the balance of power a little.

Final departure time is now midnight and there were two freighters out in the bay waiting for us to get out of the way so that they could have their turn at the jetty. This allowed me time to have a few beers with my friends in Palm Lodge, and I was glad about that. I reckoned that we were now six weeks from home, only another six weeks of that selfish overbearing loudmouth, Boom Boom and his equally selfish sweet-smiling sharp-eyed little bint, only another six weeks of surliness from the Admiral, before I can write to the company about him.

As far as the rest of the voyage was concerned I was afraid of the pain of my loneliness increasing when we get to Madang, and Sulawesi; the memory of our happiness there is extraordinarily vivid. Lesser memories may swim into your mind like shoals of little fish, but those that really matter can bite you like sharks.

**Saturday 10th January** To get out of Kimbe meant a tight turn of the ship stern first away from the dock, to get in line with the buoys showing the way past two small shallow coral reefs close inshore. The long arms of land half enclosing Stettin Bay seemed to open out for us as we sailed across and out into Bismarck Sea again. The heading was north north east at 020 degrees, and we had the Williansez Peninsula on the port side, and sailed along quite close to it.

Toward the end of Williansez Peninsula, and just past Kimbe Island to starboard, we turned north west and later will make a sharper turn to the south west when we have rounded Cape Hallman. The sea was smooth as blue ice, and in the bright sun the cumulus cloud patterns made the sky truly beautiful. The slightly darker cumulus base in the ocean trade wind belts is approximately two thousand feet above the sea, and today were the purest white cauliflowers that I had ever seen. I was transfixed by this sky, as I usually am when sailing tropical seas and oceans, and allowed my imagination free rein.

From Pilot Kimbe to Pilot Lae, New Britain to the mainland of New Guinea was three hundred and thirty six miles, and we should be there by noon tomorrow, Sunday. The weather was set fair, the air temperature 86 degrees Fahrenheit, and when I heard of the gales and snows in the northern hemisphere I counted my luck that I am in the southern tropics, but I would do that of course, without the gales and snows in the north.

I have just become aware of a face at my window which surprised me, because my window is forty feet above the deck, before I realisied that they have slung a plank on ropes from the top in order to chip off rust from round the windows. It was Big Vanya, the Russian Bear, grinning at me with what looked like a large lump hammer in his great fist. The more noise he made, the bigger his grin; I hoped that when he finally gets to Admiral Geoffrey at the end of the voyage, he does not forget that lump hammer. I also hoped that those ropes did not give way under his weight, because I felt safe somehow with Big Van aboard (As long as he keeps grinning at me.)

There has been some discussion about whether we will need visas for Indonesian ports. When we went to Indonesia we certainly required visas, and the first time, on our way ultimately to Bali, we got to Hong Kong before we realised the fact. I well remembered the Chinaman who ran all the way across Hong Kong to get them for us, because time was of the essence. If all those Chinese in Hong Kong with British passports had been allowed into the U.K. the country would soon be prosperous as rarely before; they never waste time, they really work and that is why they are hated in countries like Malaysia, and barely tolerated throughout the South Pacific where they have collared most of the trade from the locals. You only have to walk down any main street in these islands, say Luganville, Espiritu Santo, and every sizeable shop is owned by Chinese. They keep much to themselves, and by this they seem to create prosperous communities within communities wherever they settle.

Some years ago we made some very good Chinese friends in Penang, friendships which lasted, but they never mingled or socialised with Malays, and whenever we dined out with them, there were never Malays present. I am sure that it would be the same with the Indians in Fiji, but we never got to know them in the same way; there is no more exclusive community than Indian ex-pats anywhere in the world.

I have said that while I watched the clouds this morning I let my imagination run wild, and of course, that we were here together. I felt that anything more that the world had to show must not be squandered because I am alone. I felt that I must capture it all for both of us, miss nothing, waste no impression. It must be stored and be available for recall because Esmé can no longer witness it for herself. We all need to replay the good things, so that we can live with the rest. She no longer has to live with the rest, but would surely want to share the good things.

During the afternoon we passed the Vitu Islands, Garove and Unea, the latter looking like a great big boil with three heads. Garove has an enormous bay which occupies more than half the island, formed when the sea broke through the crater rim of a large volcano, and filled it. Nowhere beneath us is the Bismarck Sea more than nine hundred metres deep. Tall Dark Dem'yan has been busy with the charts and the ruler, working out our course to Indonesia after we leave Madang; this voyage, among all these islands and reefs, must be about the trickiest on the whole globe to navigate. Tall Dark Dem'yan is one of the politest and gentlest of men, always ready to show and explain what he is doing, in contrast with his captain, who really resents our presence.

On the extreme south western end of the island of New Britain was Cape Gloucester, and here Mount Langila was still an active volcano which rumbled and burped from time to time and emitted clouds of gas, rather like Boom Boom Anthony's belly.

All the time that we were in Kimbe the ship, specially Monkey Island, was covered with mega flying ants, flies and other 'burgs' of different sorts. The Americans emptied aerosol after aerosol of repellant over themselves, including their hat, shirt and trousers. Autun worked wonders for me, as it always did for us both, and ants would rendezvous in squadrons, and zoom down until they got near my skin, and then do a frantic level-off and re-climb. It was very impressive, and the protection lasted all day, now I knew what was meant by that 'all day protection' that I see advertised for women. I wondered if Autun would repel Boom Boom Anthony or perhaps kill him, it says on the aerosol to keep out of the way of children, and he most certainly is a spoiled child; I must try.

When I went into my cabin this evening I had a shock, there were two great big feet just outside, Big Van was working his way along with the lump hammer, and I waved up at him, he was a curious sight, because all his tools were festooned around him on strings so that he did not drop them on people below. I wished he would untie the string and drop that lump hammer right on Admiral Geoffrey's head with its dyed black hair. If Big Van is there tomorrow I shall suggest it, I know he would approve.

**Sunday 11th January** At 7 a.m. we left Bismarck Sea, still on a south eastern course, passed through Vitiaz Strait, between Talokina and Vinbot Islands, six miles apart, and re-entered the Solomon Sea, and began to sail round the large spur on the northern side of the main island of New Guinea which points eastward, the Huon Peninsula, changing direction to due south opposite Fortification Point. We motored pleasantly within four miles of the Peninsula, with high mountains inland, the Rawlinson Ranges, not as high as those in the central and southern highlands which are the highest in the world after the Himalayas and the Andes.

We passed Finschafen which the Germans tried to make into a capital but were driven away by malaria at the turn of the century. It was used by the Americans as a base and staging post for troops passing through to fight the Japanese to the west. They were caught unawares by the sudden end of the Second World War, and dug a vast hole here, and bulldozed millions of dollars worth of aircraft and other war equipment into it and buried it, another Million Dollar Point, though this time on land.

After two hours we reached Cape and the small Tami

Island to port, on whose reefs was a wrecked coaster, then made another change of heading to south west on 240 degrees, and began to sail into the huge Huon Gulf in which lies Lae. Here we shall load two thousand tons of palm oil and all the empty containers we have on board will have to be relocated on the ship, because they have been wrongly sited.

The calm sea of yesterday changed to a light chop with white horses and the glorious ocean sky is now full of lowering black clouds, but in this part of the world rain clouds never stay long, and are very soon burned away by the tropical sun, or blown away by the trade winds. I watched as nimbus became solid rain, but within less than an hour the sun broke through, nimbus became lovely white cauliflowers again, fair weather cumulus, and even the sea flattened. Nature puts on these shows for us and we should not take them for granted, fail to observe and appreciate them.

On the bridge this morning, Admiral Geoffrey was abominably rude to Russian Iosif. I have said that he bullies Iosif, who can barely speak English, but understands it well enough; the more I watched what goes on up there the more I hope and pray that Russian Iosif can control himself. This morning he showed his anger to me, and if that shit of a captain pushes him much further there will be trouble. If Iosif lets fly his whole career could be in jeopardy, and working on this ship is so valuable to the Russians; Admiral Geoffrey's would destroy anybody who stood up to him.

The problem was that Admiral Geoffrey thought that he saw an oil slick issuing from the stern, and demanded to know why Russian Iosif had not reported it. I could not see it and nor could Iosif, who tapped his forehead indicating that our dear Admiral had flipped his lid. I shall try to ascertain from Bright Eyed Bearded Henry if there was a leak of oil, when he next emerges from the engine room.

Admiral Geoffrey was quite right to ensure that leaks do not occur in territorial waters, such as this Huon Gulf, and I remembered rubbish was chucked when we were close inshore off Espiritu Santo; but there is a reasonable way of enquiring about things, and this man does not know how to speak to people in his authority.

As you approached the port of Lae the bright blue sea gave way over two miles out to what looked like thin green pea soup. This was due to the silt brought down to the sea by the Markham River, whose source is up in the highlands. Lae itself is the capital of Morobe Province, which includes Madang, Wau and Bulolo, the centre of the 1920's gold rush, to the west, and the Huon Peninsula to the east.

We glided into the port of Lae in mid-afternoon, and the jetty could take two ships the size of this one; it was a straightforward docking with one tug pushing us sideways. The agent came aboard and warned us about walking alone in Lae, and told us that an American woman got mugged returning to the dock here because she got lost at night.

Although it was Sunday they got to work immediately with unloading the empty containers, and loading cocoa via the Ro-Ro at the stern, the fork-lifts going inside laden with sacks of cocoa and copra for the aft hold. The sacks of copra this time were on pallets, and there were a dozen men in the hold, slitting the sacks, and emptying them on the top of the loose copra from Kimbe and Rabaul. The use of open topped containers in the previous ports seemed a much more efficient way of loading the copra.

Black clouds were gathering to the west now, and you could smell the tropical storms well ahead of their arrival.

While the rain held off the work went on, and the eighty containers taken off here in Lae will be replaced by eighty more which are damaged, for repair back in Europe.

Papua New Guinea is a large country of mountains, forests and wide fast flowing rivers, of which the Sepik is the best known. When we came here in 1990 we spent several days up the Karawari, a main tributary of the Sepik. Each province has its rivers, and apart from the Markham River, Morobe has the Butibum, and in Lae there is a Butibum Road and a Butibum Market. I wondered if there was a Butibum Bar, if there was you could probably have fun there should you be so inclined.

**Monday 12th January** I checked into the Lae International Hotel for one night, and then did a little tour to The Rain-forest Habitat, where they have created a mini rain forest under a huge plastic net, with a lake. There were twenty-two species of birds, mainly parrots and pigeons, all with fantastic colouring, and two Birds of Paradise which were very shy and rarely seen, they are a pair of Reggiana Birds of Paradise, but as yet have not procreated. There were butterflies, turtles and skinks, and the whole project was not only for tourism, but used as an education centre in ecology, biology, botany, conservation and forestry.

The Australian War Cemetery nearby with nearly three thousand graves, evoked the same feelings as those at Gallipoli, in France, in the Philippines, the Solomons and elsewhere.

The Lae International Hotel provided South Pacific Lager on draft, very cold, and in the impossible heat of Papua New Guinea was pure bliss. The people want to help, and it was good to see the Papuans drinking in the bar. They are totally unlike the other South Pacific islanders; they are short, they have long foreheads, very long noses, and long chins, accentuated in the men by pointed beards. I had a room away from the main complex, and walking to and fro I was arrested tonight by the sound of the bullfrogs. We had heard bullfrogs in Bali and Mauritius, but they were like schoolboy tenors compared with these Pavarottis. The noise they made was out of all proportion to their size, like cicadas when you see the originator of the sound you cannot believe it. I would love to have a bullfrog or two in the garden at home, it would be such a powerful reminder of past memories, of hot topical nights, of heady scents, and the promise of tomorrow just the same.

**Tuesday 13th January** I have not mentioned Fat Mona for some time. We spend less time sitting on the bridge deck now, because we dock in a fresh port almost every day. She appeared at meals and her decision to avoid the evening meal has been reversed, she now eats rather more at night than at breakfast and lunch combined, and that is quite something.

After the credit card disaster in Auckland, her Camcorder has got moisture inside it, her knees were giving her trouble because they 'dislocate'. I am not an orthopaedic surgeon but I would have thought that that was a pretty rare knee problem, perhaps she meant her knee caps. She found the heat intolerable like Tina, and her ankles swelled up when she walked.

Last night she and Alec dined out with the agent, together with Admiral Geoffrey and Chief Officer Jack, and her artificial pearl necklace broke, so they all spent time on hands and knees on a pearl hunt. It was a late night for her and she made a brief appearance at breakfast this morning, because she must not miss a meal at all costs, and went straight back to bed immediately afterwards.

When they all returned from the tour of Lae yesterday I offered them the use of my room, everybody was very hot and sweaty, and by the time they had washed, attended to their eliminations, raided and virtually emptied the little fridge, made lengthy phone calls to America and dumped their bags, we all went down to lunch. I called at the reception desk on my way to ascertain the cost of the phone calls. Americans away from home make very strange calls for no reason at all, often about games of cribbage, and of course THE FOOD.

Tina's call was to her brother, asking about her sister-in-law, who was in a home with Alzheimer's Disease. 'Are you certain she is taking all her medication dear?' Americans really believe that medication cures people.

I have written about the butterflies in Papua New Guinea and here in the garden I have seen two breathtaking specimens; they both had wing spans of five inches, one of them turquoise lagoon blue with a black surround, and the other beach sand yellow in the sun, also with black surround, together on the same hibiscus bush. I have checked in a book of butterflies in the shop here, and the blue beauty is called Papilio ulysses, and the yellow Papilio euchenor. They made my day and I cursed that I did not have my camera with me.

Back on River Tweed I found that copra loading continued and saw Trinity House Paul down in the hold, taking readings with his moisture meter. Copra must not be allowed to get damp, and all the way home constant tests will be made in all holds containing it; with copra humidity is all-important. With palm oil temperature is paramount, because if allowed to cool it will become semi-solid and impossible to unload.

While we sat on the deck or stood on the bridge whiling away the time, there was continual activity on main deck and below. They nursed this cargo like a precious child, and believe it or not by the time we reach

Europe they will have painted the whole superstructure of this ship; this is necessary on every voyage, such is attack by rust.

River Tweed, with all the cargo now aboard, is well head down, bulbous bow out of sight, and we will see how she rides the South China Sea, the Indian Ocean, the Red Sea, the Mediterranean, and the Bay of Biscay on the way home.

**Wednesday 14th January** Early this morning I stood on Monkey Island and watched the end stages of the copra loading into a deep hold fifty feet immediately below me; they have been working all night to get it all aboard before we sail at 9 a.m. I saw a line of seventeen men, stripped to the waist, standing along the edge of the hold, each with a full sack between his knees. They reached for a knife from the back of their waistbands, cut the string of the sack, tipped it forward and emptied it into the hold; and then they fetched another, and then another. Their backs glistened with sweat which ran down in rivulets.

I felt that little had changed as far as these men were concerned, since the days of the great sailing ships, and the early-century ships of steam. They must have loaded like this in the ships that Conrad described, just sacks and men and sweat. The cranes and the tractors that bring the copra to the shipside may be different, but the final loading is the same here in Papua New Guinea as of yore, totally labour intensive. There is no shortage of labour, it is dead cheap; if one man dropped out there would be thirty to step forward and take his place.

River Tweed had two friends with her at the dock, one was the Cape York of the Austral Asia Line flying the Monrovian flag of convenience, a nice compact freighter this, of good proportion and nice and clean overall. The other ship is a filthy oil tanker, the Sancova, also Monrovia registered. I watched her dock earlier, and then as they prepared to unload the oil; they brought wide bore pipes to the side of her, arteries of wealth and power, and virtually life itself.

As we edged out astern and then turned, the silt billowed to the surface. The mouth of the Markham River was only half a mile from the dock and the silt was such that when the pilot tried to take us out into the bay on a different line nearer to the coast, River Tweed almost ground to a halt. Somebody on the bridge suggested that if the fucking propeller got stuck in the mud we would not go anywhere, and you could not dispute the wisdom of that.

Eventually the ship ploughed through to clearer waters in the bay, and we picked up speed quickly to eleven knots. Russian Iosif felt that he had an ally and friend in myself, and indeed he had. This morning he confided to me that with the load equally distributed fore and aft, and with the central No. 3 and No. 4 holds virtually empty, River Tweed was bending in the middle quite considerably, and the bend was dynamic. I immediately thought about what happened to those bulk carriers the Derbyshire and the Kowloon Bridge, and wondered whether here would be my way of achieving oblivion.

As a result of the loadings at Kimbe and Lae, River Tweed was now quite deep in the water, and head down by a metre, and Chief Officer Jack reckoned this was alright for a coastal run like this, Pilot Lae to Pilot Madang, only two hundred and twenty five miles, but it must be corrected for the long run to Singapore. This should be achieved by filling the midship holds with more copra. We are now to pick up steel rods and two tractors in Singapore, which has infuriated Chief Officer Jack, because had he known this in Kimbe, he would not have blocked the Ro-Ro inside with two hundred tons of cocoa. It is very strange that nobody on this ship, or seemingly in London, really knows what we are going to do from one day to the next.

We have sailed out of Huon Bay the way we came in, and made quite a change of direction after passing Cape Cretin and Tami Island, from due north to north west, from 0.7 degrees to 340 degrees, all of four points, and after one further turn to the west during the night we shall arrive at Madang at around 6 a.m.

I noticed that when we left Lae this morning the gangways along the sides of the main decks were littered with lengths of wood and copra sacks, left by the stevedores. Later in the morning, I watched as they went overboard, and later still we ran into dozens and dozens of planks floating in the sea from other ships, and sea birds were using them as rafts. It explained why the beaches of the world are lined with pieces of wood at the high tide mark. Wherever you go there is always wood, and unfortunately plastic.

At dinner Eric made the fundamental statement that although people talk about 'the romance of the islands', they really are not romantic at all, because of the heat, the 'burgs' and the 'parverty'. Tina said that for her the romance was diminished by the fact that the natives had no conveniences. I had to make a quick decision as to whether to keep my mouth shut, or remonstrate. I did neither, but I did ask Eric why he came to these places if he felt like that, and he said that he liked to travel. I asked Tina if by 'conveniences' she meant shithouses, their thunder boxes or holes under the palm trees, and she said that she meant other things as well. (Presumably iced water, 150 channel T.V.s, big gas-greedy air-polluting automobiles, air conditioning, microwave cookers, and vast shopping malls).

I think that these people travelled in order to impress their friends when they got back home, and also because it made them feel superior. It transfused their comfort as 'haves' to see native folk as 'have nots', and thereby perpetuating the Great Divide of Us and Them, and Us could well be written U.S. They did not think that they were in any way arrogant or ungrateful for what they had. They have worked hard and earned it, and anybody could do that if they wanted to; these people on the islands did not need to live in heat with 'burgs' and be poor; this is what they want, and the Americans so wanted to believe that.

I have become allergic to people who propound, day after day and week after week and month after month a philosophy which was anathema to me before I started, and I am seriously considering flying home from Singapore. What really got to me was their hypocrisy, their pretence; if they did not like what was here they should admit it and keep away, but they want it both ways. They can only really accept the comfortable world, and poverty is uncomfortable; which is why they are not interested in India, and they are afraid of China.

To simmer down after dinner, I headed for the bridge where I found Chief Officer Jack on watch. He is always good company, and I asked him if he could navigate this ship if anything happened to Admiral Geoffrey, and he said that he certainly could and would if I could just arrange for the Admiral to have a coronary thrombosis, a lethal one tonight. Such was the love and respect our Admiral earned from his Chief Officer, and several others.

River Tweed's menu in Madang is eighteen hundred tons of copra, seven hundred and twenty tons of tinned tuna fish (to be kept at 5 degrees centigrade) and eighty tons of cocoa. All the empty containers must be removed so that the crew can get at the holds. This voyage is beginning to be like a game of Musical Containers, without the music, and many too many containers.

While we were talking on the bridge, there were storms all around, beyond the horizon the lightening flashing in the clouds, but also occasionally in the sea, as if somebody held a giant torch beneath it, and was switching it on and off. The full moon came up five points abaft the starboard beam, and I had never seen anything quite like it, because it was bright orange. It was like sunset in reverse, but without the same intensity of light. As it climbed, the moon became yellow and then when it had climbed high enough, it gave us its usual bright white floodlight. I watched all this through my binoculars with the magnification turned up ten times and was enchanted by the colour change. I did not remember seeing this in quite the same fashion previously on the voyage.

**Thursday 15th January** Just after sunrise we reached the outer lush little islands of Madang, and the pilot guided us between two of them into the absolutely delightful harbour. The early morning sun seemed a trifle bleary, and the light was very soft, which much suited this lovely place, and there were hundreds and hundreds of large fruit bats, the biggest I have ever seen, flying around like crows. It is the many small tree-covered islands that make Madang so attractive, as it sits above Astrolabe Bay; there are over a hundred of them, and it is a place of rivers and small lagoons and bays. As we glided past the Madang Resort Hotel, I thought that my heart must burst with the pain of the memory of 1990.

I saw the long rickety jetty where we stood and waited for the little motor boat to take us out to the islands, and I went to that special place which we all have in our minds which is utterly sacrosanct. This early tropical morning the beloved image I saw on that jetty, of my elegant lover and the dearest and best friend I ever had melted my heart, and the thaw waters seeped into the very substance of me in perfusion most perfect.

The chord progression of the music of the love we had, the swell of it filled me to the brim with such a tumescence of feeling, such immoderate excitement that I felt whole again just for that moment. Deprived of her nearness for the rest of my life I wondered what will be left for me when magic dreams lose their spell, or, unchained in their infinite realms like cherished melodies and fragrant perfumes on the wind, they fly away and are gone for ever.

After a straightforward docking I went to the Madang Resort Hotel, which had not changed much, arranged a tour of Second World War sites, and had a meander round the little town with its cricket oval, at the side of which towers one of the biggest banyan trees I have ever seen. I am sure that the Australians must have encouraged the natives to play cricket as top priority from the start of their stewardship of the country.

I had a couple of beers and a sandwich in the open-sided coffee shop, which I remembered so well; my shipmates joined me before going on a tour of the villages in the afternoon. Fat Mona has had yet another disaster, she went into the sea wearing her watch, which has now stopped; I am sure that there will be further disasters before we reach Europe. She had a problem with her nose which caused her to sneeze frequently. Normally the sneeze reflex involves a forceful involuntary exhalation through the nose to clear mucus from the sinuses; Fat Mona brings her larynx into it as well, and gives a great bellow on the end of each sneeze. This, with the shower of mucus, especially in the Dining Saloon, makes you wish that you carried a shower cap as well as ear plugs or were elsewhere.

The stevedores here were much better organised than in Lae or Kimbe; they were waiting for the ship to tie up, with their tractors and lorries at the ready, a full container of copra, nine tons on each, parked in line ahead. They all wore yellow hard hats and they were correctly positioned, one man to each corner of the containers for the hooking of the chains of the crane.

With eighteen hundred tons of copra to shift into the holds, they will be hard put to finish by tomorrow evening; we are due to depart at 10 p.m. for Tarnate of the North Molucca Group of islands, just to the east of Sulawesi in Indonesia. We shall not now call at Manado, at the northern tip of Sulawesi, and after Tarnate, it will be Singapore for refuel and repairs, and then home.

I opted out of having dinner with the others, and went to the Madang Resort with Trinity House Paul and Chief Officer Jack, and we had a very pleasant evening. The local agent joined us, and we sat out in the garden drinking South Pacific Lager; it was a lovely warm equatorial night and two hours passed almost without notice. There was much talk between the two officers about the ship and especially the captain, neither of them will sail with him again.

Before we left the bar, we became involved with members of the Russian crew and the stewardesses, and I had to be very careful to avoid drinking the vodka which flowed. They drank fast and enjoyed themselves, in spite of Admiral Geoffrey sitting across the bar with Chief Engineer Bill. They said what they think in Russian, which Geoffrey did not understand, and neither did I, but it seemed that a lot of it was very uncomplimentary.

I sat there thinking how different was my scene when last I was here, and how life changed that Sunday morning at home in June 1993 three years later, when the magic of our lives suddenly stopped, our party suddenly ended, and our stage suddenly emptied. I was suffused with grief and longing, with the pain coming like bayonet thrusts in my gut, and it went on an on.

**Friday 16th January** Andrew picked me up at the hotel and took me on a tour of war relics. The Nissan four wheel drive had the sort of air conditioning that converts your rivers of sweat into glaciers in seconds, and we made a turn off the main road five miles from Madang, drove along a very rough track in the jungle, until we could go no further. We then walked through veritable clouds of mosquitoes to a Japanese bomber, with twin radial engines, sitting upright and completely enclosed by trees and bushes. It obviously crash-landed, but the swathe it would have cut through the jungle had long since been obliterated. I took photographs of the bullet-ridden fuselage, and we got back to the main road, and proceeded to Alexishafen. On the way I noted a 'Top Up Primary School', and equated this with the expensive school which I attended, where you were well advised to keep your bottom down at all times to avoid trouble.

At Alexishafen we viewed an American tank, and then Andrew took me to the Look Out at Amron, which is half way up Mount Nobanob. It was from here that the local heroes kept watch on the Japanese and reported back to the Americans inland, and the big mango tree under which they stood was still there, heavily pregnant with mangoes. Andrew took me to a gun emplacement on a beach, and then to the Coast Watchers' Memorial, a tall white concrete obelisk on Coast Watchers' Point built in 1959, a lighthouse commemorating very brave men, many of them dying appallingly in the hands of the Japanese. My tour ended in time for lunch back at the hotel, and I shook hands with Andrew who was one of nature's gentlemen, and wished him luck.

Before lunch I was sitting at the bar quenching yet more non-existent thirsts, and saw Fat Mona walk across to the Reception Desk, and watching her from behind I realised what it was that made her walk so strangely. As you watch a woman wearing shorts or a swim suit walking away from you, she puts one leg forward and that buttock lifts up, then the other. Fat Mona seemed to have two buttocks on each side, an over and an under buttock, so that she had four in all. When she put her left leg forward, two buttocks one above the other lifted, quivered and shook, and similarly the right side. It was an arresting display of buttockry and of the sheer dynamics of bum- mobility. It is always advisable to keep your eyes open when sitting at bars quenching non-existent thirsts, for all sorts of experiences await you, some that you never imagined.

Before dark the fruit bats, thousands and thousands of them, seemed to mount a farewell fly-past for us, and then at around 10 p.m. the last container was hoisted aboard and clamped in place, and we were off to Indonesia.

We left the dock and sailed out of that perfect place through Dallman Strait, a mile wide between Coast Watchers' Light and Kranket Island. Out into Bismarck Sea we sailed, on a heading of 60 degrees, and later we will turn due north and pass through Isamlud Strait, but before we do that I shall be asleep in my bunk, trying so hard to dream the right dream.

**Saturday 17th January** After breakfast and Know All Jane's Oration, we made a further turn to port of two points opposite Cape Gir Gir, at the side of the Sepik estuary, and then had the amazing experience of sailing into the silt flow from this great river seven miles off shore. The bright clear blue sea changed to dull turbid green with great suddenness, with a sharp demarcation line of tree branches, bushes, and other debris of all kinds. The Sepik is one of the really great rivers of the world, and it took the ship over two hours at a steady thirteen knots to sail across the effluent, and the change back to clear blue was much more gradual to the north west. While we crossed the river effluent, it was interesting that the propeller churned up blue water from deeper down; the silt flow can therefore be only a few feet deep. Twelve miles to starboard of us lay the long line of the Shouten Islands, five discrete volcanoes fifteen miles apart from each other, Ban, Blupblup, Wey, Koil and Vokeo; they looked just like the line of tits on a sow's belly.

There is now yet another change of itinerary, we are not calling at any Indonesian ports at all, but going straight to Singapore; Pilot Madang to Pilot Singapore, two thousand eight hundred miles, which will take eight or nine days, and the radar has now packed up. I was on a mystery ship on a mystery voyage across mysterious seas and among mysterious lands. The only certainties were that the Admiral was a paranoid shit, four of the passengers were crashing bores, and everybody else on the ship was utterly delightful, and a total pleasure to be with at all times.

As far as the ward round went Fat Mona has developed no further problems yet, but Tina is suffering from a slight throat discomfort, and has brought out a box of 'larzenges' from her pharmaceutical portmanteau. Eric has not really been quite the same since he left his hearing aid for the right ear in a shirt pocket, and it did not survive the washing machine some weeks ago.

The discussion at lunch concerned Singapore, because that is the next and last stop, and the engine will be repaired there, which might take a week. Esmé and I preferred Hong Kong to antiseptic Singapore, and when I voiced that Tina disagreed firmly, she said that she liked clean places, where they spoke English, in 'Harng Karng' they met people who did not speak English and the place seemed dirty, and they did not really like the Chinese anyway. When we first went to Hong Kong some twenty years ago it was the most vibrant and exciting place we had ever seen, far more so than Singapore; there was something about China and India that frightened these Americans, and I was not sure what exactly it was. I supposed in China it was the 'carmunism', and in India perhaps the 'burgs and the parverty'.

There will be a long sail now along the northern coast of Papua New Guinea, and then Irian Jaya on a north west heading of 300 degrees, which will not change for twenty-four hours. We have left behind us the island of Kairin, and small brother Wallis, and the coast of the mainland was eighteen miles away on the port beam and will remain so. The sea appeared full of timber here, there were branches and whole trees floating past all the time, washed down from the wide rivers.

Up on the bridge this afternoon Tall Dark Dem'yan explained that there was a blockage in the radar between the aerial and the receiver, and it was unlikely to be put right before Singapore. He was poring over the maps and plotting a course through the dozens of islands at the southern end of the Philippines archipelago, which seems to hang down the Pacific like a great peacock's tail. Here was where the good navigator came into his own; he could save fuel and money for the company by getting it right. I expect Admiral Geoffrey will countermand Tall Dark Dem'yan, but I know that as navigators they simply do not compare; I also know that Admiral Geoffrey will take any credit whatever happens, but he will be quick to apportion blame if things go wrong.

At the moment it was easy, we sailed along the edge of the New Guinea Trench, which borders the Caroline Basin, we keep mainland New Guinea in sight to port, and will not change our heading for a long time yet, but in another three or four days it is going to get very interesting, especially where the words 'uncharted' and 'unsurveyed' keep appearing on the charts; and River Tweed is now well down in the water with only one engine and no radar.

**Sunday 18th January** At breakfast we were discussing the fact that we had passed the border between Papua New Guinea and Irian Jaya in the early hours, and I said that I was quite surprised when I first heard that New Guinea was the second largest island in the world after Greenland. Know All Jane corrected me and said that it was the third because Australia was bigger. Boom Boom Anthony, who likes to trip her up himself if he possibly can, told her that Australia did not count because it was a continent. She then turned to me and said that anyway New Zealand was bigger. Boom Boom said that that did not count either because it was two islands. I have now demoted Jane as a result, from Know All to Flawed Genius.

After this triumph I went up to the bridge in high exultation, tripped over the step, and my seafaring cap from Santo, of which I have told you I was rather proud, fell off, which was not the most dignified way for a mariner to enter the bridge. I have mentioned earlier that River Tweed had the facility to control the pitch of the propeller, either from the bridge or the engine room, depending on the mode switch on the bridge consol. It seemed that this was unusual, and other officers here had not met it on other ships. I wondered whether it was built into this ship and her sister-ships to cope with arctic conditions when they were Russian owned. If you altered the pitch control to 0, the propeller revolved at the same speed, but the ship did not move. Normally, as this morning for instance, the pitch was set at 60% to give us a steady twelve knots. Trinity House Paul said that on the other ships he knew the pitch was fixed, and the speed simply altered by increasing or decreasing revolutions

A warning was received this evening of tropical typhoon 'Katrina' from Brisbane. It is presently stationary near Cairns on latitude 16, longitude 148, with winds of fifty knots and it should not affect us. The sun did his dive behind clouds tonight, and because of that, the cumulus masses were blue grey, but the light behind them gave them a brilliant orange-gold edge, it was as if a supreme artist had etched the borders of every puff and every billow with the greatest loving care. It was so evanescent, this gilt-edged beauty, that there was barely time to register it in my mind before it was gone

*From Madang, Papua New Guinea, we drove along a very rough track in the jungle, until we could go no further. We then walked through veritable clouds of mosquitoes to a Japanese bomber, with twin radial engines, sitting upright and completely enclosed by trees and bushes.*

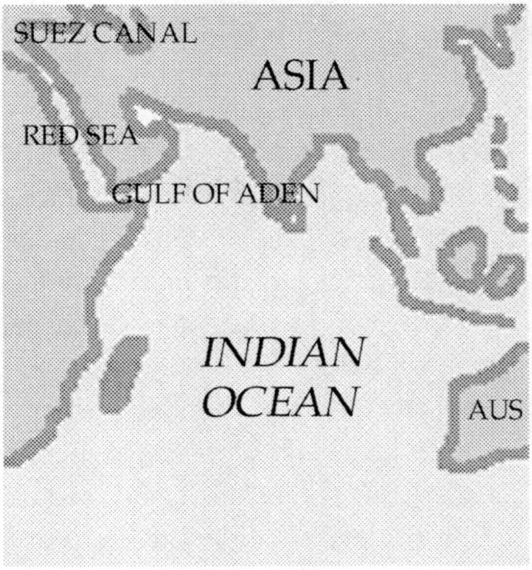


# Chapter 11

## Southern Seas

**Monday 19th January** We shall soon leave the South Pacific for good, and this part of the voyage to Singapore will take us through the Celebes, Sulu and South China Seas, and they are grouped together in this chapter under the heading of Southern Seas, although, strictly speaking from now on we shall be north of the equator. At 7.50 a.m. we did, in fact, cross the equator, and I was surprised that it had come quite so soon. You thought of countries like Indonesia as being so far to the south, but they are not, and it impressed yet again upon you the fact that so much of the world's land is in the northern hemisphere.

Today we have left the Bismarck Sea, and returned to the Pacific Ocean, but after a short time we shall leave it again and enter the Celebes Sea, and then after that, the Sulu Sea.

**Tuesday 20th January** The sun seemed reluctant to put in an appearance this morning, and I had the curious feeling that it was so late that it might never enter the day. When it did come it was the red end of pink and shone through the stratus like a lantern through slats.

There were six small fishing boats ahead crossing from starboard to port, a little fleet of them, white and with four booms on each side. Each had a man in its wheelhouse and another sitting half way up the mast, presumably watching for fish shoals. In the early morning light they made a pretty picture, and I wondered what fish they were after. The ocean here is three thousand metres deep, so presumably they were not looking for deep sea fish, and they were too small for tuna.

Rust removal continued, and I have learned that the instrument of torture with rotating spikes on the end of it is called a needle gun. I still think that the best comparison as far as the noise is concerned, is with a heavy machine gun just by your ear.

These are days and nights of sea and sky and not much else, until we wend our way through the islands of the Philippines. I am reading '1915' by Lyn Macdonald, which rivets me, and next I will probably go to the Far East with 'Life and Death in Shanghai' by Niem Cheng. If ever I make another cargo ship voyage, it will probably be to the Far East; but I must check the captain and fellow passengers first. Just imagine going again with Admiral Geoffrey, Boom Boom Anthony and Flawed Genius Jane.

The biggest school of dolphins yet cavorted around us just before lunch; there must have been a hundred of them and good leapers to boot. I wished I could take a couple home and put them in our geriatric plunge; what marvellous company they would be, I could talk endlessly to them, they like talking, while I drank lager on the balcony. They could make love, and there would be little dolphins jumping all over the place.

At 4.30 p.m. there came up, two points off the port bow, the island of Morotai, part of the huge Indonesian Archipelago which stretches from Irian Jaya in the east, to

Sumatra in the west, the biggest archipelago in the world. They are lands of colour, of gamelan music, of dancing, and of rather serious folk, of Hindu, Buddhist and Muslim belief. We went there first to Bali, and were especially fascinated by the music and the art, but in a strange way I do not sense a pull to go back, as I have to the South Pacific Islands or the Far East. Perhaps after this voyage, that too will lessen; I think that it will, because portering your loneliness about the globe does not in any way seem to diminish it, and that was what I set out to do.

**Wednesday 21st January** Each day began with the sun coming up over the starboard quarter, today he had on his yellow shade for a while, and then he took it off quite quickly and was naked white. Days start with promise, it always seems better in the morning; the problem is so often the remainder of the day. At 7 a.m. nine miles from the Indonesian island of Kadurang, we changed from the course we have been on for the past three days, turned three points to the west on 274 degrees, and will continue this for eight hours before turning north again, as we wend our way through this northern Indonesian group. Thirty miles to the south west is the warning of a Dangerous Large Explosive Dump. You console yourself that ultimately all the metal shit that is dumped during wars into the seas will rust and disappear, leaving the coral that forms on it and the fish that spawn around it.

There was a bad weather area about twenty-five miles long over the bow, which took two hours to work round to the port beam, and as it did so the sun shone from starboard and a gorgeous rainbow appeared, very flat and shallow, a low trajectory rainbow. River Tweed gets more head down as we use up the water and fuel from the aft tanks, and with a Force 5 blowing she is taking the sea on her nose; every now and then she rises up and gets a biff in the bust. The spray provided transient rainbows, and Russian Iosif and I stood on the bridge and watched this lovely coloured aquadisplay. He told me that rainbow shapes vary immensely, and in the Atlantic he has seen rainbows circle the bow like coloured coronets. Russian Iosif is a quiet studious man who maintains his dignity in spite of his bullying captain; I admired him for I know that long before now had I been Iosif, I would have told the Admiral what I thought of him and lost my job.

While I was on the bridge, I heard the dulcet tones of Fat Mona. They were dulcet because she was two decks down; when she reached the bridge she handed me a piece of paper with the name of the Russian doctor who is a member of the crew. It appeared that he earned considerably more money crewing on River Tweed in four months, than he earned in a year of state medical practice in modern Russia; I would like to talk to him, but he speaks very little English. Admiral Geoffrey must delight in having power over somebody who has been better educated than himself, and that could be his problem with me.

The Lunch Time Lecture today was begun by Boom Boom Anthony and finished by Flawed Genius Jane, because Anthony could not wait any longer to get his snout in the trough. Surprisingly, it took the form of a Poetry Reading; there are no more guide books to learn up, and they read from a book they had bought in Papua New Guinea. I felt that I had had enough of being educated and made myself scarce.

At 4 p.m. we crossed the Fifth Parallel, changed course two points to port, and proceeded to the north west on a heading of 310 degrees. During the night the biggest island of the Philippines Archipelago, Mindanao, will be to the north of us. In 1988 we never came further south in the Philippines than Cebu, and missed Mindanao; it is the island where Muslims predominate, and it is different from the rest of the group.

After passing the Sarangam Isles, eleven miles to starboard, we entered Celebes Sea at 6 p.m., and shall sail across it during the night, keeping some fifteen miles from the southern coast of Mindanao. Our speed has been further reduced to ten knots to relieve the load on the single engine, and I hear that the ship may be in Singapore for a week or more for extensive repairs. This is unfortunate, but I shall find a hotel for a few nights to have a rest from lectures, and to renew acquaintance with draught Tiger beer, and telephone my loved ones.

Sometime tomorrow morning we should enter Moro Gulf, which lies in the crotch where the long Sulu Archipelago joins Mindanao from the south west. We shall then escape from Celebes Sea through the ten mile wide Basilan Strait between Basilan in the south and Zamboanga in the north; Zamboanga being a sizeable city on the end of the Zamboanga Peninsula

Tonight I felt that the calm of the Celebes Sea should be complimented by Rachmaninov, so after watching the sunset, a good one lasting over an hour, the red ball drop was only the start of the show, I listened to his Second Symphony and Second Piano Concerto.

**Thursday 22nd January** In spite of Admiral Geoffrey's anxieties about getting through the Basilan Strait, this was accomplished without difficulty. It is ten miles wide, and although there were several ships of varying sizes we did not collide, even without the radar. We passed through at 12 noon, and saw Zamboanga City to the north, but did not get a view of Basilan City on the other side because it was misty. There are many islands dotted around, some with tempting long sandy beaches, and it was a pity that on this voyage River Tweed did not have business in the Philippines.

The Strait quickly opened out on the westward side into the Sulu Sea, and during a hot afternoon we cruised west north west on a heading of 290 degrees at the surprising speed of 13.2 knots, on our one tired engine. Both Celebes and Sulu Seas were extraordinarily calm; there was a soft wind on the starboard bow, very little cloud, just some wisps of gossamer thin cirrus high in the tropical sky, and peace reigned supreme. This peace was disturbed by Flawed Genius Jane who decided that I needed a private Supervision or Seminar on the subject of the Sulu Sea. I cut her short by telling her that there was only one thing we needed to know and quoted:-

'There are plenty of ships in the Sulu Sea
There's a ship for you and a ship for me.'

Her eyes flashed like bayonets in the sun, peace was restored and she returned to her book.

I am much enjoying Nien Cheng's 'Life and Death in Shanghai'. She gives a very personal picture of the horrors of the Cultural Revolution, and in many ways the book is similar to Jung Chang's 'Wild Swans', though that covers three generations. Shanghai fascinated me as a boy in the nineteen-thirties, the International Settlement, the Bund and the Wangpo River. We were able to see a good deal of Shanghai, old and new, on our tour of China in 1993, when it was growing at such a rate as to make Hong Kong seem pedestrian in every way. I well remembered us sitting in the lobby of the Peace Hotel, and Esmé absorbing the history of the place, Noel Coward writing 'Private Lives' there and the last young Emperor, who really wished to be a westerner, dancing in the ballroom on the top floor. Walking along the river then and back down the Bund, you could vividly imagine the cavalcade of life and events that those elegant western-style buildings had seen; from the prosperous days of the International Settlement, with most European countries trying to get a foothold, through the Japanese atrocities in the late nineteen-thirties and the Second World War, the advent of Chinese communism under Mao and the Cultural Revolution which was part of it, to the present day explosion of business, trade and banking, and the stock exchange, which in a year or two would be the busiest in the world.

Because he had severely reprimanded us for spending too much time on the bridge, before dinner, I asked to see Admiral Geoffrey, and was granted an interview in the radio room on the bridge. I asked if I could have a time in the day when I could come to the bridge to read the charts; he said that I could come to the bridge provided I only stayed fifteen minutes, which was all I needed. I fully accepted that he was anxious about getting through Basilan Strait, but it was not what he said to us, it was the manner in which he said it. None of the other officers were as concerned about this as he was. He is frightened to death about shipping density, he will never delegate responsibility and he has two officers, Chief Officer Jack and Tall Dark Dem'yan, who could see him off the seas when it came to navigation; he probably knows that, and that is why he cannot let go.

Everybody got badly sunburned up on Monkey Island today, and Fat Mona looks like a lobster. She is looking for somebody to take her to afternoon tea at Raffles Hotel in Singapore, because she thinks her husband will be on duty, but there are no takers at present. She is currently reading 'Evita' which holds her attention, she is fascinated by Eva Peron, and keeps singing 'Don't Cry for Me, Argentina' while she reads. She asked me if I could ever marry a prostitute, and I told her that if I fell in love with one and she with me I probably could, referring of course to the distant past when testosterone was still one of the hormones coursing through my bloodstream. She asked whether I would be worried about 'clap', I reassured her that it was very treatable even in Eva's day, and she seemed reassured at that.

Fat Mona identifies herself with the characters in the books that she reads in an extraordinary way; Kenneth Williams worried her to death. I cannot remember when I last met such a feeling, uncomplicated girl. All she needs to do is stop over eating, get down to one buttock on each side, and only laugh when she hears something really funny.

She was just about the only person on this ship who had not seen the dolphins, because she is always in the wrong place when they appear. Yesterday she had just gone down from the deck to her cabin to do some ironing when they appeared, so I got Tall Dark Dem'yan to telephone her from the bridge, and she bowled up the stairs and saw them. When she learned that I had arranged the phone call, she advanced across the bridge and gave me a great big kiss. She would have embraced me, but with her massive knockers her vestigial arms were not long enough; it was like being kissed by a large open-mouthed lamprey, bless her.

**Friday 23rd January** Today's sail should be interesting. At 4 a.m. we passed Bancoran Island, heading 256 degrees westward across Sulu Sea, and as I reached the bridge before breakfast for my permitted fifteen minutes chart read, there was a turn northwards to 283 degrees. This sea has been shallow most of the way so far, varying from five hundred metres to one hundred and ten metres, and the charts are studded with shoals, vaguely outlined. Eventually we shall see ahead the enormous Philippine island of Palawan, shaped like a mammoth penis pointing down in a south west direction for hundreds of miles, and we shall have to find a way round the southern tip of it between islands and shoals and cope with strong currents. I am glad that I shall not be on the bridge because Admiral Geoffrey is already nervous as hell, and we are a hundred miles away yet.

Perhaps we shall run aground on Ellis Shoal to the south, I would like that, especially if River Tweed is a write-off and Admiral Geoffrey gets court-marshalled and hanged, drawn and quartered, with myself holding Big Van's coat while he does the drawing and quartering, the great Slavonic sod.

On the radio this morning the news was of hijackings in the South China Sea, which is the next sea we shall cross. Pirate activity during the last four months has affected seven ships, two of them container ships and all of them have disappeared, and this has happened to one hundred and twenty-six ships during the last year. Because of this River Tweed has gone into anti-pirate mode; this is evidenced by two powerful hoses tied on the main deck rail amidships, one to port and one to starboard, and these will squirt into the faces of the pirates should they dare approach. Exactly what good two water hoses will be against Kalashnikovs, machine pistols, and stun grenades gives food for thought.

Straits and reefs and shoals and islands and seamounts, and now pirates, I would half pity the Admiral if he had not been such a swine to us for so long. Looking through the window of the bridge I noted that he now has different shorts on, perhaps the increasing anxiety has caused the worst to happen.

At 11 a.m. we were abreast of the small atoll of Roughton Island, a very small atoll sitting in the middle of a vast lagoon. Sulu Sea here was dark blue, and the lagoon was very bright green in its periphery near the reef, and darker green nearer the island, with two sandbanks. This spectrum of colour, dark blue through light green to dark green, with the bright yellow sandbanks as they reflected the noonday sun was very striking, a perfect transition from Oxford blue, through light jade to yellow via emerald. I simply stood on Monkey Island and gazed at it, and was sorry when we left it behind. The course changes from 283 degrees to 256 degrees to 243 degrees to 200 degrees gets us round the big island of Balabac, through Nasubata Channel, before we turn west again on 252 degrees opposite Ellis Shoal. We have gone through eight points on the compass in circumventing the island, and all around the chart shows strong currents, hidden shoals, one Danger Channel, the Limbucan Channel, which we have avoided by going west of Limbucan Island.

As we sailed into Balabac Strait, and then out into the South China Sea the sun was blistering hot, there was not a cloud in the sky, some turtles passed by to starboard, for the sea is quite shallow here with surface marine farms marked by red flags, and shoals galore, and we have prepared ourselves to deal with any pirates who fancy us. I shall stay very close to Big Van, and will offer to hold the lump hammer while he gets going with the needle gun if necessary.

FRAIL ELDERLY ENGLISH DOCTOR
ATTACKED IN SOUTH CHINA SEA
PIRATES BOARD SHIP
SAVED BY BRAVE RUSSIAN CREWMAN
THREE PIRATES DEAD
UNUSUAL INJURIES TO LOWER BOWEL
(Headlines in South China Morning Post,
22nd January)

In addition to the fire hoses on the main deck there are now four spot lights on each side, which will be lit every night while we are on the South China Sea, so that any half blind pirate pissed out of his mind can find us without any difficulty. I expect Admiral Geoffrey will blow the horn all the way across too, to make doubly sure that they do not miss us. He should put up a notice outside his cabin, which he likes to do, and this should read 'Blackout All Lights, No Noise, Speak in Whispers, Fart Silently' (that might be difficult for Boom Boom Anthony), and we should hare across the South China Sea as the big old Queens did across the Atlantic in the Second World War.

There is a new chart on the charthouse table, I crept in to look at it and then I crept out again, like the cat in the crypt, though with a different purpose. The northern half of the South China Sea is labelled one large Dangerous Ground; there are more Marine Farms well out to sea, and many shoals closer inshore, Big Bonanza Shoal, North and South Furious Shoals, and Emerald Shoal. This whole group of shoals is named Sunken Barrier Shoals, and all around here is shallow water; it must be an absolute haven for fish.

I finished this day at sea with Sibelius and then, for the turn in, Schumann's Piano Concerto, melodic, soothing and hopeful, and written by a man who ultimately lost all hope. Sibelius can increase my sadness and depression like no other composer save Mahler, but his music is commanding; you cannot listen to it and do other things, think other things, muse, the music of Sibelius is by no means and never musing music. He makes you listen to him but I feel that had I known him, I would not have liked him much. He was a conceited man like Wagner but unlike Wagner he was not a promiscuous racist. I would want to ask Sibelius how he could have deprived the world of his eighth symphony by burning it before anybody could judge it, because he didn't think it was good enough. Mozart would have irritated me I think, the bloody little genius, it all came so easily to him. I might have liked a pint with Schubert, but not Elgar; I feel that Elgar was probably a pompous reactionary, having graduated from fairly small beginnings he resigned from his London club when Ramsey MacDonald was elected a member. I am sure that I would have been able to relate to Beethoven, who, I feel, had to work hard to reveal the songs in his heart, and what songs; possibly Tchaikovsky with his weaknesses, and sensitive Chopin certainly, and Brahms perhaps. Schumann would have come across as a bit of a weirdo, as certainly would Liszt. I know I would have got along with Rachmaninov, with that lovely ugly face.

**Saturday 24th January** When we passed through Balabac Strait yesterday we were within thirty miles of Sabah, the part of Malaysia which is the northern end of the enormous island of Borneo, and here the Philippines and Malaysia are that close.

At 4 a.m. we passed Charlotte Reef, at 6 a.m. Louisa Reef, the only land anywhere near us today. Russian Iosif who has read Conrad, pointed out on the chart the 'Alternative Course to Hong Kong in the North East Monsoon for Low Powered Steamers'; some of these charts are old and Iosif loves them. I could not help noting that the 'Alternative Course' advised for those old steamers now passed over a big ammunition dump at a depth of only six hundred metres, possibly Japanese but more probably American. Most of the metallic detritus dumped in the sea at the end of the Second World War is harmless to sea life, but amongst it there are unknown numbers of drums of chemicals which are not, and in time all that will pollute the sea. Here, with all the carefully attended marine farms immense and long term damage could be caused, not only to the farms, but to the coral reefs and their fish. You just hope that nature will always heal all, cure everything, and that must include the damage that it does to itself, which is probably greater than anything that man has so far managed, global warming included.

There was a mid-morning change of direction southward of about one point, to a heading of 233 degrees. The wind has dropped, even the slight breeze on our stern, and the heat is quite oppressive. I spoke to Bright Eyed Bearded Henry who emerged from the engine room for a breath of air on Monkey Island, and he was very pleased with the way that the one engine was performing, giving us thirteen knots and occasionally up to fifteen. It is not evident on the charts, but he felt that River Tweed must have a favourable current under her stern.

Tonight after dinner, I went up to Monkey Island and I realised that I had much underestimated the anti-pirate defences. There were four lights on each side and five hoses, all switched on; it was a striking display of light and water against the background of the bow-wave foam. The jets from the hoses arced thirty yards into the sea; I would still back the Kalashnikovs, but it was a right pretty sight tonight and no mistake.

*The detritus of WW2 litters the islands and the seas that surround them. This American fighter remains where she was force landed in the Solomon Islands.*

*Rabaul, Papua New Guinea, the pilot turns to come aboard with smoking Mount Tavurvur in the background. On 17th September 1994 at 7.30 a.m. Tavurvur erupted and covered a large part of Rabaul with volcanic ash in no time at all, fortunately nobody was killed.*

# Chapter 12

## Singapore

**Sunday 25th January** We maintained a steady south westerly course across the South China Sea, making a slight one point correction southward to avoid Diana and Jackson Riffen Reefs; I wonder if they discovered them together and decided to have one each, or whether Jackson discovered them and gave one to Diana. Past these small reefs barely above the level of the water, we were back on line at 230 degrees.

We shall enter Singapore Strait during the night and sail the Middle Channel, after passing the two islands Pulubintang and Pulubatam on the port side near the mouth of the Strait. The alternative is the South Channel, but the Middle Channel is slightly deeper, offering fourteen fathoms, which should be enough to keep old River Tweed from bumping along the bottom. Singapore Strait is another of the navigation areas on this round-the-world voyage where Admiral Geoffrey may have to change his shorts in a hurry, but now that we are virtually banished from the bridge I will not be able to hear him snapping at his officers, or making sarcastic remarks to the likes of Russian Iosif.

The Breakfast Symposium today was geographical, and conducted by Boom Boom Anthony with interjections from the Flawed Genius. The subject for discussion was 'The Continents of the World', and fairly soon we got stuck on Oceania, and Boom Boom and the Flawed Genius started arguing. Boom Boom insisted that Oceania was a continent in its own right, the Flawed Genius in the teaching of modern geography disputed this, and Eric and I, whose last geography lesson was before either of them were born kept very quiet.

We shall see no land until we get into the Singapore Strait, but Russian Iosif promised me plenty of ships. The main traffic to Singapore is from the north east, from China, Taiwan, Japan, Korea and all over the Far East, to Australia and Africa, with much less coming as we are from the South Pacific.

There was a Force 5 blowing today from the port quarter and River Tweed was on a bit of a roll, so that my ironing session this morning took a little longer. It was made more difficult by the fact that somebody seemed to have parked their chewing gum on the iron, or something equally tacky, so that my lovely stylish off and on drives did not have the full flow and follow through for which I was justly famous at cricket, and more recently at ironing; in fact, in one of my drives, a straight drive right down the board actually, my follow through was so full and flowing that I let go of the iron, and it crashed against the wall of the cabin. When Tina asked me later if I had noticed that the flex had come loose, I said that it was perfectly alright the last time that I used it, and suggested that she should discuss it with Jane who did more ironing than myself, (what with Anthony's habits at trough).

I learned quite early at the great public school which I was privileged to attend, that owning up to anything was fraught with peril and, at that school, pain; and so I have made a point since then never to confess to anything or admit to anything where there may be the slightest risk of opprobrium. Of course, if there is any possibility of acclaim I will be right there smiling in the front row

The heat was oppressive hereabouts because the following wind had now dropped, and the metal of the ship acted like a radiator for the equatorial sun. You had to find small spaces on the deck where the superstructure gave a little shade, and move around to stay with it. Whenever I went to the bridge to check the charts, the cool air conditioning was very refreshing, and I tried to skulk down in the chartroom so that Admiral Geoffrey did not know that I was there, but he really misses nothing, the beady black-eyed tyrant, those awful eyes that glisten with lust when he looks at the Flawed Genius. I wondered what his wife was like, I know that his daughter ran off and married a van driver which infuriated him, I would not blame her, I would marry a one-eyed doubly incontinent dwarf in order to get away from a father like the Admiral.

**Monday 26th January** The sun dragged itself up over the port quarter with white clouds washing its face, and all around us were ships from many countries coming and going in the early morning light. I knew that Singapore had become the world's most important shipping cross-roads and was the largest container port in the world, but here were mixed cargo ships, tankers which looked a mile long, car carriers, gas carriers, which I had not seen before, and giant container ships which dwarfed us. River Tweed joined this early morning get together rather tentatively I thought, as if she felt that she was hardly good enough, and was certainly not dressed properly. Some of these ships, especially the big container carriers looked right spick and span in their bright and varied liveries. If you stood up there on Monkey Island this morning, and turned through three hundred and sixty degrees, you would see fifty ships and that was twenty miles out at the mouth of the Strait. It made the parties at both ends of the Panama Canal seem small; I shall be interested to see what Suez will be like.

The exodus from Singapore in a never-ending line of ships was on the port side, with us going in to starboard were ships of all sorts, and as we got nearer Singapore there were more ships cheek by jowl than I have seen since Portsmouth on D-Day minus One in 1944, and perhaps more than that. Going alongside us was a clean and green mixed cargo ship with a bright orange funnel, Hamburg registered, and I asked myself why were German ships always the cleanest and best kept of all.

Behind all this was the Singapore backcloth, a forest of high rise buildings built at random. From the outer harbour it was nothing like as exciting as Hong Kong as I remembered, though the shipping was just as concentrated, if not more so. As we glided gently in we were passed by a Bangkok registered oil tanker with a big hole in the bow, and three gas carriers which have four to six big domed gas containers on the decks, and presumably more below, and I wondered what gas they were carrying.

Fussing about among all these ships were the fuel bunkers looking like miniature oil tankers with very low gunwales, and a little superstructure with a funnel at the stern. They seemed much more attractive and efficient than the flat barge 'placenta' which fed River Tweed at the Pacific end of the Panama Canal, and the moment we dropped anchor, we had one alongside evidently anxious to get pumping; it will take ten hours to fill River Tweed's bunkers, and by now she is pretty thirsty.

Watching all this from Monkey Island we were thankful for a breeze from the east, because the thermometer read 96 degrees Fahrenheit on the bridge deck. Changi Airport was to starboard, and we could see planes coming and going every minute or two. I believe that this is the second new airport since we first came here in 1979; that is not really surprising when you look at the rate of growth of Singapore, from the port and naval base and the post-war wreckage of 1946, to one of the biggest and most thriving City States in the world in little more than forty years, and continuing to grow all the time.

I doubt if I have truly had an original thought in my life and I am filled with admiration for Sir Stamford Raffles, who came here and founded Singapore while he was in Borneo at the turn of the century. He must have seen the possibilities, geographical and otherwise, and acted on them. Many fail to see opportunities, and many of those who do fail to act upon them, but not so Raffles.

When we finally came to rest and the anchor descended, the agent who came aboard offered to take those of us who wished ashore in the launch. I opted for this and very soon wished that I had not, and had waited until tomorrow when River Tweed would dock for a few hours. Descending that ladder was alright if you hung on with both hands, but getting on the launch was a different exercise. There was quite a chop in Singapore Strait, and at times something like a four foot discrepancy between the bottom of the ladder and the little deck of the launch. I felt I was much too old for this, but with considerable Chinese assistance I boarded the launch, and it ploughed and rolled its way to the jetty, which took some twenty-five minutes. Mr. Boon Fat Chan to whom life seemed to be hilarious, was the agent, and I was deposited at the Royal Peacock Hotel in the middle of Chinatown, and this was a Chinese New Year's Eve.

The Chinese New Year's Eve is very important, this was the year of the tiger and we were lucky to be able to share in that. The Chinese make our New Year's Eve with 'Auld Lang Syne' and people kissing other people's spouses whom they may not always like very much, and everybody yawning and longing for bed, seem rather contrived. This place was alive with lights and dragons and lanterns and illuminated tigers, everybody getting pissed out of their Chinese minds on Tiger beer. There was nothing wrong with that, and it will go on for days on end. I wished I could stay longer, Chinatown was alive tonight.

**Tuesday 27th January** Having said that Singapore is antiseptic and dull compared with Hong Kong, I much enjoyed my walk to the centre this morning. I was very struck by the attractive old colonial style buildings, most of them built between 1880 and 1930. Many had survived the last war, and have been kept in good condition, and the Central Fire Station, the old Central Police Station, now the National Archive, Stamford House, both very French looking with shutters over the windows, the Convent of the Holy Infant Jesus, built between 1890 and 1910, with attractive cloisters, were well worth a visit. There were two old rather decayed buildings housing the Jubilee Electronic Company and the Singapore Lorry Drivers' Association, and St. Joseph's Church, and beside it a small church built in 1916 with different shaped windows on each of it's floors, which gave it an interesting look. I headed for Raffles Hotel and found that it had been completely rebuilt recently, taking two and a half years to complete. It was now a huge hotel and shopping plaza, very expensive-looking but attractive on three floors around squares with tropical bushes and trees. You got the impression of white buildings with dozens of dark green painted balustraded balconies. I had a beer in the Writers' Bar where many famous authors drank; I hoped that I would get inspiration, but it was not as forthcoming as it was for the likes of Somerset Maugham.

I could not help noticing that almost every man in the street was jabbering into a mobile phone, and many of the women as well. I felt that they never put them down, they always had them to their ear, they probably slept with them by their ear in case they talked in their sleep. As far as other bodily functions were concerned, urination should be no problem, though the men had better think what they were doing and be careful about the zip if they did it one-handed, defecation should be alright, you could wipe yourself one-handed, but tearing off the paper might be a problem; if you just tugged at it with your one available hand it might not tear off, and you would end up festooned with it, wrapped up like a mummy. As far as making love went, my generation was always taught that Real Gentlemen should stick strictly to the Missionary Position and take the weight on their hands, except in very friendly circumstances where elbows were allowed. If you used one hand it had better be the stronger one, and what about Colonel Condom's eighteenth century invention to protect his troops from venereal disease? How would you get that on at half-time? I wondered if mobile phones had taken the place of sports cars such as E-Type Jags with long bonnets for those men who suffered from penis envy.

I saw a Burmese Restaurant down a side street, with the name of 'Butifull Myanmar Restaurant' and simply had to go in. In Singapore, if you asked for draft Tiger beer, you were brought a two and a half pint pitcher unless you specified otherwise, and there was nothing much wrong with that when you have just walked two miles in a temperature of 88 degrees Fahrenheit. The menu was most promising, among the 'soops' was the 'Soop of the

Gourd'. I did not really fancy that because the only gourds I had seen were ensheathing the pricks of savages, and I felt that the soup might taste a little too gamey. Myanmar Soop Noddle seemed a better bet. I chose not to do so, but had I wished I could have ended the meal with 'Myanmar Hottea refilable'. As an experience Butifull Myanmar Restaurant was much more interesting than the Dining Saloon on River Tweed, with Admiral Geoffrey glowering in the corner.

In the evening I repaired to the restaurant which I had discovered the day before, and they presented you with the 'Straits Times' as you arrived. As I supped from my pitcher of draft Tiger, I noted that a James Brown, inflicted with the title of 'The Godfather of Soul', had been admitted to a South Carolina Hospital to shake an addiction to pain killers; I could not help thinking that any addiction, in my own case of course alcohol, did not need shaking, but suppressing.

I skipped the pages devoted to the question of whether Presidential zips remained done up and I lighted upon a most interesting paragraph on page 24. 'Lover Ditches Pregnant Woman aged 60 After Discovering Her Age'. This sportsman, a mere stripling aged 58 had put his bun in that aged oven, the oldest recorded, without knowing the age of it. When he found out, he just had to return to his loving wife Vera, (it would be Vera, wouldn't it?) and his adult children who 'fully understood him'. (I bet they did). What got me was his statement that the whole thing was due to 'a multitude of pressures', the poor lamb.

**Wednesday 28th January** I returned to the ship this morning, which was now tied to the dock for twenty- four hours, for the loading of Backos, or Hy-Macs, as we know them, and heavy metal pipes destined for Hamburg. Tomorrow River Tweed will return to the outer harbour and anchor there while the engine trouble, which is much more serious than expected, is dealt with. There were strange men in the ship, six German specialist engineers, and Chief Engineer Scottish Bill told me that we shall be here for another full week. Singapore will be pretty dead for the next three days and will return to normal on Saturday. Presumably there will be a water taxi service for those who wish to go into the city from the ship.

When I made a comfort stop in a public loo near the dock this morning, I had a very pleasant surprise. As I approached my stall I saw on the wall in front of me a quite delightful work of art. It was a coloured drawing, half size, of a gorgeous girl with black hair falling over her shoulders, well endowed indeed with all the angles right, and a flat belly sloping, with all the gradients right, down to the hummock of love topped by an enchanting little tussock of black love hair. It was extraordinary for two reasons; firstly it was on the wall of a public building in a city where just thinking about farting in the street gets you fifty lashes, and actually doing it the gallows next Friday, and secondly, just below that dear little quim were not the lips of heaven roscid with the linctus of love, but a big willy sticking out in expectant mode with a supporting baggage of which anybody could be proud.

Now, I will not say that in the changing rooms of university and hospital I have not seen bigger weapons, and indeed two members of the St. Bartholomew's Hospital hockey team, the two full backs as it happened, could have attended any Fancy Dress Ball anywhere in the world without having to dress up at all, as petrol pumps. This willy on the wall, though, could have held up its head, and indeed was so doing, in any company or competition anywhere. I do not remember seeing a better illustration of hermaphroditism previously, nothing crude, everything in proportion, and most artistic to boot and I almost forgot to pee. I do not normally spend much time in loos, though my wife always grumbled that I did, but I will say that a desperately needed pee is one of life's fundamental pleasures, and you would not cut short a good lay or break off a good crap, at any rate before you have finished the sports pages, so why not take your time over a pleasant slash and look around you; actually and regrettably, I have little choice these days

Back on the ship I found that we will move out to an anchorage in the Western Anchorage for the repairs to continue, and that these will take another ten days. I shall probably remain on board rather than make more trips ashore, because I have seen enough of Singapore.

This anchorage is out in the Strait but away from the main shipping lanes, and we have all around us many ships at anchor, and one wondered what they are all doing. They could not all be waiting for berths, and perhaps a lot of them have the same type of problem as River Tweed; there are literally hundreds of them. A little way to the south of us there are several 'Three Football Pitch Oil Tankers', low in the water and waiting to discharge at the long oil jetties on an island in the Strait, which also had a refinery on it as well as hundreds of storage tanks.

There were others, obviously empty, lying off and waiting to fill. I supposed that Singapore had now become overall the busiest port in the world, with its wide deep waters, and its geographical situation on the globe, ideally placed between east and west with unparalleled facilities for the handling of containers, of gas, and oil. I wondered what it would be like in twenty years' time; the mind boggled and I trust I shall not be alive to see it.

**Friday 30th January** Rain clouds covered us as we lay at anchor with engines silent and Chief Officer Jack was worried about River Tweed dragging her anchor and drifting into other ships moored close by; they were so close that I felt that if I stood on deck and held out a plate, I would have no trouble getting meat and two veg for dinner. Because Admiral Geoffrey was absent I spent the morning on the bridge sitting in the pilot's swivel chair in the port wing, and watched the movement of the ships. I felt that I could sit there for ever with my binoculars scanning this extraordinary scene. Late morning one of the oil-stained specialist engineers sent out by River Line, and a Malaysian assistant, came up to the bridge to make a phone call back to U.K. to ask for instructions. He told me that the damage in River Tweed's gear box was the worst he had seen in all his experience with P. & O. and latterly River Line with one exception, and that was in another River Line ship which had to go all the way round the world on one engine, because the other was damaged beyond repair.

He confirmed that the problem was poor maintenance by the previous owners, and insertion of poor quality spares before River Line bought the ships. They now had the gear box completely apart and knew what had to be done, and his phone call was to get permission to proceed with repairs; I overheard him ask whether the owners required photographs of the damage and photosonic tests for the benefit of the insurers, and they did.

It was the opinion of several of the officers that River Line bought these ships cheap from near bankrupt owners, and were now reaping the rewards. Presumably the insurers will raise premiums to a point where they become impossible because of previous claims; I have been Medical Consultant to Life Insurance companies for years, and I know the game. Not much will happen for the next week; they hope to finish the work by next Thursday, and do sea tests that day, and if River Tweed passes these we shall finally be on our way on Friday. Meanwhile I must try to dodge a threatened Lecture by Boom Boom on 'The Religions of Papua New Guinea'.

**Saturday 31st January** Fat Mona arrived on Monkey Island this morning with her new and expensive binoculars, which she bought in Singapore two days ago. It was a damp and very warm morning and when she looked through the binoculars she was desperately disappointed because she could not see anything clearly and she was near to tears; she said that they were faulty and quite opaque, and was completely serious. After I had wiped the mist from them her happiness was unbounded.

All my shipmates are today visiting the Botanical Gardens and the Singapore Zoo and I decided to stay shipboard. I feared that the List of Future Lectures must now include 'The Flora and Fauna of Singapore and the Malaysian Peninsula'.

**Sunday 1st February** Today I have to report a collision in the Northern Anchorage between two ships at anchor. They were too close and a sudden change of current caused one of them to swing round and catch the stern of the other, causing considerable damage to the rudder and propeller. This seemed to be a subject of mirth for Admiral Geoffrey as did the message that a Filipino crewman had gone overboard in the Baltic Sea from M.V. Hope, plying between Lithuania and Rotterdam. These two pieces of news really made the Admiral's Sabbath. It was a great pity that there were no public hangings in Singapore this weekend because that would really get him going.

When they returned to the ship last night from their day ashore there was a crisis because Fat Mona was too scared to step across from the launch to River Tweed's ladder. She stood on the bow of the launch shaking like a mountainous pink blancmange and refused to move. Fortunately her husband Alec was with her, and somehow he managed to pour her over and onto the bottom step of River Tweed's ladder. Boom Boom and the Flawed Genius elected to remain ashore but I knew that they would be collecting material for many more Lectures, and that filled me with dread.

I was informed by Chief Officer Jack that the German engineers, who are living aboard while they fix the engines are drinking up all the beer, and Admiral Geoffrey has forbidden Purser Alec to replenish the stocks, which is not surprising, because he himself only drinks wine.

The movement of the ships held your interest. There were giant container carriers, supertankers and large white cruise liners coming and going all the time. This morning we had a visit from the rubbish launch, and the crew tipped a skip full of decaying food and all sorts of other things as well into another skip on the launch many feet below. One of the ropes holding the skip came unhooked, and half the trash went into the Singapore Strait; if anybody reported it there will be floggings tonight and no mistake, and Admiral Geoffrey no doubt will rub in the salt.

**Monday 2nd February** I found it very peaceful here at anchor, and I was not quite sure why. I sat for hours watching the shipping, each ship a little world of its own with its little population, and each person with their own happiness', worries, fears, disappointments, loves and hates. I wondered, while I scan all these ships with my binoculars, how many of them hide tragedies, how many people in them in this wide seaway today were running away, trying to escape from something or someone with which or with whom they could not cope. Seafaring remains a profession in which few questions may be asked so long as the work is done; as in no other profession people tend to mind their own business.

I imagined what secrets these ships around us must encapsulate, and secrets are integral to human life itself; no tyrant or bully in the history of mankind has ever managed to stop people thinking. I knew that I would love the sea and seafaring, I have known that all my days since childhood, and now I have the opportunity to indulge it, but it is a life best kept for the lonely and the solitary. You should not embark on a voyage like this expecting to indulge in gregariousness, or make a quantity of new lasting friendships. You may do that but most likely you will not.

It is best to do this sort of thing with an absolutely open mind, and of course a need to see the world for yourself, but unshared, with only yourself to consider, and that is why I am on this ship, and why that wheezy old Captain Campbell, the agent through whom I booked this voyage, was so right when he told me that I would be most likely to meet other lonely old folk and I would find that that would be the best for me. If only that had transpired instead of my being limited to the two couples that I have here with me, who after all have each other, I know that I would have been much better off; perhaps next time I will be.

**Tuesday 3rd February** This morning I learned about liquid gas carriers, supertankers, and the factors governing the way that ships swing at anchor from Russian Iosif, during his watch. Big gas carriers do not carry the gas in separate round tanks, the whole ship is one large tank and the domes that stick up above the deck are merely upward extensions to create more volume. They carry liquid gas and are considered perilous to work on by many sailors, including Russian Iosif, who gave oil tankers a wide berth also.

We watched the supertankers leaving the oil terminal in a steady stream, very low in the water and drawing up to sixty feet compared with River Tweed's thirty. Iosif talked about the Torrey Canyon disaster of the 1960's off the Cornish coast, she was just about the first giant tanker to run aground, and he said that if the owners had been prepared to summon tugs when the Master first radioed that he was in trouble the ship would not have gone onto the rocks; they jibbed at the expense involved with tugs. It took six miles to bring one of these giants to a halt, and if you tried to do it too abruptly by going fast astern, the shaft and the propeller would disappear astern as from a rectally eviscerated mammoth; the captain of the Torrey Canyon did not have six miles. I had noted that at anchor some of the ships around us were pointing one way, and others at right angles, and in my ignorance I asked Iosif the reason why. He said that those which were empty were governed by the direction of the wind, while those that were laden swung with the current.

Apart from the large cruise ships, there were other white ships looking very smart, and like embryo cruise ships. They left Singapore in the early evening and returned early the next morning, and they are floating casinos; gambling is forbidden in Singapore. These ships take people out of territorial waters for a night's gambling, and the ticket costs several thousand dollars before you even start playing, and on New Year's Eve they were charging ten thousand Singapore dollars per head. The Chinese are inveterate gamblers, it is part of their soul, but perhaps what made a night on these ships even more attractive was the inclusion in the price of the ticket of a luxurious cabin and a woman to go with it; I am not quite sure whether a good lay would compensate for losing all your money though it would surely garnish a win.

The grapevine quivered tonight, and if we were anywhere between Espiritu Santo and Papua New Guinea there would be a beating upon the natatambol tree which told me that very possibly the engine trouble cannot be fully dealt with here in Singapore. I am told that the German engineers have the necessary expertise to put the gear box right but have not been given the facilities, and that we may, after all, have to limp home on one engine, and that the fortnight spent here has been a total waste of time and money.

Chief Officer Jack is certain that had River Tweed remained at the dock when we first came here the necessary work could have been carried out, but not anchored out in the Strait, and that River Line's determination to cut costs has brought this about. It is looking as if it will be the end of March before we reach Europe. It was Alec Waugh, who wrote in his 'Hot Countries' that the charm of travel is intrinsic to itself, to be pursued as art for art's sake. Stuck out here, anchored in this sodding strait for who knows how long, I am beginning to think that there is much to be said for my local pub, though artistic it most certainly is not.

**Wednesday 4th February** The news from the engine room this morning was better, and some hope is restored that we shall be able to go home on both engines, but it is not yet known when we will sail. It is very frustrating to have ships anchored beside you for a while, and then move off again.

Mr. Boon Fat Chan has come across in a motor launch and is closeted with Admiral Geoffrey, he is a delightful man and I would not wish that on my worst enemy, but perhaps we shall now really know when we might up-anchor and head out of Singapore Strait into Malacca Strait, and be on our way. Going through Malacca Strait will bring back memories of childhood, and the tall polished shell case in the hall, full of walking sticks and malacca canes. I expect one of my ancestors brought them back from Malaya, and probably used them to flog the natives into submission; some of my ancestors were not very nice people.

There was an informal party this evening to celebrate a birthday, and I grasped the opportunity to talk with

Barry, the River Line trouble-shooter, who has been aboard since Papua New Guinea. He talked much about the big tankers and those which have gone aground, like the Torrey Canyon, and he filled me in on the three other major disasters, Amoco Cadiz on the northern coast of France, Exxon Valdez off Newfoundland and Brer in the Orkneys, and the only one of them not due to human error was the wrecking of Brer. He told me of a big container carrier which hit a small island at twenty-four knots because the watch was asleep, and the rest were at a party; the cost was seven million pounds and he was working for the company at the time. He saw Exxon Valdez a few years ago, completely repaired and refurbished; he said that she was the biggest and most beautiful ship that he had ever seen, and he has seen quite a few.

**Thursday 5th February** The days pass, and they are working twenty-four hours a day down in that engine room. Anchored out in the Strait, I yearned for the open sea now with the soft shine of sapphire, and the glint of diamonds, and distant lagoons with the throb of emeralds in the sun. We still have sunrises and sunsets, with the clouds seeming sometimes to burn like rubies themselves, and glow with the purity of pearls; we still have much of nature's jewellery even anchored here.

I know that as we cross the Indian Ocean we shall regain it all, and our sail home will be blessed by undiminished lights of beauty much of the way, though we may perhaps have to look a trifle harder for them the further north we go. The carpet and drapes of gold and silver, of red and yellow and green and blue will gradually fade, but we must ever be grateful for the witness of it all, and store away safely the memory of it if we can.

There were three islands in line off Singapore City across the strait, Pulau Sebarok, Pulau Jay and Pulau

Bukam, all of them oil terminals, and Bukam a large refinery as well. The big supertankers took no more than twenty four hours to load, and then glided majestically out into the Strait, usually five or six of them each day, and it blew the mind to imagine what would be the effect on Singapore if one of them went aground here and leaked its oil. You would think that by the law of averages, with all his traffic, one of them soon must.

Instead of the intoxicating perfumes of tropical flowers upon the wind of the evenings, we have here on River Tweed the strangely pungent smell of the copra wafting up from the holds, difficult to describe but I can best liken it to the smell of stale and sour pina coladas left unfinished from last night, and today this has been modified by the stink of the garbage from the skip near the stern, the 'poubelle boat' having failed to give us a call today as expected.

Tina is now worried that she might inhale some lethal microbes, and spends much more time in her cabin than on the sun loungers on the bridge deck, also she has been told by one of the officers that the copra breeds a small fly, the bite of which can cause urticarial wheals. As far as catching diseases by inhaling from garbage goes, I was reminded of the belief inculcated in my childhood that you would catch diphtheria if you stood over drains. As a result I had nightmares for years about being held with my face over drains until I reached puberty, when other things became the subjects of my dreams, rather more pleasant things if I remember rightly, but it was a long time ago

**Friday 6th February** The orange solar fireball rose in quite a hurry into an early morning sky without cloud today. It was as if it had a return ticket, because it was exactly the same traveller as I saw last night going the other way though more slowly. I wondered where it spent the night, and what it had been up to while I was trying to dream my pathetic dreams. At breakfast there were only Eric, Tina, myself and Admiral Geoffrey, alone as usual at his corner table, the other senior officers with the exception of Chief Engineer Bill try to give the Admiral a wide berth at meal times, eating earlier or later if they possibly can. He never speaks unless spoken to, and usually gives curt cut off monosyllabic replies. This morning two of the American fools tried to get him into conversation about his job as ship's captain, in spite of his previous rudeness to them, and the gist of what he said was that he had the power to limit the sale of alcohol to anybody and to put anybody off the ship if he chose, for any reason. I wondered where was their dignity in trying to speak to him at all.

A very dirty, rusty oil tanker named Nike, suddenly flew the blue and white flag just beside us this morning, which denoted that divers' inspections were taking place, and there were several motor boats sitting under her behind, and much activity. After a couple of hours they all departed, the blue and white flag was lowered, and Nike pulled up her anchor, and off she went leaving us quite jealous.

The major world ports such as Singapore never sleep; they are perpetually alive and awork. There is a whole world populated by small boats revolving around the bigger ships, supplying their needs inward and outward, a huge floating service industry. Among all this there must be the pursuit of crime and its rewards. I wondered how many of these ships anchored around us, even River Tweed herself, were at this very moment concealing contraband. If you were smuggling drugs here you would have to be very careful, for they kill you if they catch you. I think they hang you, but perhaps in special cases they might give you the choice of being shot.

**Saturday 7th February** Small boats seemed to be visiting River Tweed with increasing frequency. There was a fuel bunker boat last night, pumping in another fifty tons, no more because the fuel tanks allowed the oil to pour for'ard and we were head down as it was. There were provision bringers, garbage receivers, boats bringing spare parts for the gear box and mechanics to work on them, and River Tweed was regularly circled by pilot and police boats, watching out for the chucking of rubbish overboard.

This morning a boat took the shore goers across to Pasu Panjang wharves for a day in town. At breakfast poor big Olga, the senior stewardess, presented Admiral Geoffrey with the list which he had asked for of the names of the crew and other staff, and the amounts of money they wished to be advanced from what they have already earned on the voyage so far, so that they could make purchases in Singapore. He flew into a rage in front of us all in the Dining Saloon, and shouted at her that all money earned on this voyage was his money and his responsibility until the home port was reached, and asked what they wanted it for. He refused to release it and she was extremely upset and crying. She told me later that this had not happened on previous voyages with different captains.

We have been joined in the Western Anchorage by a pretty little orange coloured tanker, Jakarta registered and named Kunti, and fairly close by there is an enormous bulk carrier with bicycles parked by the superstructure which they needed to get to the for'ard holds. Chief Officer Jack, who has worked on bulk carriers, said that in a fog it becomes impossible to see the fo'c'sle, even with binoculars. This ship of the Navix Line was the biggest ship that I have ever seen, and with no derricks amidships, which super-tankers need to lift the pipes, bulk carriers are the sleekest of the giant ships.

**Sunday 8th February** The ward round today has revealed that Tina was upset by the fumes of paint and fuel which creep beneath her cabin door, and she thinks may be interfering with her breathing. She was also concerned that going to and fro between the relative cool of the cabin air conditioning, and the oven heat outside, and it really is oven heat on the bridge deck, might dispose her to 'infection'.

They all told me on the ward round that they had had 'sharts' for 'virus infection' because they were coming to these southern and eastern parts and would be exposed to many foreign people with diseases. When I told them that these vaccines probably would not confer any protection against the latest cloud of viruses which change by the day, they seemed angry with me.

There was one further problem on the ward round which I should have mentioned. As this is not a cruise liner but a cargo ship, the towels in the cabins were changed only once a week, which shocked Tina so much that she washed her towels every two days. She said that as far as she and Eric were concerned this was absolutely essential. I could not help wondering whether that meant that Eric had momentary losses of confidence and forgot himself. She said that the purpose was the avoidance of 'germs and infections'.

On the bridge this morning there were fewer ships around us. Little Kunti had gone, and so had that great bulk carrier. We are now promised sea trials tomorrow evening, and if all is well we shall head for the Straits of Malacca on two engines the day after. I was joined on the bridge by Flawed Genius Jane, and we discussed the port and the shipping and I suddenly realised that she was giving me a private tutorial. Perhaps I am uncharitable about Boom Boom and Flawed Genius Jane and they really mean to help. Perhaps.

Today, while on the bridge, I saw upon the charthouse table the River Line Monthly Bulletin For Captains. I was not sure whether I should have perused it, but I have believed in life that anything left lying around was fair game. There were warnings about oil spillage, and much about navigation in fog, when the ship must be put on standby, and extra look-outs posted; and the Master must be on the bridge and the engine room be alerted to change speed without warning.

There was advice and instruction about passage planning generally, and the fact that eighty percent of accidents occurred in pilot waters was emphasised. What interested me particularly was the company's concern that mail was not being collected; they could say that again, I have had virtually no mail all the way round, I supposed it would flop on the door mat long after I got home. There was more about servicing the Suez Canal, but I had to 'scarpa' because the Admiral hove into sight. After dinner I was able to have a long conversation with Chief Officer Jack and Trinity House Paul in the absence of Admiral Geoffrey; when he is there he does all the talking, mostly about himself and money.

These two, Jack and Paul talked at length about the Herald of Free Enterprise disaster at Zeebrugge, and the effect upon ships of sailing into waters which suddenly become shallow due to sand bars and such like. When the ship encountered a sand bar, the water flow speeded up, but the pressure under the ship diminished, and she would go either head or stern down. In the case of the Herald of Free Enterprise she went head down and the bow doors were left open. Jack said that in shallow water, old mariners talked about 'feeling' or 'nosing' the sand banks.

The conversation then turned to berthing big ships, and Jack had experience on the liner Oriana, just withdrawn from service; he said that on her there were only two consols on the bridge, which incorporated three radars. The Captain berthed the ship, and also controlled it at sea by moving a small lever less than six inches long. Docking was accomplished by the experienced use of this lever, which controlled vectors and thrusters aft and for'ard which automatically edged the ship to dockside. Oriana had variable pitch propellers, two of them, and the engines answered to the automatic control; tugs were used also, but were not absolutely essential. All the captain really had to do was ascertain the ship's angle to the dock, and feed this correctly into the computer, and the vectors and thrusters did the rest.

I felt that there was little difference between docking a big modern ship and landing a big Boeing on automatic pilot, and I cast my mind back to Captain Sorrell Master of the Queen Mary who arrived in New York during a tug strike. He scorned the use of tugs and took her dockside using his four screws without causing any damage. Jack said that he must have been lucky with wind and weather and that some captains might use what is known as "inspired controlled anchor dredges" under similar conditions.

We talked of the danger of 'pooping', the engulfing of a ship by a following sea, which sailors dread; any sea coming head on should always be survivable, but many a ship has succumbed to 'pooping'. I left the bridge wishing very much that I lived near Southampton, and could have a few pints from time to time with Chief Officer Jack, he is one of the great bonuses of this whole voyage for me, he has much, much more to tell me and I think that he would enjoy doing it; we get on.

Having taken the piss out of my American shipmates all the way, I have done much less than justice to their sense of humour; which surfaced from time to time though was often fairly basic. Tonight I asked for English mustard and there was only French mustard available; when it came Eric said that only a Limey would eat baby shit.

**Monday 9th February** The day started with a malfunctioning toaster, which upset Admiral Geoffrey very much indeed and he laid into the stewardesses, which he likes to do whenever he can because they cannot answer back; from then on the whole Saloon breakfasted in total silence. There is no love lost between Geoffrey and myself and I met his eyes a few times during the meal and they were black, small as agates and twice as hard.

I think that I have been less than charitable to this tortured soul, who assuredly needs help, and I will recommend, in my letter to the Managing Director of River Line that the company seeks a psychiatric opinion before they allow him to captain any of their ships again. I will not need to do that of course, if Big Van happens on the Admiral on the main deck one dark night in the Bay of Biscay, but that is unlikely for he stays on the upper decks of the ship at all times.

It would be nice to read:

UNIDENTIFIED BODY WASHED UP ON
PORTUGUESE BEACH
SEVERE FACIAL AND GENITAL INJURIES
BELIEVED CAPTAIN OF M.V. RIVER TWEED
WENT MISSING A WEEK AGO
NONE OF SHIP'S COMPANY ABLE TO HELP

Now that would be a wonderful way to end a wonderful voyage. We could get the key from Purser Alec and raid the big fridge, drink all night on deck and get rat-arsed. We could acclaim Big Vanya as a hero, though I would not like to shake his hand, his hands make York hams look like chicken drumsticks, the huge animal that he is. We might light him up and dress him overall, he would like that, especially the lighting up, and with vodka if possible.

**Tuesday 10th February** River Tweed finally hauled anchor at 11 p.m., turned, for the current had swung her to head east, and we began the long twenty-five day voyage home. On the bridge deck after breakfast this morning the forge heat of the past week had tempered, and there was quite a determined wind blowing from the north west as we left Singapore Strait and entered Malacca Strait, sailing along eight miles off the coast of peninsular Malaysia.

Making conditions more comfortable also was the cirrostratus cloud cover, a diaphanous veil which was just sufficient partly to baffle the sun, giving the whole sky a milky diffused look as if the prisms in my binoculars were made of ground glass. The common cloud sequences tend to progress from cirrus to cirrostratus to altostratus, and then, just before or during rain, there will be nimbostratus and nimbus; after two hours on the bridge deck we had the fibrous striated appearance with diffused light patches letting the sun through, of altostratus. These changes depend not only upon water content but also wind force, and as I have said there was a lively blow down Malacca Strait this morning so that as the day wears on we shall get more of the sun unblanketed. The north west coast of the Malaysian peninsula was dotted at intervals with towns and ports, and by mid-morning we had passed the sizeable town of Malacca and saw high rise blocks and an oil terminal. At this point with 'Sand Waves' ahead, and a water depth of twenty seven metres , we were eight miles from Malaysia, and seventeen miles from the huge Indonesian island of Sumatra opposite; we could see Malaysia but we could not see Sumatra. The two diesels throbbed contentedly and gave us a steady fifteen knots into this headwind on 311 degrees.

Instead of the shipping gang-up of Singapore Strait we now had plenty of space, though in this part of Malacca Strait at any given time there will still be a dozen ships and more in view to port and starboard. When we reached the narrowest part of the Strait between Tanjung Tuan in Malaysia, and Madang on Sumatra, four miles and seventeen miles away respectively, I realised what was meant by 'Sand Waves'. They are not, as I thought sand dunes on the sea floor, but enormous suspensions of sand floating just beneath the surface, up to thirteen metres deep. The colour of the sea in Malacca Strait was champagne bottle green, but these clouds of sand gave it the look of turbid urine, and they must have been due to the upward swirl of strong under-currents, for the sea here is seventy metres deep. At the narrowest point there were four buoys indicating a wreck and until very recently the mast of the unfortunate ship protruded above the surface; there was another wreck marked on the chart some twenty miles ahead of us in the middle of the shipping lane.

As we passed Port Dixon in the early afternoon there were two mosques quite close together with virgin white minarets and what looked like a Christian church, and I felt that here was another example of the way in which the four main religions, Hindu, Buddhist, Muslim and Christian still existed side by side in these countries of Malaysia and Indonesia, and indeed elsewhere. I think that this was brought home to us in India and Indonesia more than anywhere else, but it is existence rather than living together in harmony, and surely what the next World War will be all about.

Mankind will never cease to fight over the worshipping of its gods, which is one main reason why Esmé and

I became attracted to Humanism. Esmé made a study of comparative religion and always said that if she were not a Humanist she would lean toward Buddhism.

Later in the day we came to One Fathom Bank, fourteen miles long running north  south in the middle of the Strait and half a mile wide, and there was a special Traffic Separation Scheme about this, with northbound and southbound ships having to remain more than half a mile apart with the forbidden zone between them, northbound to starboard, southbound to port, as is the rule of the sea. This was beyond Port Dixon, and after it the Malacca Strait widened out and we headed away from Malaysia as the peninsula curved northward, and we kept a course some thirty miles from Sumatra on a heading of 300 degrees.

Today we have begun the longest single leg of the whole voyage, Singapore Pilot to Suez Pilot, four thousand nine hundred and twenty-six miles, which beat Dunkirk to Panama by some five hundred miles. The late afternoon sun still threw his flame down on us from a sky cloudless except for two or three tentative sheets of buttermilk mackerel, which looked as if they had been caught on a stage where they should not have been when the footlights went up. We were warned that we shall cross the Indian Ocean in the middle of the monsoon season, but so far we have had almost uninterrupted tropical high summer.

*At Singapore there were more ships cheek by jowl than I have seen since Portsmouth on D-Day minus One in 1944, and perhaps more than that. Behind all this was the Singapore backcloth, a forest of high rise buildings. I supposed that Singapore had now become the busiest port in the world, with its wide deep waters, its situation on the globe, ideally placed between east and west, with unparalleled facilities for the handling of containers, of gas and oil.*

# Chapter 13

## Indian Ocean and Arabian Sea

**Wednesday 11th February** I have mentioned some of the books that I have read on this voyage, and I have just finished an interesting novel by Bryce Courtenay set in the time of the deportation to Australia of those deemed to be unworthy citizens of Britain, and although there was a good deal of humping and bumping in the book, it was mostly of a straight-forward nature. I know that I may have disparaged the Missionary Position earlier, but it has certainly stood the test of time, at any rate for the missionaries, and I remember a certain very well known titled lady in the Gay Twenties who acquired an unparalleled knowledge of the bedroom ceilings of Bloomsbury by the use of it.

I venture to suggest that by a little tasteful invention and innovation, a change of angle of approach and presentation perhaps, not only the making of love itself may be more pleasurable, but there may be unexpected side benefits. I know of a couple who thereby discovered serious wood-worm on the under surface of their antique bedside table, which they would otherwise not have detected. While experimenting with one of the inverted dependant lotus positions one unhurried Sunday morning, in that Queen of the Suburbs, Ealing, another couple spotted a very valuable earring under the bed between the carpet and the skirting board which had gone missing three years previously. The point that I wish to make is that there is a pleasant half-way house between the unreal sex portrayed by some authors and the good old M.P. You do not have to swing from the chandeliers, or suffer the discomforts of the airing cupboard or the kitchen sink or even the stairs, but please ladies, try to think beautiful and appropriate thoughts if you can, try to forget about the supermarket shopping list or what is on telly this week or whether you should have tried that finesse at bridge last night.

The next book that I will read will be about Moghul India, and no doubt the joys illustrated in Karma Sutra will feature, but it will be tasteful if so, and no less interesting I am sure.

There will be little or no land visible to us all the way across the Indian Ocean; we may see the southern coast of Sri Lanka but there is little chance of anything else, so that books and music will come to the fore, and binoculars and camera will take a back seat for a couple of weeks. The sea at sunrise this morning would have made a Suffolk millpond on a summer afternoon seem turbulent. River Tweed's bulbous nose created a most unwelcome dehiscence, and at seventeen knots her bow waves had the look of foamed cream in the early yellow sunlight; the still wisps of cloud were as fine silk tulle. It was an early day scene that filled my mind with its tranquil assured beauty, and with overwhelming sorrow that I was seeing it alone.

As we left Malacca Strait, and headed toward the Andaman Sea, the colour of the water changed from bottle green to battleship grey, and we shall march with the northern coast of Sumatra, out of sight to port since Cape

Jangoan Jamboya early this morning. At approximately 6 p.m. we shall change heading level with the island of Pulau We at the extreme north of Sumatra, and sail due west through Great Channel on 270 degrees, between it and the tiny island of Pulau Rondo, two and eight miles distant respectively.

Away to the north of us and out of sight lie the Nicobar Islands, yet another infamous penal settlement with the Andaman Islands, at the time when the East India Company controlled the trade of all this part of the world, and men waxed fat by forcing the sales of opium to China and elsewhere; we shall pass forty miles to the south of Pygmalian Point, the southernmost tip of the Nicobars as we negotiate Great Channel.

You have a feeling as you sail across these seas that you are less isolated, although you may not see land you know it is there, unlike the Atlantic and Pacific the Indian Ocean did not seem to portend such boundlessness, although I well remembered our 'away from it all' feeling when we first flew to the Seychelles, and were told that we were one thousand miles from any other land.

The tropical sun on this latitude seemed as hot as anywhere along the way, and my shipmates are permanently larded with 'sun blarck' so that they look as if they are about to swim the English Channel covered in goose fat; they are terrified of skin cancer.

We rarely see Fat Mona these days; she appears sometimes in the afternoons, for she does not rise until noon, and spends a little time with us on the bridge deck, and I think that the heat of the day is too much for her. She flops and pants and sweats on her sun lounger like a big over-heated female Labrador. I know that she badly wants to get home now, and I doubt whether she will sail the seas again; she wants to start a family, and at her age she should get on with it, though the mental picture of Fat Mona at near term defies even my imagination. If her gods were unkind enough to arrange a multiple pregnancy the farrowing would have the aura, proportions and general atmosphere of the farmyard, and the air would be rent not by cackles, but by screams hideous upon the ear.

At 4 p.m. Pulau We loomed through the off-shore mist to port , a big mountainous island and the point just past which we shall turn to the west; the sun will plummet tonight over the foremast, while the moon, his face red from hurrying, preserves a decent interval before vaulting over the stern and the chimney stack, and I will stand up there right between them like a referee in a contest between two real beauties.

We passed between Pulau We and the Rondo Islands at 6 p.m. two miles from the former and eight miles from the latter, which consisted of a round hump with sheer cliffs, vegetation covered and ten or eleven discrete vertical rock pillars of different heights sticking up out of the sea looking like the teeth, some broken, in the lower jaw of a prehistoric monster. We were still in Great Channel, and it must be aptly named for there were many many ships here from tiny fishing boats, some without canopies, and diminutive motor coasters to bulk carriers.

**Thursday 12th February** We have ahead of us now two days of ocean sailing, and this morning there were white horses on the waves, but they nodded gently and gracefully as if in greeting, and River Tweed had no more than a pleasant pitch.

At breakfast Boom Boom Anthony announced to the class that he had a cough, and as if to demonstrate his problem achieved a forced expiration with mucous accompaniment to silence a male voice choir in full song, but without any transtussive bafflement with his hand; consideration of others is no part of Boom Boom's make up. This was repeated through breakfast, and I felt much relieved that Fat Mona did not rise before high noon, for had she been sitting behind me in her sneeze mode I would have been truly in the eye of two storms with only one way to go, and that would have been upwards.

Big men always seem to talk louder, cough louder, sneeze louder, snore louder, and as far I know fart louder than others, though I must say that I have never loitered long enough to calibrate the last of those and prove that point. I hope Boom Boom recovers very quickly, or, preferably bursts both lungs simultaneously and drops dead, and then the Admiral can console the Flawed Genius in his cabin, and perhaps I can catch him doing it and sell him the photograph, but of course keep the negative.

Fat Mona appeared momentarily on the bridge deck this afternoon, and confirmed my suspicion that the dreaded mal de mer had struck again. She stood by the rail and said that she was ill to the point of vomitation as soon as we left Singapore, and has not had a proper meal for three days nor been able to read. She then clutched her stomach and did a fast waddle to the door leading to the stairs.

Purser Alec confirmed earlier today that they are anxious for Mona to get pregnant as soon as possible and are waiting before 'going in for it' until she has finished her anti-malarial pills. By the look of her today I think that they will have to wait longer than that; Alec weighs eighteen stone and more, and having that bouncing up and down on your stomach would test a fully fit Mona, let alone one in the grip of vomitation, and, speaking purely anatomically, her behind would make any other approach somewhat problematic.

We have now left Great Channel astern and are ploughing our way across the open Indian Ocean at a madly gay 16.4 knots, due west on a heading of 280 degrees, and if River Tweed keeps this up we shall pass close by the bottom of Sri Lanka at 8 p.m. tomorrow and reach Suez Pilot on Sunday 22nd February at about 10 p.m.

The ocean floor is markedly level between Sumatra and Sri Lanka, varying only between three thousand and four thousand five hundred metres, no mountain ranges or great rifts and trenches beneath us. I felt that most of the ship's company were now looking forward to Le Havre; certainly the stewardesses and crew were, and at Le Havre the bastard of an Admiral will have to shell out the money they have earned, which for the Russians is considerable, with the crew earning much overtime by painting ship. He will hate to let them have it, having refused them the chances of shopping ashore all the way round, and it will be given with right bad grace.

There were stellar dust storms in the heavens tonight, and then the moon climbed his ladder and shone a liquefying light, as if to lay that dust and wash it away. Some nights the heaven seems impossibly high, but tonight I felt that I could almost touch it if I stood on tiptoe up there on Monkey Island.

**Friday 13th February** I fear that Boom Boom Anthony and the Flawed Genius may be planning a Continuing Course of Revision Lectures. Imagine having to sit twice through 'Social Development and Gradual Emancipation in the Custom Villages on the New Hebridean Island of Espiritu Santo', or 'The Exploitation and Isolation of the Kanaks in the Early Industrialisation of the South Pacific French Colony of New Caledonia', or even 'The Inexorable Deterioration in Racial Relationships Leading to Open Conflict in Independent Fiji and its Influence in the Ultimate Decision to Return to the British Commonwealth'.

I wondered if they really were Official Guest Lecturers, and if they will pass round the hat at the voyage end; if they do I will know just what to put into it. I must go carefully through the small print of my contract with River Line, and if nothing is written there about Lectures, I will demand a rebate for being bored out of my wits by these two arrogant intellectual snobs.

There were clouds aplenty today providing transient relief from the tropical furnace of the sun, and also a pleasant north west breeze over the starboard bow, but between noon and 4 p.m. it was really too hot to sit out on the decks, and the choice for myself lay between the air conditioning of the cabin and the bridge. Although I might spend up to an hour at a time sitting in one of the two pilot's chairs in the wings of the bridge, Admiral Geoffrey has ignored me when he comes up there. We seem to have reached a situation of armed neutrality, and it will much suit me if we never speak to each other again. The ships pass to port going east, and at over sixteen knots nothing has overtaken us to starboard since we cleared Sumatra.

The extreme south of Sri Lanka must be one of the busiest corners for ships in the world, and we shall pass, after dinner this evening, the tiny pimple of Dundra Head, just seven miles to starboard and if the weather is good shall have a good view of the lights of the Sri Lankan night; that will probably be the last view of land until Aden, for I doubt whether we shall see any of the Maldives, which lie west of the Indian subcontinent and Sri Lanka.

I dwell with much sadness upon the little pretty lands that we have left behind us, and which in all probability I will never again see. I think not only of their beauty, but of their peoples and their customs, ways of life and of adopting and modifying the habits brought to them from the west, and while adapting to that the way that they have retained many of their rituals. Upcountry in many of these islands circumcision is still the most important ritual in a man's life, and often it takes the form of a kind of supracision, the foreskin being cut off and the healing edges sprinkled with irritating substances to form a raised ring of scar tissue proximal to the glans, in order to enhance sexual pleasure for the women.

When you thought of the resort in the modern day in the west to flavoured condoms and the like to enhance sexual pleasure, you realised that these primitive people were way ahead of us when it came to increasing sexual joy for each other; they discovered almost at the beginning of their history how to grow piston rings on their willies.

At 9.30 p.m. the lighthouse on Dondra Head became visible to starboard, at first I was not quite certain whether I could see it or not, I just knew it was there and there was the very faintest glow in the sky in the same direction. It took one and a half hours to sail past the southern extremity of Sri Lanka, more and more lights became visible and then I could smell the wood smoke, quite pungent in the offshore nightwind even seven miles away. I felt suddenly very close to Esmé then, for she so loved the Indian subcontinent, and in spite of its independence Sri Lanka seemed such an integral part of it.

As we sailed past at seventeen knots I was sure that I could smell flowers and spices as well as burning wood, I was convinced that I smelt sweet night flowering jasmine right out in the Indian Ocean, such was my imagination, but it was nice. Russian Iosif was on watch on the bridge and he was most keen to point out the towns of Weligana, and Galle which has a sizeable port. He is now quite at ease with me and cracks jokes in broken English, and I have to be very careful to try to sense the punch line when it comes. Iosif is quite personable, with his close cut hair, new grown moustache and 'Cigar' eau de toilette; I have grown to like him immensely and shall miss him at the end of this voyage more than most.

Iosif checked the course on the chart with me, recorded our time of passing Dondra Head Light on it, and an immediate change of heading from due west on 269 degrees to west north west on 282 degrees; he told me that we now have four clear days sail to Aden, and bid me 'night night', which he had just learned.

Before I went to bed I climbed up again to Monkey Island for a last look at the twinkling Sri Lankan night, and was immediately born high upon a swirling vortex of memories. They swept me round the corner to the east, and jettisoned me just up there on the left, and it seemed like yesterday, but of course it was hundreds and hundreds of miles and many years ago, on a virgin white solitary beach near Covelong where my love stood in the high midday sun, wet from the sea and happy like a child, because she had just swum in the Bay of Bengal; since childhood she had always wanted to swim in the Caribbean and the Bay of Bengal. Her childlike wonder and enthusiasm for new experiences that her world had to offer, stayed with her until the end of her life, and if you lived with her and you loved her, you were perpetually and gratefully infected.

If you cannot dream the dreams that you want to dream, wishes are the dreams that you can control, so that if I cannot dream the good dreams I can always wish the good wishes; I wished very much tonight that I was back on that beach at Covelong all those years ago, and that was a good wish indeed.

**Saturday 14th February** This morning we have passed ninety miles south of Cape Comorin at the southernmost tip of India, and then sailed across the Lakshadweep Sea towards the top of the Maldives. If I were to write a twenty page Epic Poem of Love and Romance I might begin thus:-

They swam and they surfed
Made love in the sun
On the shore of the
Solomon Sea
or, to be more local:-
They swam and they surfed
Made love in the sun
On the shore of the
Andaman Sea
but any romance would fade I think if I wrote:-
They swam and they surfed
Made love in the sun
On the shore of the
Lakshadweep Sea

Any sea bordered by islands of such beauty as the Maldives should be worthy of investigation, whatever its name; I have not seen them myself but my friends tell me that I should go there without fail. The islands hang down the ocean from the Seventh Parallel North to the First Parallel South, like a huge bunch of grapes, five hundred miles of them, each one an atoll ringing a central lagoon, and the reefs and fish must make for a snorkelling heaven.

We shall pass through the stalk at the north of them, Eight Degree Channel, to bring us back into the Indian Ocean and into Arabian Basin and then the southern edge of the Arabian Sea. This morning an S.O.S. was received from M.V. Ever Mighty, named, in this case I think, after Allah rather than Jehovah, because it was an Iranian ship which had lost a man overboard off the coast of Tanzania in Somali Basin, well to the south west. I worked out, with three weeks to go, that we have crossed seven seas so far and there are more to come, but we shall be repeating ourselves when we re-enter the Atlantic, and so our score of three oceans is complete.

Poor Fat Mona, is still in a decline; Purser Alec told me that during the hours that she spends out of her bunk, which get fewer and fewer, she was most 'iffy', I was unfamiliar with that diagnosis, but it suggested the widest parameters; he tapped his sweaty forehead as if the disease had ventured above the diaphragm and higher than that. She has not appeared for two days either on deck or in the Dining Saloon, so perhaps at least she may be achieving an involuntary and minuscule shrinkage of the corpus; but when she wraps herself around the Giant Burgers again, that will be reversed with interest, for after each bout of sickness Fat Mona exacts the most terrible revenge for the wasting of her trough time.

It will be midnight and after before we leave Lakshadweep Sea and pass through Eight Degree Channel between the two topmost atolls of the Maldives; ships, now that we have rounded Sri Lanka are few and far between, many will have peeled off to the south making for South African ports and the Cape, and those that we do see are mainly eastbound, sailing from Suez and Aden to Singapore, Australia and New Zealand.

There were cloud banks in the sky tonight and every now and then they parted to reveal ravines, and you could see the stars at the bottom of these briefly, and then like a peep show they would close again. It was as if someone in a hurry had thrown diamonds into the bottom of canyons without care or concern for their value; there was neither order nor pattern to them at all, it seemed such a waste. I felt that I would like to collect them up and display them properly according to size and brilliance.

I spent the greater part of the evening talking to Dishy Pyotr, the ship's Officer Electrician. He had tried to make my T.V./Video work, and he stayed for a beer and a talk. He is a highly intelligent and well-educated man and his wife is a teacher in the University of Murmansk. Life is hard for young people in Russia today because the pay is so low; Pyotr regards himself as very fortunate to be on the pay list of River Line and to have regular work, though he does not like leaving his wife and nine year old daughter. He and his wife met at University and have been married ten years, and they love each other 'too much'.

We talked of many things, he is depressed about Russian politics and what will happen when Yeltsin goes. He writes poetry and was very interested to know that I was writing this book. Like myself, he suffers from psoriasis, because, he says, he is a very emotional man, and that gave me food for thought; I told him that psoriasis also attacked intelligent and clubbable people, and he liked that.

He said that he and his wife, apart from being much in love, liked each other and were good friends, and asked me what it was like to lose the person you loved the most. I could not really begin to tell him, and he fully understood why. He is aged thirty with his life ahead of him, and after he left I sat thinking about him and his wife and daughter, and worried about what was the Russian future for those intelligent young people, and felt guilty about the opportunities which life had given to myself. As a result of this unexpectedly pleasant evening, I now knew for whom those fires behind Dishy Pyotr's eyes were banked, and that was nice indeed.

Pyotr was very attractive and seemed quite unconscious of it, and I could see the ache and the shine of mental fornication in the eyes of Little Anna, the youngest of the stewardesses, when she looked at him, and, to my utter disgust, Flawed Genius Jane gave him the eye whenever she could, and tried to monopolise him at the barbecues.

**Sunday 15th February**. Eight Degree Channel was safely negotiated at around 2 a.m. this morning without hitting any of the atolls, and so it should have been at a width of over thirty miles. This morning we had a bright sun smiling down upon us as we entered the Arabian Basin, the cloud formations were vapid and small, and there was a friendly breeze, not insistent enough to cause more than a wrinkle on the surface of the blue sea. Having come to the end of the last of the books that I brought with me, I did a trawl of the ship's library; much of its contents did not interest me, but I found a book by Evelyn Anthony which I had not read, I thought I had read them all. 'The Occupying Power' will be a bonus, and hopefully get me to Aden without too much talk of the old bang-bonk-bangity-bang

Looking over the rail of Monkey Island there were many small fishing boats about, not in flotillas, but lone, and it always amazed me how far out to sea they ventured in their need to catch fish. They must be out of communication with the shore for days on end, and some must disappear without trace over the years. The growth of tourism will help, but life is hard for the island folk, the living they get from fish must be pretty poor on the islands of the Maldives. The same applies to the islands of the South Pacific, where I was told very firmly that the money from tourism was not fairly dispersed among the people, but plundered by the few at the top. The weather has been set fair most of the voyage, but I would not like to be far out to sea in these small fishing boats when the squalls blow for real.

'Today is the Birthday of Admiral Geoffrey' and he celebrated after breakfast by following me to my cabin, and telling me, with his black eyes blazing a foot from me, that he was banning me from the bridge for the rest of the voyage, because I was still spending too much time there in spite of his earlier reprimand, and interfering with the normal navigation of the ship. This meant that I would have to sneak into the chartroom when he was otherwise engaged. The officers on the bridge told me that the Admiral considered me to be 'A dangerous man, and dangerous cargo', and laughed their bloody heads off, the disrespectful devils. To be a dangerous man at the age of seventy-seven with every joint and muscle stiffer than a lover's dick, takes some doing I can tell you

As we sailed north east the ship's clocks were retarded every other day by one hour, which played games with the sleep centre and the metabolism, not to say the eliminations. I shall soon find myself rising when I should be reclining, and receiving insistent calls to stool in the middle of the night. I hoped that when I reach home I would be able to get through a game of tennis without interruption.

We were making good time, rarely less than 16.5 knots and should see Aden during the afternoon of Wednesday 18th February, leave the Arabian Sea and enter the Gulf of Aden having sailed blithely over Owen Fracture, a gorge in the sea floor deeper than the Grand Canyon but much narrower, one hundred miles from the shores of Arabia. We shall sail through the Gulf of Aden and then the Red Sea and the Suez Canal, but somehow the prospect of this did not fill me with the anticipation that perhaps it should have done. I have always wanted to sail through the Suez Canal, as the Panama Canal, but the Middle East generally did not have the same thrill, ancient Egypt apart.

It is not so much the politics, although there is potential for trouble there, the Third World War in all probability, but the colourlessness and cheerlessness that the general adherence to fundamental Islamic faith conveys. The South Sea islanders have absorbed the teaching of the Christian missionaries, digested it, and changed it into a happy go-go singalong theme in their lives, and this applied very much also to the islands of the Caribbean.

Esmé, who made a study of comparative religions used to ask why these happy folk loved to thank their god for what they had, when that god had given them so little, placed them firmly on their rung of the ladder with so little chance to step up. I suppose it is all about knowing the possibilities, and the restlessness of ambition, the forsaking of the peace, of the contentment with what you have for the strife to attain what you see others having. The truly awesome, and for many repulsive law of human survival dictates that there shall ever be the few riding high in comfort upon the backs of the many who live in discomfort. I am quite sure that Christ did not approve of that, though the Parable of the Talents has always offended me.

I looked in wonder at the firmament tonight, most of the clouds had business elsewhere, the moon too, and there seemed room enough on that stage up there for everybody to shine, no need to jostle, there was happiness there, they were all smiling. At the end of this day of bad beginnings, I listened to the First, Second ,Third and Fifth Mozart Violin Concerti, which brought to earth some sweetness and light, to go with those stars in the heaven.

**Monday 16th February** One of Tina's worries is that the iron has got sticky again, and she looked around the table at us, and insisted that it was due to the printing on somebody's tee-shirt. I did not wear tee-shirts, my bust is too big, but I did see one in Singapore which declared 'We did it in the Cable Car', perhaps I should have bought that and gummed the bloody iron up for good and all.

I really cannot wait to get back to real people and to happenings that are vital to us all, such as the Queen Mother's fracture, and the movement of Presidential zips. With regard to the latter, I was interested in an opinion poll among American women, published in a respectable English newspaper that somebody had brought aboard. In answer to the question 'Would you sleep with the President?' 80% of them ticked the 'Not Again' box. There will be one more full day in the Arabian Sea and then we shall have land within fifty miles of us on either side almost all the way home, though we may not see it, the Red Sea and the Mediterranean are wide enough to give the impression of oceans I am told, and the only land we shall see in the Mediterranean will be Sicily with luck, and then Gibraltar.

**Tuesday 17th February** It was all pure 'white mares' tails in the wind' first thing this morning, swirling and whirling across a sky of mallards' egg blue; and then they had gone, to grace some other heaven as if shooed away by the sun.

I wheeled my sun lounger into the few feet of shade cast by the ship's superstructure and settled down to another hard day's seafaring, reassured by the knowledge that Purser Alec had delivered another two cases of beer to my cabin before breakfast, to help me through the fire of the day and quench my thirsts, existent and non-existent, and by the look of it, this day will be a right scorcher.

Admiral Geoffrey came to the starboard wing of the bridge and looked through the window, and I seriously wondered why he was so daunted by my presence on the ship, afraid even, and what was it that caused him to dislike me so much, evidently from the start of the voyage. I did not realise this until we were across the Atlantic, for he did not speak to me until his sneer about my son's geographical education.

This was quite a new experience for me, and as his anger toward myself escalated, so did his fawning over my shipmates. The officers on the bridge assured me that he sneers about the other four just as much as he rails about myself. None of those officers who covered the watches had sailed under Admiral Geoffrey before, nor met him, and three of them together with Purser Alec and Bright Eyed Bearded Henry, the Second Engineer, were determined that they never will again.

By noon the sky was quite cloudless except for an unusual ring of puffballs all round the horizon, just above the sea, like ping pong balls perhaps, rolled to the rim of a huge round table on a cloth of blue baize. I think that they were desperately trying to get out of the sun but there was no escape for them, and now they would be destroyed one by one like white rats with a terrier in a ratting pit.

I had a talk on deck this afternoon with Johnny, Henry's wife. She was a cheerful intelligent woman, very friendly, who read much and as I have said, well understood my loneliness. All the other passengers and officers were fond of her, and although it was not in her remit, she was always anxious to help us all to get as much out of the voyage as possible. We talked about assessing others, and came to the conclusion that you could learn as much if not more about a person by what they did not say, by their silences in given situations, than by their talking. If you wanted to know what was in somebody's heart and soul, you could learn more if you could reach behind their talk, and you could more easily do that by watching them when they were silent, while others talked, by listening to their quietness as well as their sound.

Because of the language difficulty some of the Russians on board did not talk much, but I felt that I knew them very well, people like Russian Iosif and Dishy Pyotr, and Tall Dark Dem'yan, with whom I have spent much time. I have thought a good deal about this long voyage and how it could have been made more enjoyable. Apart from a change of Captain, I would have welcomed two more passengers, preferably from the U.K. and the sexes would not have mattered; it was unfortunate that the other three British folk had to cancel at the last minute. Having said that nothing has happened to make me wish that I had not come on the voyage; the plusses have outscored the minuses, I have met some very pleasant people, and four months have passed away astern that I shall not have to sail through again.

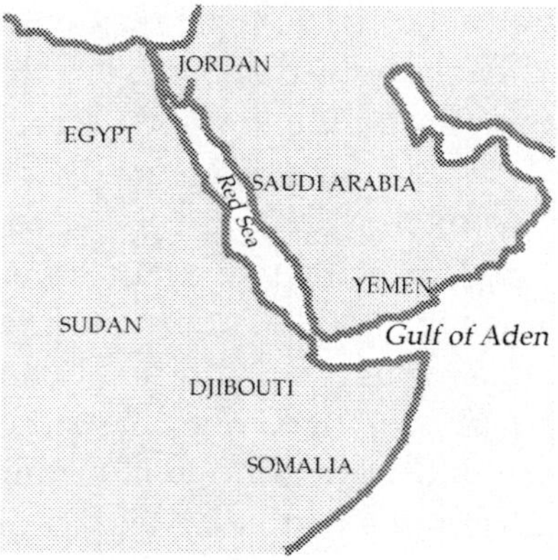


# Chapter 14

## Gulf of Aden and Red Sea

**Wednesday 18th February** The wind this morning has veered through 180 degrees, and instead of coming over the starboard bow now blows from the port quarter, and that without any change of heading from 280 degrees. This should give us a slight increase of speed, with the currents unchanged, and meant that we should pass Raas Caseyr on the point of the left shoulder of that troubled country of Somalia, at about 2 p.m. on our way into the Gulf of Aden.

We should pass Raas Caseyr ten miles out, and although there will be counter-currents inshore they should not affect us, but there will be irregular tidal streams of up to two and a half knots, and north east monsoon winds with west and north west sets as we round this corner of the African continent.

River Tweed sailed over Error Seamount without scratching her bum although the name suggests that somebody did, and at 1.45 p.m. we saw the coast of Africa to port, long low mountains behind and much sand and some vegetation on the seaward slopes coming right down to the shore. As we sailed round into the Gulf we could make out little detail in the mist of the afternoon, but the sight of the land was strangely welcome for the Indian Ocean had seemed endless, with not another ship in sight since we left the Maldives behind us.

Fat Mona seems to have recovered somewhat, and she has joined us on deck these last two afternoons, and making up for lost time with the camcorder, whirring away at anything in sight and much that is not. She has sufficiently recovered to resume reading Stephen King, and is now exercised to get her legs nice and brown so that people will know that she has been to the tropics when she gets home. She has spent so much time in the cabin that the sun will have to work overtime because she has much femoral acreage to tan; it was a good thing that she did not want those four buttocks done as well.

Flawed Genius Jane had a long chat with the Admiral by the port rail on Monkey Island this afternoon, they appeared most happy and animated, and her eyes never left those black marble chips that he calls his eyes. Boom Boom Anthony had better watch out, or he will find that his little minikin really will finish the voyage beneath our pot-bellied sea dog. His stomach was a little smaller than Boom Boom's but bore many scars and looked like a map; I hoped that they were knife wounds, and I would not be surprised if they were. Jane threw her head back and laughed with great gaiety into his face at everything the bastard said, and I nearly catted all over Fat Mona, which would have been a pity, with her near as dammit ready for the Giant Burgers again, and all those unopened sauce bottles waiting for the smack of her hand at trough in the Dining Saloon.

I hoped that the next scar on Admiral Geoffrey's belly would be a post mortem scar and very soon, and how would I love to make it-while he is still alive, with a blunt and rusty bread knife, slowly.

As we passed the northernmost point of Somalia, Aluula, there was a change of heading from 282 degrees to 273 degrees, and we shall sail due west just north of the Twelfth Parallel through the Gulf of Aden until we make the Straits of Bab El Mandab at about 8 p.m. tomorrow, which will lead us into the Red Sea.

**Thursday 19th February** The sun joined me on Monkey Island at 6.15 a.m. this morning, and the air was warm already. The wind had shifted across the stern and was blowing from the starboard quarter. I loved the tropical early morning at sea, even without the heady fragrances as the flowers open out for the sun on land.

The ship was quiet at sunrise, there was no noise of hammering and drilling which came a little later when the crew started their daily maintenance tasks. There was just the contented beat of the engines and the quiet answering rhythmic vibrations it produced in the ship's structure. There was usually little to catch the eye except for the sea and the sky, but this morning there was a large school of porpoises leaping past the bow and playing along the port side, miniature whales and I wanted to ask them where were their big brothers. It seemed strange that you could sail all the way round the world without seeing a whale, but they presumably prefer colder waters.

The course of the ship will take us to within twenty miles of the Port of Aden, but this will be too far away for us to see, and after Aden the depth of water all the way through Bab El Mandab and well into the Red Sea will be between fifty and sixty metres only, and the two channels to east and west in the Strait seemed close as on a single carriageway road, when you looked on the chart. Here indeed was another of nature's shipping narrows, and made ever more congested by the development of the oil industry in the Middle East.

There were monsoon currents in the Straits of Bab El Mandab of up to three knots. From June to September they flowed south east in the Red Sea and east north east in the Gulf of Aden, and the reverse from October to April, the changeover month being May. When we go through the Straits tonight we shall pass within five miles of the Yemeni island of Mayyum to starboard and within ten miles of the African mainland, which here will be Djibouti, and we shall have passed the Port of Djibouti sitting on the southern shore of the Gulf of Tadjoura, which is a diverticulum of the Gulf of Aden to port.

**Friday 20th February** We went through Bab El Mandab last night at 9 p.m., it was a pitch black moonless night and all we saw were two revolving lights and a few onshore lights on Mayyum to starboard, and were joined by six or seven other ships at a distance; most of the traffic seemed to be Red Sea bound.

This morning there was a strong head wind, the clouds were low and the sea slate grey. There was a change of heading to the north in the early hours, and we were now sailing at sixteen knots up the middle of the Red Sea on 330 degrees. We have passed a chain of Yemeni islands to starboard, starting with Avocet Rock, followed by Centre Peak, Jabal Zubayer, Saddle, Rugged, Haycock and Quoin Islands; all these lying some twenty five miles off the mainland, and once passed we shall see no more land for three days until near to Suez. I had not fully appreciated before the voyage began that the ship travelled along a series of straight lines at different angles. There was no helmsman turning a wheel to steer us round rocks and islands, like a wing three-quarter round a full-back; it was all much more geometric.

Boom Boom Anthony had the bloody nerve to launch forth into an Unpublished Breakfast Lecture on the subject of 'The Influence of Immigrant Populations Upon the Gaining of Independence of Certain States'. I could not tell you what he said because I did not listen; it came quite out of the blue and surprised and obviously bored Flawed Genius Jane, who liked to give the lectures herself and could not think one up.

Boom Boom chided me for not taking enough photographs, and proudly told me that so far he has used up well over forty rolls of film, each with thirty-six exposures, and I will bet that they will form the basis of many, many Illustrated Lectures back home, although many of them are of far away shores in semi-darkness. He and Jane have already written a twenty-five page pamphlet about the voyage which they plan to distribute among their friends.

I spent time on deck with Fat Mona who seemed depressed. Apart from her problems with mal de mer, she was deeply upset by the way Admiral Geoffrey had treated her Purser Alec from the moment they joined ship; they, neither of them could understand it, and were desperately worried that he would give Alec a bad report for the voyage, which could jeopardise his future, and which would be totally unfair and without basis. I promised her that I would support Alec, along with the Russian officers whom the Admiral has bullied all the way, in the letter that I shall write to the company about the Admiral's behaviour toward myself. I was not in any way vulnerable, but they were and he knew it. Watching Admiral Geoffrey bully Alec reminded me of Big Lenny being bullied by the farm owner in Steinbeck's "Of Mice and Men".

Although the day has been overcast without any sign of the sun, the ambient temperature has not fallen below eighty two degrees Fahrenheit, but the north westerly head wind, high enough to make standing at the rail on Monkey Island difficult, made for the first cool day for three months and was an unwelcome portent for the near future.

**Saturday 21st February** The sun came up in such splendour at 5.45 a.m. this morning, as if to make up for his poor showing yesterday. The first sunball rose quickly above the dipping horizon over the starboard quarter, vermilion-red before changing rapidly in a few minutes to blinding white through all the yellows. He tried to get behind those nebulous slats to start with, as if wanting to see and not be seen, but they would have none of it. They parted and told him that he had nothing to be shy about. I think he will stay with us for the day.

It was at the beginning of a day of tropical promise which you felt you must share or it was wasted, and this morning I half wanted the sun to go away, and be replaced by comforting heavy curtains of low black clouds. There is a strange comfort in dark skies at times; that surely was why Goya painted blackness, as happiness ebbed away beyond his reach. Perhaps I had these feelings because I was almost back to my domestic dungeon.

The Red Sea is not really an ellipse, it has dilatations and narrowings all the way so that it is really like a caterpillar with two horns at the northern end, the Gulf of Aquaba leading to Aquaba and Eilat to the right, and the Gulf of Suez to the left, which will take us to the southern end of the Suez Canal.

We have had Ethiopia and then Sudan to the port of us, and that huge country of Saudi Arabia to starboard. Earlier this morning we passed Sarasan Bank, fifty miles to starboard with breaks and coral heads, and Port Sudan one hundred miles to port. At 4 p.m. we were level with the large Saudi Arabian city and port of Jiddah to starboard, fifty miles to the east. River Tweed punched through the

Force 5 sea with her head well down and maintained fourteen knots. I could sense a feeling among the officers stewardesses and crew that they could not wait to see Le Havre; they felt that the job was done, and unloading would be the responsibility of the new crew. When we sail into Le Havre there will be no flags flying, no confetti, no streamers, and no bands playing; just general relief for them all.

*At the entrance to the Suez canal. Unlike Panama the Suez is one way with alternating convoys of some twenty Northbound and Southbound vessels.*

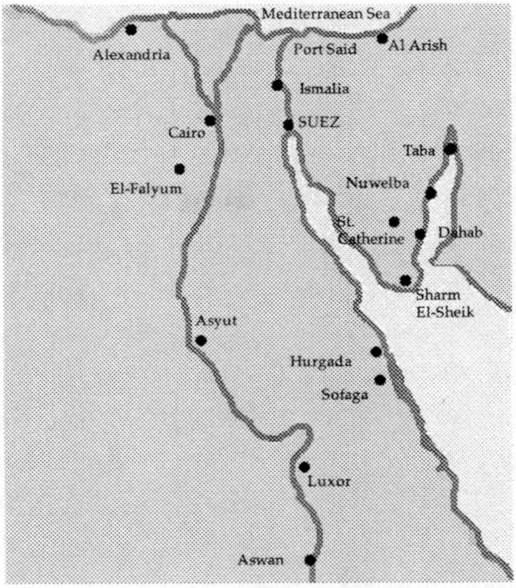


# Chapter 15

## Suez

**Sunday 22nd February** A notice has appeared above the loo in my cabin instructing me to place in it 'Only the Products of Bodily Functions and Toilet Tissue - No Paper Towels, Detergents Etc.' The key word to this Admiral's Edict seemed to be 'Etc.'. I assumed that as I was not in the habit of menstruating, using condoms or stuffing The Times down the hole I could ignore this notice, and I wondered who had offended, and how, to produce it. Tina was long past menopause but was on HRT, and the Flawed Genius was in full womanly flow, so it could have been them. It could also have been Fat Mona and Alec, or Johnny and Henry. I hoped very much that it was not poor old Fat Mona.

The expected time of arrival in Suez Bay is 4 a.m. tomorrow morning, and we may or may not go through the Canal the same day, depending on the shipping traffic. Later this evening we will enter the Gulf of Suez through the Strait of Gubal, leaving Shaker Island just to port, and the Strait here is fifteen miles wide. Further north, going up the Gulf of Suez, we pass the shallows of Felix Jones Patches, where the Gulf is only ten miles wide, and after them Moresby Shoal. Egypt will be all around us, Sinai ahead.

The wind was still blowing this morning, but there were fewer white horses than yesterday, and by the middle of the morning the sun was strong and the sky virtually cloudless, so that it was pleasant sitting on the bridge deck with the sky azure and the Red Sea indigo, and this pleasant breeze in our faces. Chief Engineer Bill came along and told us that the air conditioning had now been switched off for the rest of the voyage, confirming that we go ever northward toward the winter of the Northern Hemisphere, and very soon it will be sweaters and slacks on deck.

The Suez Canal is older than Panama, it was opened on the 17th November 1869, and under the Convention of Constantinople of the 29th October 1888 it was declared open to all nations, and would not be blockaded except in time of war. The whole Canal area was designated a Free Port. Of recent memory the Suez Canal was closed in 1956 and re-opened in 1957 having been nationalised by Egypt. It was also closed at the start of the Arab-Israeli War in 1967 and re-opened in 1979, when extensive re-dredging and widening was carried out until 1982.

Pilotage is compulsory to go through, and the maximum draught for ships is 12.8 metres, beam 64 metres and no restrictions on length. Ships with a beam of between 61 and 64 metres can only go through if wind and weather conditions are favourable, and for them the maximum beam wind is ten knots. All projections, ladders and derricks must be inboard, and bow anchors have to be held ready to let go.

I was sure that River Tweed fulfilled all these conditions with something to spare, but we must all keep well away from the bridge in view of Admiral Geoffrey's nervousness at times like this. The officers tell me that on every ship on which they had sailed through Suez which carried passengers, they were always welcome to stand on the bridge so long as they kept out of the way. I will be better on Monkey Island, I do not want to stand too near the Admiral when he is nervous for obvious reasons, I remembered Basilan Strait in the Philippines only too well.

At 10 p.m. we sailed firmly into the funnel that is the Gulf of Suez, there were lights along both sides, and there were the red flames of the burning off of gasses in the refineries, some five miles distant on either side. We passed Waly, Amal, Nessin, Morgan, Badri and Ramadan oil fields. It made you realise that this part of the world is sitting on a sea of oil, a sea of liquid black gold.

**Monday 23rd February** We had to arrive at the top of the Gulf by 4.15 a.m., and failed by about thirty minutes, which meant that we would spend today anchored in Anchor Position No. 10 of the twenty eight positions in the waiting area in Suez Bay, and will go through the Canal with tomorrow's convoy. There were two southbound convoys and one northbound per day, twenty ships in each, and I counted sixty ships waiting in the Gulf around us. Today's convoy will commence entering the Canal at 11 a.m.

Several small motor launches have come alongside this morning, and men tried to board, presumably to sell to us or steal from us. We were warned that Suez was possibly the worst place for thieving on the whole route, and to keep all doors firmly locked. Big Van was down on the main deck ready to smash the fingers of the fellahin if they tried to get over the rail. His trousers stopped short at the calf, and with a large ring in his ear and a red bandanna round his head, he looked just like a pirate himself, the great Russian yeti; I shall miss him.

At 10 a.m. we were told that we would, after all, go through the Canal today, and within half an hour we up-anchored and were on our way. As at Panama we sailed along a channel marked by buoys, past Newport Rock and into Newport Rock Channel. This Channel took us to the mouth of the Canal which was to starboard, we had to turn through 30 degrees, and the depth here was 33.5 metres. We followed the Channel and entered the Eastern Channel of the Canal proper with the city of Suez and a tall Signal Tower on the port bank. We were some way behind the convoy which had gone ahead, and the last ship of it was out of sight.

We passed several dredgers, and, like painting the Forth Bridge, keeping the Suez Canal clear was a continuous process. To starboard there was endless flat desert of stone, sand and yellow dirt as far as the eye could see, with just a hint of mountains very far away. To port there was habitation, there were date palms and small fields of vegetables, much greenery due to the fact that the Nile was only sixty miles away. A wide tarmac road ran with the Canal, but traffic was sparse and mainly oil tankers.

Unlike Panama the Suez Canal is one way, and we must have been the last northbound ship of the day, very much a straggler and our speed was five knots. After some three hours Eastern Channel opened out into Little Bitter Lake, and our course was marked by concrete buoys. Little Bitter Lake was wide, but nothing compared with Great Bitter Lake into which it leads. In Great Bitter Lake there was two way sailing, and during our time in the lake we counted twenty one ships passing us on the port side going south; container ships, oil tankers, car carriers and mixed cargo ships at fixed intervals. One big container ship was anchored in the Eastern Channel and pointing the wrong way; its steering had failed, and this

Canal was no place for that to happen. There were small dhows with fishing nets piled on the stern, and all round the western shores of this big lake there were buildings, houses, blocks and hotels, far away in the distance.

There were checkpoints, five of them on the west bank of the Canal, recording the size and time of passage of each ship, and River Tweed was recorded as she left Great Bitter Lake eventually, and entered the Eastern Branch of the next part of the Canal.

Ismailia eventually appeared to port, preceded by the impressive white stone memorial to the Dead of the First World War, and we noted many pock marks from shells on it, and wondered in which war that occurred. A mile or two further on, on the bleak desert to starboard there was the memorial to the dead of the Six Day War of 1967. This was modern and fascinating, it was in metal and a huge exact replica of a bayonet fixed to the end of a rifle.

Ismailia was an enormous city and we seemed to take ages to sail past it. There was the luxurious villa of the President, a sports complex, and newly built housing blocks. Everywhere there were dredgers at work, and every few miles they were shoring up and repairing the bank on both sides of the Canal. In this stretch the Canal had clear-cut edges much of them bricked, which made it seem narrower, and it meandered, which surprised me, because I had imagined it to be a straight cut through the desert; perhaps rock formations dictated changes of direction, or they were following the contours of the land.

The transit time for Suez Canal was twelve hours, compared with eight hours for Panama, and they both had a lake half way, but Panama had locks and was two-way all the way. There was a cooling wind on the deck and sweaters and anoraks were essential; Fat Mona wore two sweaters and a heavy greatcoat which had a fur collar, which she must have inherited from her grandmother

At one point there was a loud report from Fat Mona's sun lounger when she changed position. I accused her of farting, and she said that if she really had the sun lounger and the mattress would now be half way to Cairo, and I could well believe her. Flawed Genius Jane has been taking copious notes all day, and even went down to the bridge to get more paper in mid afternoon. That boded ill, and I knew that now we could be inflicted with Lectures morning, noon and night, covering the whole history of the Suez Canal, Egypt and its people.

The Suez Canal by night was less than arresting, the road along the West Bank had graduated to motorway status, and the yellow lights of it and small conurbations along it accompanied us to port. On that forbidding desert to starboard there was little light indeed, just scattered yellow winks here and there, and a road far away in the background without much evidence of traffic on it. You were bound to make unfavourable comparison with the excitement of Panama by night, or by day for that matter, but I was glad that I did not fly home from Singapore and miss this experience of the older of the two great canals of our world.

At 9 p.m. the lights of Port Said danced to port, miles and miles of them, and we picked up speed and breasted out into the Mediterranean Sea of such very happy memory, I felt that I had just begun the last lap; 'Five Days to the Rock, Four Days to the Dock' as seafarers say when they leave Port Said for home; one more sea, one more strait, one more bay, one more channel.

I bade goodnight to Boom Boom and the Flawed Genius, who were munching sandwiches to assuage their hunger, the five course dinner being a mere distant memory of three and a half hours ago, left Monkey Island and went to bed; it had been an interesting day.

# Chapter 16

## Mediterranean Sea

**Tuesday 24th February** We were now heading north west on 288 degrees, the diesels were giving us 14.2 knots and the sea was calm. Egypt had fallen away on the port quarter, and the next land that we pass reasonably close to will be Malta, but out of sight fifty miles to starboard in two days time. Far north of us before Malta, are Cyprus and Crete.

Now that the Iraq crisis seemed to have passed, albeit temporarily, we need not have worried whether River Tweed would be delayed in some way in the Red Sea or the Gulf of Aden. Tina was sure that we could have been bombed or torpedoed.

BRITISH CARGO VESSEL SUNK IN RED SEA
AMERICANS MISTAKE FOR ENEMY SHIP
NO SURVIVORS
LAST VOICE HEARD INSISTING
A 'PERTAYTER'S A PERTAYTER'

The air and sea temperatures this morning were the same at sixty six degrees Fahrenheit. A distress alert has been received from Rescue Co-ordination Centre

Southern Norway/Stavanger, a ship M.V. Kurdayogi has blown up and caught fire in the North Sea, three men killed and thirteen survivors picked up by M.V. Rosa Tikano heading for Las Palmas. M. V. Rosa Tikano has been congratulated upon the excellent assistance offered.

We have three thousand three hundred and ninety miles to cover, three thousand three hundred and ninety miles from Pilot Suez to Pilot Le Havre, for it is there that the passengers will disembark and the copra will be unloaded under the latest arrangements.

We realised that River Line was anxious about time when we unexpectedly got on the end of that convoy through the Suez Canal; I would dearly love to know how much that 'sweetener' cost the company. It was a lovely Mediterranean day, sky literally without cloud and sea a slightly creased indigo carpet, no warnings on the charts today of wrecks, shoals or seamounts, just some tunny nets closer to Libya, but these will be well marked. The heat from the sun was sufficient to allow reading on deck in spite of a cheerful and energetic little seawind on the starboard bow. As you sailed further northward each day, you knew that as far as sitting on decks bathed in sun was concerned you were on borrowed time; you had already stolen a southern summer from your northern winter.

**Wednesday 25th February** Yesterday's creased indigo carpet was now without its creases, and we slid along as across a pan of blue oil. As we passed well south of Greece there was a cold wind astern, the sun had paled, was reluctant, gloomy unsure and wintry, generous still with light but parsimonious with warmth. It was so unlike those summer suns that smiled upon Corfu without fail when we went to the taverna in Kassiopi year upon year, and felt that we had discovered paradise; it seemed so long ago that I could almost be persuaded that we never went there. Memories like that develop gaps and deficiencies which vary; upon times you have to play games of hide and seek when you do not particularly wish to play, the memories hide and you must seek.

To the south of us there were Herodotus, Archimedes and Epicharmos Seamounts, none of them more than one hundred metres beneath the sea, and we shall cross over Herodotus Rise as we pass south of the Greek mainland. The depth of the Mediterranean averaged one thousand to two thousand five hundred metres all the way from Suez to Gibraltar, and our heading of 290 degrees will take us through Malta Channel, between Malta to port and Sicily to starboard twenty-five miles from each, around noon tomorrow; we shall sail between Medina (Malta) Ridge and the Ionian Abyssal Plain on the sea bed and leave the shallows of Medina Bank to port.

Flawed Genius Jane is having a birthday party before dinner in the passenger lounge, and I know that Admiral Geoffrey will be there. They do not even have to rely upon a look across a crowded room, they will be able to stand together and look into each other's eyes, black marble into black obsidian.

Fat Mona asked if she could consult me on the bridge deck this afternoon where I was having a post prandial nap, wrapped up in a thick sweater and Rohan anorak. She asked me what where the symptoms of early pregnancy, because she thought that she might have 'fallen'. She was two weeks late with her 'curse' and stopped taking the anti-malarial pills three weeks ago. She said that they had only 'done it' once after that and if she was pregnant Alec's nickname would have to change from 'Smoko' to 'Bonko'.

She could of course have been pregnant, she was feeling sick, there was nothing new in that for her but the sea was dead calm, and her titties were pricking. I advised her to keep a close watch on her private parts and to let me know at once if they became purple, so she will probably spend the rest of the voyage squatting over a mirror, bless her. It would be wonderful for them both if she were pregnant because it is exactly what they want, and it would make the voyage seem more worthwhile for her than it has hitherto.

The Birthday Party was well attended, Flawed Genius Jane, the Birthday Girl, appeared in a sari which she bought in Singapore, and attempted a bare midriff. This was a mistake for two reasons; firstly she had no midriff, with her legs ending in her armpits, and secondly her overeating had produced a roll of fat where her midriff should be. She was very brown and looked half Indian, perhaps she is, the self satisfied little squaw. Admiral Geoffrey made no speech, but presented her with a gift from River Line, and sealed it with a kiss.

Back in my cabin I had to neutralise all this somehow with music. I chose the Violin Concerti of Mendelsson and Brahms. Esmé often said that the Violin Concerti of Brahms, Beethoven, Mendelsson and Bruch generated within her such exquisite feeling that it transgressed the boundary between pleasure and pain. She said that at that point there really was no difference, because you were at the summit of sensation, you could go no further.

**Thursday 26th February** There was a storm in the early hours of this morning and water swilled the decks when I went to investigate. The rain clouds were disappearing fast, and we were soon back to mares' tails and cotton wool and cauliflowers; Biscay storms were forecast, but we were three or four days from there as yet.

The sea today had a mild chop, and I was interested when Chief Officer Jack showed me the rough guide to seas and swells which they use. As already discussed the wind was measured on the Beaufort Scale of 0 to 12, above 12 was hurricane force. The sea Scale measured 0 to 9, wave height 0 to 14 metres, over 14 metres was termed 'phenomenal', and this did not measure the waves from trough to peak, but the upper part of them only, which could affect the ship. Swell Scale also measured 0 to 9, Low to Heavy, 0 to 4 metres, and this was a measurement of trough to peak. Above four metres was considered 'confused'.

I am reading a good yarn at present, about life in the Middle and Far East from 1944 onwards. I have reached page ninety without a smell of sexual intercourse, but I fear that in another twenty pages somebody may have 'done it' to somebody else, and I think I know who will 'do it' to whom, and from the look of things now she will do it right back, and that will be tasteful and timely for the reader for a change.

At noon we were in the middle of Malta Channel, and on the starboard beam there were the oil rigs of the Vega Oilfield some seven miles away. Sicily, out of sight to starboard brought back memories most clear, of a ridge with glorious Greek temples at Agrigento, a campsite among the antiquities of Syracuse, and the attractiveness of Taormina in the southern Italian sun. Malta to port conjured up a vision of almost treeless sunshine, and meals at the Churchill Restaurant in Sliema, with dishes that I could even now remember, and the friendly people, and their extraordinary loyalty and bravery during the Second World War. We must now be sailing over some of the wrecks from that famous Malta convoy which hardly had a chance. The northern coast of Malta was just visible enshrouded in mist on the port beam, and then during the afternoon we sailed the Sicilian Channel. Away to the north east was Terrible Bank and Adventure Bank, and nearer the shores of Sicily in the north and the African mainland to the south there were Marine Farms and tunny nets to avoid.

Fat Mona told me that she was experiencing lower abdominal pains, 'like she was going to come on'. I earnestly hoped that she was not going to inflict an abortion upon the ship's company, because I was no medical expert in those areas of the female body, having preferred always to venture and dally there only upon purely social occasions. She tried to speak to her mother on the mobile telephone every hour on the hour, but we were not close enough to land for her to do so, and she will probably have to wait until Gibraltar.

The poor little darling was most troubled in her mind, and I have reassured her that it is very common to have congestive pelvic pain in the early days of pregnancy. I have said at the start of this book that you can give weighty reassurance from a position of relative ignorance when you are a distinguished physician, and be believed without question. I was.

At dinner, Admiral Geoffrey came in late as we were finishing. He looked at Flawed Genius Jane with lustful eyes of jet, and thanked her for the party last night, without acknowledging the rest of us. She signalled back at him, doe eyes of dark sloe at pure jet, the treacherous little tart. As soon as River Tweed docks at Le Havre she will have less use for him than for yesterday's Tampax, I can tell you. At least I have maintained honest and dignified hostility toward Admiral Geoffrey, while she has played him all voyage like a cunnystruck cod, entirely for her own ends.

At 9 p.m. we passed the Italian island of Pantellaria to port, and then we sidled past Cape Bon which is the nearest we get to Tunisia, only ten miles away. Now there were six more sailing days left on this Cargo Boat of the Southern Moons, ugly old River Tweed, she with her belly full of palm oil, copra, cocoa and coffee to be off-loaded in European ports, and then off she will go again, pregnant with manufactured merchandise, on another lap of the oceans and the seas, under the suns and the moons and the stars, to the little pretty lands far away. I shall think of her upon times, indeed I will, and of my friends in Santo and Honiara and Rabaul and Kimbe and Lae and Madang, most certainly Madang, where they understood my heartbreak; you are bound to warm to folk like that if you are where I am.

**Friday 27th February** Before morning light, we sailed past the Gulf of Tunis which embraced Carthage and all its magical history, and the Lake of Bizerte, a graveyard of White Russian ships which sought refuge there following the Russian Revolution. At 8 a.m., level with the Tunisian Isle de la Galite which was clear to port, we changed heading to the south west on 263 degrees. We ignored the warning that the waters in Canal de la Galite are dangerous for trawling, we were not going down there, and we carried many things on this old ship but no nets. By mid-morning we shall pass the border on the mainland of continental Africa between Tunisia and Algeria.

My thoughts were wistful on the rail this morning, the sea and the clouds were iron-grey, the officers were back in black trousers, and passengers were wearing drab anoraks. I went back to that tumult, that riot of brilliant colour around Baie des Citrons on New Caledonia, to those poincianas on Espiritu Santo, which coloured you scarlet as they involved you in their fire when you stood beneath them. I really felt that they had gone from my life for ever now, but there is something reassuring and comfortable about colourlessness when you feel low, you do not want the challenge of colour then; I have found that out for myself these last three years.

I regret that the painful pricking in Fat Mona's bristols has increased, and this morning she noticed spots of blood on the toilet paper. I hoped desperately that she would not abort in the Bay of Biscay; with all that tossing, pitching and rolling about she well could. I hoped that she was just having a wishfully delayed period, because I would not want to be involved in Fat Mona's abortion.

I have now reached page 230 of the book that I am reading, and it cannot be long now before they 'do it', because, the 'flame of the desire that he has kindled deep within her' has now licked where it should not have licked, and she is as 'soft putty moulded to the curves of his long muscular body', the randy cheating little bitch, with a loving husband and six year old son waiting for her in Hong Kong. I will bet you that by page 330 he will 'slide into her' because that is what they all do, do they not? Mind you, having kept her waiting until page 330 she might have gone off the whole idea of him, narcissistic creep that he is.

We ploughed on through the Western Mediterranean at a steady 14.2 knots, and are due to pass through the Straits of Gibraltar early tomorrow morning. Like the Suez Canal at the other end of this big land-locked pond, I am doing it for the first time in my life.

**Saturday 28th February** River Tweed has safely navigated the final conduit of this long voyage, and as she breasted the buffets and billows of Biscay Bay, and headed for the home straight of the English Channel, we were back in the waters through which we westward sailed four months ago, and have come full circle. I was left with my thoughts and reveries and memories. I have rounded this planet by its seas, and it is ever a smaller place for me now.

Would that I had not to travel alone.

# Postlude

I have travelled twenty-eight thousand three hundred and thirty nautical miles, crossed three oceans and twelve seas of all the colours blue and all the colours green, and I have seen the beauty of the evening, of the night, and in the morning which is beyond me to describe with any justice. I have touched eleven ports upon nine islands where I have seen flowers of such colour to make you close your eyes lest the brilliance blind you, and inhaled scents of such fragrance to hypnotise your brain into a torpor that permitted no other sensation.

If you asked me what else I have achieved by this voyage, I would find you hard to answer. Having wanted to sail the seas of the world since I was young, I suppose that I have achieved that, and reaffirmed in my mind the sheer beauty of nature unbridled and all its bounty; that never changes, nor ever will it.

I have seen parts of the world that I have never seen before, places and peoples of which and of whom I have read and never thought that I would see. I have asked myself if I have now seen all that I want to see, and I think that the answer to that is that I have.

I have met shipmates like Chief Officer Jack, Russian Iosif, Tall Dark Dem'yan, Dishy Pyotr, Young Trinity House Paul, Purser Alec and his Fat Mona, together with Bearded Bright Eyed Henry and his slim Johnny, none of whom would I have known had I not sailed on River Tweed. I have met the folk of the islands, whose cheerfulness seemed so much a part of the tropical sunshine.

I have had to find new resources and resilience within me which I knew not existed. I have had to deal with people and situations aboard ship that I did not expect, and I have had to cope with the absolute loneliness that confinement with total strangers and the inability to communicate with those whom you love, who love you and who understand you and the way you feel, confers. The fact that the most important person on any ship, the Captain, who controls your life in all ways was, in my case, a constitutional psychopath, at times caused me to draw upon qualities in my character that I had forgotten were there, such as inexorable and unshakeable self-control.

If the purpose of changing the horizon of my loneliness was to diminish it, then this voyage was a failure; if it was to help me to want my love less and to reconcile myself to living without her, and to be less bitter about her suffering, again it was a failure. Strangely the unexpected gain from the whole odyssey was a discovery of disparate strength and fibre within myself at an age when late self-discoveries of any sort are somewhat unseemly.

I truly know now, that nothing can faze me, disturb daunt or even wound me. I think that I have found another makeshift self for the short term, if that is possible within the blurred periphery of personhood, and if I cannot soon die then I suppose that this revelation is a good thing, because my real self died with Esmé in that lovely long, hot and cruel summer of 1995, and however good a helmsman I might be, I would eternally be rudderless and adrift on a sea with horizons aplenty, but never a shore.

# Postscript

Admiral Geoffrey was sacked by the Company following complaints about his behaviour on the voyage by three officers and three passengers.

Purser Alec has been on extended sick leave since the end of the voyage.

Chief Officer Jack has left the Company and has a shore-based job as Captain on the Isle of Wight ferries.

Chief Engineer Scottish Bill, Bearded Bright Eyed Henry and Johnny, Tall Dark Dem'yan, Russian Iosif and Dishy Pyotr and not forgetting Big Van and his needle gun remain with the Company and are all back at sea.

Trinity House Paul had a good report and is heading rapidly toward his Second Mates' ticket.

Eric, Tina, Boom Boom and the Flawed Genius returned with relief to God's Own Country and continue to enjoy their lives of happy plenty, comfortably insulated from 'all that parverty'.

Fat Mona is not as yet with child, but she and Alec continue to 'go in for it' with commendable persistence, determination, optimism and enviable frequency.